DOES PEOPLE DO IT?

STORIES & STORYTELLERS
TERESA MILLER, SERIES EDITOR

Also by Fred Harris

Does People Do It?

A Memoir

FRED HARRIS

UNIVERSITY OF OKLAHOMA PRESS : NORMAN

Library of Congress Cataloging-in-Publication Data

Harris, Fred R., 1930–
Does people do it? : a memoir / Fred Harris.
p.   cm. — (stories & storytellers ; v. 5)
Includes bibliographical references and index.
ISBN 978-0-8061-3913-5 (hardcover)
ISBN 978-0-8061-8663-4 (paper)
1. Harris, Fred R., 1930–   2. United States. Congress. Senate—Biography.
3. Legislators—United States—Biography.   4. United States—
Politics and government—20th century.   5. Oklahoma. Legislature. Senate—
Biography.   6. Legislators—Oklahoma—Biography.   7. Oklahoma—
Politics and government—1907–   8. Oklahoma—Biography.   I. Title.
E840.8H28A3 2008
328.73092—dc22
[B]
2007029514

Does People Do It? A Memoir is Volume 5
in the Stories & Storytellers series.

The paper in this book meets the guidelines for permanence and durability
of the Committee on Production Guidelines for Book Longevity
of the Council on Library Resources. ∞

For my parents,

Fred B. Harris and Alene Harris, now long gone.

They did the very best they knew how.

"Does people do it? If people does it, *I* can do it."

—Ralph Harris

Contents

Prologue
Does People Do It?

I am sitting in my Dale Hall Tower office on the west edge of the wonderful, spreading main campus of the University of Oklahoma in Norman. I am nearly seventy-six, and I am here because I accepted an invitation to teach for fall semester 2006 as a Distinguished Visiting Professor of Political Science at OU, my alma mater. (I probably would have agreed to work for no pay just to be called "distinguished," though I was careful not to mention that to the OU official who offered me the position.) Here, in a building named for the late E. E. Dale, that great old ex-cowboy historian who was one of the best professors I had as an OU student, I feel that my life has sort of come full circle.

It was in the fall of 1948, fifty-eight years ago, that I first entered the University of Oklahoma as an apprehensive political science and prelaw freshman. I was straight out of the small, somewhat limited high school at Walters, Oklahoma, and the only person in my immediate family to go to college. Enrolling at OU was something like parachuting into an unknown wilderness without a map.

But I drew strength from a personal attitude I'd picked up early: Does people do it?

I mostly got this attitude from a favorite uncle, Ralph Harris. He and the rest of my dad's brothers were like brothers to me. I grew up working in the fields with them. When I was a kid, we were known as the Haybaling Harrises in Cotton County, Oklahoma. We baled local farmers' hay for hire. I started my first regular job in the crew the summer I was five. Daylight to dark, I rode around and around on the plodding horse that powered our old-time haybaler. My wage for that first work was a dime a day.

Back then and always, Ralph Harris was lean, strong, and tough. His mother, my grandmother—we called her Ma—nicknamed him Rooster, I guess because he was always up early, scratching for a living. He and the others called me Bud, and we all called him Hammer. He had penetrating gray eyes that most of the time shone with his funnier-than–Will Rogers humor but glared with dangerous steely anger if you ever made him mad.

Hammer would fight. The year before I was born, my dad was sharecropping on a dryland cotton and maize farm outside Mule Shoe, Texas, for a landowner Daddy ever afterward referred to as Old Man Cope. In the neighborhood, Daddy later told me, there was an insufferable bully "who needed his ass whipped," but he was too young for my dad to take on. So, Daddy mailed a postcard back to Walters, Oklahoma, and told his younger brother, Hammer, to come out and take care of the job for him. Hammer hitchhiked his way to Mule Shoe and soundly "frailed the bastard's knob" in an arranged fistfight until the young bully'd had enough and "hollered calf rope," as they used to say. Job done, Hammer hitchhiked back home to Walters.

In his late teens, Hammer would work in the fields all day, then, one night a week, walk three or four miles into Walters, pull on skimpy boxing trunks and scuffed-up, faded red, eight-ounce gloves, and earn a couple of dollars as a winning buzz-saw prizefighter in a makeshift ring on the local Wollam Theater stage. Early afternoon on one such fight day, Hammer lost his temper with a troublesome horse he was harnessing and hit the horse in the jaw with his right fist. The horse wasn't hurt, but Hammer's fist was busted. Still, he didn't want to give up the prospect of winning two dollars in the ring that night, so he tightly taped the broken hand and fought anyway, one handed, really, and won the money using only his left hooks, uppercuts, and jabs.

"Whatever your job is," Hammer would tell you, "go about it like you was killing snakes." He always did. And he would tell you, too, when you were working with him, as I did in the hay fields and, later, following summer wheat harvests all the way up to North Dakota, "Don't ever let me hear you say 'cain't.' I hate to hear that word. You think 'cain't,' you do 'cain't.' You think 'can,' you do 'can.'" Another thing Hammer used to say was, "I may give out, but I won't give in, and I won't give up."

He doted on me. When I was in the first grade, I was thrilled when he showed up unannounced one day at my rural Lincoln Valley School in his blue Ford V-6 sedan. He got me out of class, and bringing a single-shot 410-gauge shotgun for me, he took me with him as his sidekick to an exciting community rabbit drive, followed by a sumptuous fried-chicken-and-potato-salad "dinner on the ground" prepared by local women.

Years later, when I ran for president, Hammer was a Rock Island Railroad brakeman in Cedar Rapids, Iowa, and his wife, my aunt Wanda, ran the one-desk office of a little local private aviation company. They proudly hosted a great outdoor campaign rally for me at their rural home, on the south edge of Cedar Rapids. That night, an Associated Press reporter traveling with me asked Wanda what she and Hammer did. "You might say that we're in transportation," she said.

Twice during that early winter campaign in Iowa, before I had yet accepted Secret Service escorts, Hammer served as my chauffeur, driving me in his car from one side of that presidential first-caucus state to the other, to and from important campaign events. One of those times, he and I did not get back to his house until maybe two o'clock in the morning. Aunt Wanda was asleep. Hammer and I were worn out, but he cooked us a little snack of scrambled eggs, and we sat down at his kitchen table to unwind. This was just after a mercifully unsuccessful assassination attempt had been made on the life of President Gerald Ford. Hammer was dead tired, and he said to me, wearily, "Bud, I don't think it's nuts trying to shoot these politicians; I think it's their kinfolks!"

But truth was that he loyally and deeply believed in me, and he desperately wanted me to win the presidency. For one reason as, seared by the Great Depression and knowing what it was like to need work, he expressed to me that same night in his kitchen, "You get that job, Bud, you'll be fixed for life."

Hammer had run away from home when he was seventeen. He'd headed out west to Los Angeles, hitchhiking and hopping freights to get there, hoping to find a way to make a living. Times were extra hard in those Depression years, and he later told me, "Bud, my shoe soles hadn't hardly hit the pavement out there before I run out of what little dab of money I'd saved." He was anxious to find some work, and work was scarcer in Los Angeles than he'd figured on.

One morning, he made his way to a nearby jobsite where a dam was being built. He presented himself to the straw boss who he'd heard was looking for an additional man to run a fresno, a big one-man dirt-moving scoop pulled by a team of horses, sort of the bulldozer of those days.

The straw boss sized up Hammer's skinny frame with a clearly skeptical eye, then told him, "Son, you work for me, you gonna have to move such and such cubic yards of dirt a day; whatta you say to that?"

Hammer's response: "Does people do it? If people does it, *I* can do it." He got the job. And he did the work, too.

Does people do it? I learned that early, primarily from Hammer.

I graduated the University of Oklahoma College of Law in 1954, pretty much broke and with a wife and young daughter to support. I started practicing law in Lawton, Oklahoma, barely knowing how to find the courthouse. Could I make myself into a successful lawyer and a solid and productive local citizen?

Does people do it?

When, sadly, the local incumbent state senator succumbed to a brain tumor and I was encouraged to become a candidate for that position, at age twenty-five and only a year and a half out of law school, I wasn't sure I knew how to run a winning two-county political campaign or, if I won, how to really make a beneficial difference for other people in that job and become a sound and effective state senator.

Does people do it?

At age thirty-three, having visited Washington, D.C., only twice, mainly as a tourist, I had to work at imagining myself as one of only one hundred members of the United States Senate when I announced my candidacy in 1963 for the office left open by the death of the larger-than-life Robert S. Kerr, who'd just been called "the King of the Senate" by *Time* magazine. Was I heavy enough to win Senator Kerr's seat? If so, was I prepared enough to make a lasting and meaningful contribution for my country and to be a successful senator?

Would I be able to educate Americans sufficiently on the intertwined problems of race and poverty that so much engaged my energies and attention, in the Senate and on the 1967 Kerner Commission, and help animate national progress on these terrible, endemic national problems?

Could I reform and rebuild the Democratic Party when I became its national chair in 1969?

Could I make a worthwhile impact as a serious 1976 presidential candidate, win or lose?

Does people do it?

After I quit the Senate and left Washington, could I write constructive, and instructive, books about politics and government that someone would want to publish—or read? Could I become a tenured full professor of political science and usefully teach what I knew? Could I write novels?

Does people do it?

In spring 2006, my wife, Margaret Elliston, and I were stepping up our physical training for an upcoming two-week European bicycle tour we were scheduled to ride, mostly along the Danube River, from near Munich down to Vienna. She and I were not altering our routine much because we had been long-distance biking (as well as cross-country skiing and snowshoeing) for years, and we had ridden in a similar two-week European bicycle tour, this one in Provence, the year before. But a friend of ours, who didn't know all that background, asked me—I was seventy-five at the time—about the planned Danube ride: "Fred, can you hold up for that?"

Does people do it?

All my life, I have always sought, been stimulated by, new challenges. And when faced with one, I have always been like the little boy in the story who needed, wanted, some way, to get over a difficult high wall he'd come to: first, he threw his cap over; then he *had* to go over after it.

I have always instinctively decided on a goal before I knew for sure how to achieve it. Then, after making the decision, it was for me, as my old mentor in the Oklahoma State Senate, Don Baldwin of Anadarko, used to say, "a case of 'ground hog': climb a tree or get eat by the dogs"—a case of have-to.

Can I write a personal memoir that other people might find engaging and of some useful inspiration or application for their own lives? I hope so.

Does people do it?

DOES PEOPLE DO IT?

1

—∞—

Before the World Changed

I FLAT HATE TO MOVE FROM ONE HOUSE TO ANOTHER. Always have. But I never thought much about why I felt that way so strongly. Not until a few years ago, when I started gathering material about 1930s life in the small southwestern Oklahoma town of Walters, where I was born and grew up. Before I got sidetracked into writing my first novel, using the 1930s material, I had in mind writing a limited nonfiction memoir to be called "Before the World Changed," that is, before World War II.

So, on a sort of research trip to and throughout Walters, I undertook a memory-jogging drive up and down my small hometown's streets, accompanied by my wife, Margaret Elliston. And as she and I slowly wheeled along, I soon found myself, like a tourist guide, pointing out to her various houses, one after another, where I'd lived as a boy.

Margaret interrupted with an obvious question. "Why in the world did you all move so much?"

That caused a stunning realization to hit me for the first time in my life: in the stretch from fall 1937 to spring 1948, when I was between the ages of seven and seventeen, my family and I lived in twelve different Walters houses. *Twelve!*

It averages out to slightly over one move a year, all in the same little town of about two thousand population. Thinking about it some more, I realized that for my earliest years—from my birth year, 1930, to 1937, when we moved into Walters to stay—I could also count at least seven other houses we'd lived in, all but one in my home county, Cotton County, Oklahoma, and most of them near Walters.

With all that seventeen-year—1930 to 1948—commotion, no wonder I've always hated to move!

But why did my family change residences so often? I had no idea. Neither did one of my sisters, Loretta Sue Stauffer (named after the movie star Loretta Young), who still lived in Walters. Both our parents were by then dead, and so were their brothers and sisters, my uncles and aunts. Most of our parents' contemporaries, too. We couldn't ask any of those people. But my mother's closest friend, Lil Williams, was still alive, though quite old and in a Walters nursing home. At my request, my sister Sue went to see her, to ask her the question on our minds. Lil Williams's response was that our mother, Alene Harris—who, as Sue and I already knew, could do almost anything, including painting, carpentry, and wallpapering—would soon improve and brighten up each rented house we moved into; the landlord would then raise our rent, and we would thereafter have to move on to some other place and start the cycle of "fix up, then move" all over again. Maybe that was the reason.

But one friend I later told all this to said, "Fred, each time you came home from school and found that your folks had moved away again, leaving no forwarding address—how come you didn't finally get the message?" He was joking, of course. So was another friend who told me, "It's a damned good thing you didn't get elected president of the United States; it would have bankrupted the country to make national monuments of all the houses you lived in!" *Fred Harris lived here, and here, and here, and here, and here. . . .*

Ticking off the nineteen houses that my family and I occupied from my birth until I graduated from high school, I find that I have vivid memories connected to virtually every one of those places, including, even, my seven earliest homes, before the Walters twelve.

The recollection of our very first house, though, is not properly mine but my sister Kathryn's. I was born in an unpainted two-room, clapboard-sided frame house on unpaved South Boundary Street at the south edge of Walters at about 5:30 A.M. on November 13, 1930. Mama pointed out the house to me years later. It was located on the east side, the "right" side, of the railroad tracks, but just barely. The next houses west, across the tracks, were in what people disparagingly called Snuff Ridge. Residents over there were looked down on some, though they were surely no worse off economically than my parents. Like my own folks, people who lived in Snuff Ridge were poor and working class—and white. No African Americans lived in Walters. Originally, they may have been barred from doing so.

My little birthplace house has long since been torn down, but my older sister, Kathryn, now gone too, claimed in a handwritten family-history sketch that her own earliest recollections were of that two-room house—a kitchen and one bedroom—and the early morning hour when I was born there. "I would have been nearly three years old," Kathryn wrote. "Some say that I could not have remembered at that young age, that I must only remember what I've been told. This is not true! I apparently woke up during the birth or shortly afterwards. I remember Mother in the bed and Daddy and the doctor there. I remember standing up and holding onto the rail of my white-painted iron baby bed and Daddy and / or the doctor trying to get me to lie back down. I was facing the bed where mother was, on the north side of the room. Perhaps Mother was making a lot of noise. I do not know or remember that."

My birth certificate shows my first name spelled "Fredy," with one *d* in the middle and a *y* at the end. The blanks on the form were filled out by hand, by Dr. G. W. Baker, I suppose. He was the attending physician (and our family doctor during my childhood). There has always been some question about my middle name, whether it was meant to be Ray or Roy. On the birth certificate, the name looks like Ray, which is what my dad thought they'd named me, after a Mississippi uncle of his, Ray Lee Carey. But my mother thought the middle name they'd given me was Roy, after her older brother, Leroy Person.

Until junior high school, most people called me Fredie Ray, and that was how I spelled it, but after deciding that was a little boy's name, I began rather grandly to write my name as Fred R. Harris, and, when pressed, put my middle name down as Roy. Fred R. Harris is the name I have used officially ever since. I hope nobody ever tries to overturn my elections to the Oklahoma State Senate and the United States Senate on the grounds that I ran for those offices under an assumed name.

—⚞— —⚞— —⚞—

I'm about the only one who believes that I can remember the West Texas farmhouse, near the little communities of Lakeview and Deep Lake, where we lived when I was two and where I suffered a terrible burn to my right elbow that left the bone sticking out. (And it *is* possible that I remember this house from some later childhood time when we went back to West Texas to pick cotton or to visit relatives.) I have no recollection of my awful burn experience in that house, but I can see in my mind the house as plainly as a digital color photo: it's west facing and painted yellow, and I'm on the north side of it, enjoying playing by myself in the sand.

This would have been in 1932. My dad was trying to make a living by sharecropping on a sorry, sand-hilly parcel of West Texas land. One winter day, according to what Mama told me, Daddy had taken up some hot coals from the living room woodstove and momentarily left them on the floor in a small metal tub. A little neighbor girl and I were playing cars in that room, each pulling a matchbox behind us on a string. She stepped on my box, jerking me so that I fell on my back, right onto the red-hot coals. To lift myself out, I plunged my right elbow into the fiery mass and wasn't rescued until the flesh on the elbow had been destroyed. A country doctor treated the terrible resultant wound with some kind of greasy salve, Mama said, and predicted that my elbow would always be stiff. His prediction was wrong, but his treatment somehow worked. Mama said that I was in bed so long because of the injury that I had to learn to walk all over again. But the only permanent reminders I have today of the incident are a clear, and happy, mental image of that West Texas house where it occurred—and a rather ugly right-elbow scar.

—⚬— —⚬— —⚬—

I think I was something like three (and Kathryn was nearly six; Sue, a baby, and my youngest sister, Irene, not yet born) when we lived with a Comanche Indian family—George and Mabel Coosewoon and their daughter, Mabel Jean, who was my age—in the home they owned out in the country, north of Walters. (The name Coosewoon, properly pronounced, must mean in Comanche something like "see the buffalo.") The Coosewoon house was across a bend in East Cache Creek, just north of Sultan Park. It was a white-painted frame house situated on a low hill and facing south, with brick half-pillars and a couple of juniper trees at the front steps.

During the harsh years of the 1930s, it wasn't all that unusual in Oklahoma for two families to share a house, as we did with the Coosewoons, but I've never heard of that kind of sharing occurring, back then around Walters, between a white family and an Indian family. The fact that such a thing happened says a lot about the generosity of the Coosewoons. And it shows that my folks were either not prejudiced against Indian people, as many whites were, or their poverty trumped their prejudice. The Coosewoons owned their own home; we did not have one.

One of my strongest memories associated with the Coosewoon house is of one day lying on my back in the grassy area in front of it, looking up at fluffy white clouds floating south and being able to see in the clouds absolutely perfect sculptures of objects like cats, dogs, and bears. I do not mean that the clouds looked like the animals; I mean that they were exact white *replicas* of them. I have since read somewhere that the ability of a child to see those kinds of precise figures in clouds fades at about three years of age. I don't know if that's true or not. I do know that when I was three, I did clearly see those wondrous shapes and, disappointingly, never could again.

When I was about four, we lived for a short time in another house with a different family, a white family—the Taylors and their daughter, Barbara, whom I would later date in high school. Their house was a low and wide white frame building with green trim that was a combination Conoco gasoline filling-station office, grocery, and home. It squatted on the concrete highway about half a mile east of Walters. My family lived in the west part of this house, the Taylors, in the east part. Out front, to the south, were two calibrated glass-globe-topped gasoline pumps. When a driver pulled up and said how many gallons he wanted, say, five gallons, Ol (short for Oliver, I imagine) Taylor, the house and station owner, worked a large lever back and forth to pump gasoline up into the glass globe from a below-ground tank until the level reached the five-gallon mark. Then he inserted the hose nozzle into the car's tank and let gravity drain the pumped-up five gallons into it.

My family must have shared the kitchen in that house with the Taylors, as we surely did, too, at the Coosewoon place. But I don't think we shared an indoor bathroom in either place. There wasn't one. In fact, I don't think we lived in a house with indoor plumbing until I was twelve.

After the Taylor house, and when I must have still been four, we lived briefly in what Daddy called the Hawkins place, what I call the "newspapered" house. A heavily weathered, unpainted old one-story L-shaped dwelling, it faced south on an east-west dirt country road, a couple of miles west of Lincoln Valley School and about three miles north of Walters. The house was uninsulated and badly run down. I have the feeling that it had been abandoned, that nobody had lived in it for some time, before we moved into it. The inside walls of the few rooms in this house were wallpapered with newspapers to cover the many cracks and keep out the wind. I do not know whether this newspapering was Mama's work or not. It could have been. I know that she probably could not afford to buy real wallpaper back then. She would have mixed flour and water to make a homemade paste for sticking up the newspapers, as she later did for real wallpapering.

When we lived in this newspapered house, I couldn't yet read, of course, but I fancy that I can remember looking at wall newsprint photographs of the young Canadian Dionne quintuplets, who were then as famous as Hollywood movie stars. About this same time, over at the nearby Indian-lease farmhouse on East Cache Creek where my Harris grandparents lived, my uncle Bill, nearest of my dad's brothers in age to me, tried one day to fool our young cousin Margery Lloyd into thinking that I could read. He would whisper to me the words in a newspaper comic strip, then have me repeat them aloud to Margery as if I were actually reading. I don't think she believed I could read, but I remember fervently wanting to. I could hardly wait to learn.

My dad was not farming the newspapered place but was just renting the old house alone. He was trading cattle for a living by then, buying and selling livestock, something he would do for most of the rest of his life. He had removed the rumble seat of an old Chevrolet coupe he owned and replaced it with a handmade livestock bed and sideboards; I figure that he could haul a couple of calves or four or five hogs in this makeshift pickup.

By trading cattle in those early days, my dad was able to keep food on our table, but I doubt now that there was a whole lot of it. He needed to make some extra money, too. That fall, together with Mama's sister, Aunt Vera, and Vera's husband, Uncle Buster Harper, as well as their children, my young cousins, Billy and Mary, we went out west, out on the plains of West Texas, to pick cotton, or "pull bolls," as people said. We camped in an abandoned house out there. The littler kids spent the day sitting in the cotton field in one of our two old cars. My sister Kathryn and I, during a good part of each day, worked in the field with our parents.

Mama and Daddy were paid by the pound, by the number of pounds of ripe-white cotton bolls they pulled, sacked, and weighed up. Each of them took two rows of cotton a piece. From sunup to sundown, bent over nearly double or on their knees and using both gloved hands, they grabbed cotton bolls from the dried stalks, left and right, and stuffed them into the long ducking sacks they dragged behind them from straps across their shoulders. The two of them together could often weigh up as much as an astounding two thousand pounds of cotton bolls a day! My sister and I helped. We went ahead of them, one of us with one parent, the other with the other, and ourselves pulled bolls to fill a slop jar, a cleaned-up porcelainized waste bucket we each carried. When Kathryn's or my slop jar was full, we emptied it on the ground ahead of Mama or Daddy, who, coming along, rapidly scooped up our little pile of cotton bolls and crammed them into the sack, lessening slightly the work they would otherwise have had to do.

My memory of the newspapered house is tinged with a sense of shame. I recall being awakened late one night, lying on the pallet where my sisters and I slept, to hear a frighteningly loud argument between Mama, inside the front door, and Daddy, outside on the porch, drunk. He had come home late. She had locked him out. He was demanding that she open the door. She adamantly refused. Then, all of a sudden, Daddy kicked the door in with a dreadful crash. The old door didn't just burst open; the whole thing was torn completely loose from its rusted hinges, and it slammed to the floor with an awful sound like an explosion. I raised up in alarm and discovered that I could see straight outside into the dark night. I do not remember what happened after that or how, or how soon, my parents reconciled, as they most surely did. All I remember is how ashamed I was, right then, that my family lived in a house that did not have a front door and how embarrassed I imagined I would feel the next day, or afterward, if somebody came to visit us and found that out.

Next, when I was five, we lived about seven miles south of Walters and four miles west of the town of Temple in an unpainted two-room house on the wooded east bank of East Cache Creek, on a farm we called the Pres Baten place. Our little house faced south on an east-west dirt road and was on Indian-owned land; Daddy must have subleased the house and farm from a white guy named something like Presley Baten.

Around a tree-lined creek bend west of us lived a desperately poor but marvelously musically talented family, the Langstons. They made a bare living in the woods—by chopping down trees and making fence posts and firewood for sale and by picking up pecans (all as my grandpa Pa Harris and some of his sons, my uncles, did, too, off and on). Some nights, we walked over to the Langston shack after supper and sat outside in lantern light under giant native pecan trees and listened to the Langstons play the guitar and mandolin and sing some of the saddest songs ever composed, songs like "Give My Love to Nellie, Jack," "When the Work's All Done This Fall," and "Tracing Little Footprints through the Snow"— songs I well remember yet.

West of that Pres Baten house, too, but across the creek on a log footbridge lived another very poor family, the Winfield Gillespie family. He was a drunkard who was said to beat his wife and kids. I recall that on more than one occasion, Mrs. Gillespie fled to our house with the children until her husband could sleep off a drunk. I started the first grade, at Temple, while I was still five, though I went there only a week before we moved again. Kathryn and I walked a quarter of a mile east of our house each of those first few school-day mornings and caught a school bus there at the corner. On the bus with us was a Gillespie daughter, Christine, the same age as Kathryn. That pitiful girl's fingers and toes were almost webbed, and her face was dreadfully twisted. Kathryn and I felt sorry for Christine, and befriended her. Unlike some other kids, we thought of her as a person; a lot of them—then and in the years afterward, when we sometimes saw the poor girl on the streets of Temple—called her "the pig girl," taunted her, and ran from her in mock terror.

Across the road and a quarter of a mile east of our Pres Baten home lived a Butler family in a quite attractive frame house, painted neatly in dark yellow. We all thought of the Butlers as rich, though I'm now sure they weren't, of course. There were two Butler daughters, perhaps in the sixth and seventh grades. One was blond, the other dark haired. Kathryn and I thought these girls were unbearably beautiful. Their hair was always well-brushed and shiny, their store-bought dresses, extra nice and pretty. Some late afternoons, the two Butler daughters would walk down to our house to visit. For Kathryn and me, these were almost achingly sweet occasions. She "claimed" the blond girl, I the dark-haired one. The four of us would sit together on the front step of our little house. I would hold the hand of my girl, and Kathryn, hers, while the two of them mostly talked to Mama as she sat snapping green beans or maybe embroidering a cup towel.

The Pres Baten place is where I remember my first Christmas. I woke up a little during the night before, Christmas Eve, on the floor pallet where I was sleeping. I saw Mama and Daddy quietly putting up and decorating a small persimmon tree that Daddy had apparently chopped down earlier. I watched as they then placed some oranges, nuts, and a few wrapped presents beneath the brown-leafed tree before blowing out the coal-oil (kerosene) lamp and going to bed. Christmas morning, wanting to please my parents, I feigned great surprise, never letting on that I did not believe that old Santa Claus was responsible for bringing that wondrous tree and gifts during the preceding night.

While we lived at the Pres Baten place, Kathryn suddenly became desperately ill with typhoid fever. Mama had to take her on the bus, sick as Kathryn was and running a high fever, to a charity hospital, Crippled Children's in Oklahoma City, a one-way trip in excess of 130 miles. The two of them stayed up there for something like two weeks of treatment. When they did finally come back home, Mama brought me a wind-up toy that walked. And she promptly took me and my younger sister, Sue, into the little town of Temple so that we could line up, terrified, at a small red brick building and get typhoid shots provided by a newly established public health program.

The next place where we lived, a mile and a half east and nearly two miles north of Walters, was on a rented 160-acre farm of part sandy-soiled oat field (where I was to see one of the last steam engine–powered threshing machines at work) and part weedy pasture (where Kathryn and I were to spend a lot of time, herding Mama's dumb turkeys). The unpainted two-story house faced west on a dirt road, about three-quarters of a mile south of Lincoln Valley School, a two-room country school where I would complete the first grade.

I cowboyed my way over this ten-mile move from the Pres Baten place to the Lincoln Valley farm. Daddy had me and one of his younger brothers, my uncle A. C., drive Daddy's small herd of cattle on horseback. All the way that day, a really hard fall rain beat down on Ake and me, drenching us, but I didn't care. I was happy to be riding a little borrowed spotted pony and on a real western saddle, though my feet didn't reach all the way to the stirrups. I remember feeling like the tough Little Joe, the wrangler of the cowboy song, on a rugged Chisholm Trail cattle drive to Dodge.

Lincoln Valley School was a one-story white-frame country school taught by a newly married young couple, Rodney and Nellie Patton, who lived in a small teacherage on the premises. The school's "little kids' room," for grades one through four, one row each, was taught by Mrs. Patton, and the "big kids' room," for grades five though eight, was taught by Mr. Patton. There was a small, slightly raised stage for school and community programs in the big kids' room. A large woodstove heated the school building, and that winter, when Kathryn and I, after walking three-quarters of a mile north from home, would sometimes get to school before Mr. Patton had yet built a fire; she and I would stand around shivering, rubbing our aching fingers, until he finally got one going.

I loved the first grade at Lincoln Valley School. A guy I know at Walters felt just the opposite, and he is still locally famous for something he said. The teacher asked him, "Max, can you write your name?" His reply was, "Hell, no, this is my first day of school!" I *could* write my name, at least my first name, Fredie, when I started school. I couldn't read, but I learned fast and after that could never get enough of reading.

Years later, when I was a member of the United States Senate, my wonderful Lincoln Valley teacher, Mrs. Patton (then Nellie Friels, remarried after her first husband was killed in a motorcycle accident), invited me to visit her first-grade class at Walters. In introducing me to her students that day, she said, "Boys and girls, the first year I taught school, there was a little boy in the first grade who just *loved* reading. Every day, he would finish his work as quickly as he could, so he could go to the table in back and pick out another book to read on his own. At the end of the year, that little first-grader got the prize, a shiny new quarter, for having read the most books of any student in the whole school!"

She then told the kids that that little boy was me. Getting the Lincoln Valley prize for reading was always a vivid memory for me. And maybe it started me out liking awards—and winning.

The shiny quarter became a part of "my own money" that I had begun to accumulate, along with a beginning sense of self and independence. Using the quarter and some of the dime a day I'd earned the preceding summer in the hay fields, I sent off on my own a $1.25 mail order to Montgomery Ward, filling out the form and writing out the address myself, in pencil, for a Red Ryder BB gun "with scope sight" that was advertised in the company catalog. When the BB gun came without a scope sight, I immediately wrote Montgomery Ward a postcard, requesting that they promptly send me the missing item. Instead, the company simply mailed me a second BB gun, identical to the first—this one with no scope sight, either. I gave the windfall second gun to my cousin Billy Harper.

At the Lincoln Valley farm, Kathryn and I carried our homemade school lunches in a couple of used, washed-out syrup pails. The lunches usually consisted of nothing more than sandwiches Mama made from biscuits and other stuff left over from breakfast. That really never bothered me, though I did notice, with a little envy, I'm sure, that some kids had sandwiches made with store-bought "light bread," as we called it, and a few even had store-bought cookies. One of the high points of my Lincoln Valley days occurred for me one night when I briefly excused myself from a community gathering at the schoolhouse for a trip to the outdoor toilet and surprised my Uncle Bill Harris, a few years older than me, kissing Wanda Jean Pompe in the dark near the water pump, just off the school porch. This incident was a high point for me because in return for my promising not to tell anyone about what I had seen, the mortified Wanda Jean, daughter of a local oil company pumper, volunteered that she would give me one of her chocolate cookies every school-day noon from then on. Unfortunately, this wonderful improvement in my school lunches lasted no more than a week because Kathryn soon told Mama on me, and Mama—irrationally, I thought—made me quit blackmailing poor Wanda Jean.

Kathryn wrote in her family-history sketch, "I don't remember ever feeling ashamed or embarrassed that we were poor except that Easter at Lincoln Valley when I was ashamed for Fredie and I to spread our lunch with the other students. It makes me sad to remember a little girl and boy who sat over under a tree (at the picnic across from the school) by ourselves so that the other kids would not see that all we had in our little lunch buckets was leftover homemade biscuits from breakfast with salt pork on them or maybe some peanut butter and jelly."

I don't remember feeling that way. Things hit Kathryn a whole lot harder than they did me, including, for example, Mama and Daddy's often troubled relationship. In her sketch, Kathryn said, "There are a lot of memories I will not elaborate a lot. These being fights, fusses, and problems between Mother and Daddy. Daddy was an alcoholic and a womanizer. He loved to dance and party. Mother was a nagger, very vindictive and quite bitter sometimes. I guess each one was as much at fault as the other."

Being the oldest child, Kathryn often got mixed up in Mama and Daddy's quarrels. Sue and I did not, and, lucky for us, we never developed the kind of psychic scarring that seems to have marred Kathryn's life. Not long before she died, Kathryn told Sue, "I've never lived a happy day." How sad if true.

I do remember a disturbing scene I happened upon one afternoon after walking home from Lincoln Valley School. Mama was gone. Daddy was lying face down on the bare springs of a bedstead we had put outside under a tree for hot summer night sleeping. I was shocked to see that he was apparently crying. Standing stiffly by the side of the bed was Daddy's mother, Ma Harris, a rather severe, hard-shell Baptist woman, who was trying to comfort Daddy "Now, son, she'll come back," Ma was saying, as soothingly as she could manage.

Mama did come back. Life went on.

Sure, there came a time in my early adolescent years when I was casually embarrassed about my parents, as a lot of kids become at that age. I did not know anybody else back then who had a father who drank too much. I assumed that most other families, unlike ours, had no serious money problems. I envisioned them all sitting down to every meal together, cheerful and happy, like Mickey Rooney's Hardy family in the movies. And I was even a little ashamed—Lord, forgive me—that on especially cold winter mornings, Daddy sometimes drove us to school in his cattle truck, when other kids' parents had proper cars.

But neither things like that nor Mama and Daddy's troubles affected me inordinately, as they did poor Kathryn. This was true for a couple of reasons, I think. First of all, I had my own separate life. During my early summers, I mostly lived with my dad's parents, Ma and Pa Harris, and my dad's younger brothers—Dick, Ralph, A. C., Jack, and Bill—when some or all of them were still at home. The uncles spoiled me, treated me like I was someone special, though they teased me a lot. One night while I was asleep, for example, they cut my hair short in front because it was always hanging down in my eyes. But I welcomed even that kind of attention. I was "Bud" to these uncles, a kid brother.

Back then, on my Harris grandparents' rented farm, Pa and Ma always got us up at four o'clock in the morning, well before daylight. Ma started cooking breakfast. Pa and the rest of us headed for the barn. We fed and watered the hogs and chickens and gathered the eggs. We fed, watered, and milked the cows, then ran the milk through a hand-cranked separator that centrifugally split the milk into its constituent skim milk and cream. We fed and watered the horses and mules, harnessed them, and left them standing in the lot, ready to be hooked up to the two wagons that would carry us to the hay field where we had earlier placed the baler and would be working that day.

Then we washed up and went in and sat down to Ma's breakfast of bacon, ham, or sausage; eggs; biscuits; gravy; and ribbon-cane syrup. When we had finished eating each morning, we all had to remain seated at the table while Ma read a chapter from the Bible. (She read Bible chapters to us in sequence each day, and when she had finished the book, she would start all over again at the beginning, with Genesis, chapter one.) By each morning's end of Ma's Bible reading, Pa was always starting to fidget. It was getting closer to daylight, and he wanted to be in the hay field as soon as the sun was barely up enough to dry the dew. But we all had to continue to sit still as Ma next commenced a long and detailed morning prayer. She talked to God as if he were one of her kinfolks who'd been away for a while and had to be brought up to date. Then, the instant Ma finally finished with "Amen," Pa would jump up, grab his hat, and say, "Let's hook 'em up, boys!" We would scatter at once to the horses and mules. Uncle Ake used to claim that he was nearly a grown man before he found out that, right after "Amen," you weren't always supposed to quickly add, "Let's hook 'em up, boys!"

Working as a member of the Haybaling Harrises from age five to twelve, and after that, following the wheat harvest in my dad's crew from Oklahoma to North Dakota for nine straight summers, I always had my own money—and a small personal bank account, even, from about the seventh grade on. I didn't think of myself as being especially poor or deprived. Ma Harris used to say to me, not altogether teasing, "You like us Harrises better than them old Persons, don't you?" Grandma and Grandpa Person were my mother's parents, and truth was I loved them, too. But going along with Ma, I always said I did like the Harrises better. And I was proud to be a Harris. I thought we worked a lot better and harder than most people.

Different in another way from Kathryn, I saw Mama and Daddy more positively, more as whole, basically good people, than she did. I still think of my dad as a quiet, really hard working, tough and wiry, Levis-and-boots-wearing cowboy kind of guy, generous and loyal to his friends and family, totally dependable. The bridge of his nose was fistfight flattened, and his Scots-Irish face was red from a million tiny burst capillaries, except for the starch white top half of his forehead, usually shielded from the sun by a fine Stetson hat. He was a good neighbor to everyone who knew him and had the tightest relationship with friends that I ever knew about, but it was always clear that he "wore no man's collar," as they say. I'm sure he wasn't afraid of anything that walked—on two feet or four. And he needed nothing more than a stern word or two in his low voice—a voice my own kids grew up calling, though they were referring to me, the "Fred Harris voice"—to make a frisky horse stand still for bridling, to send a snarly dog slinking off with his tail between his legs, or to quiet down a too-rowdy kid.

Daddy had been grown all his life, I think. Pa Harris took my dad out of school when he was a little boy to work him in the fields and even to hire him out to others. So Daddy had only about a third-grade education, but he always regretted that and tried to make up for it by studying our school books, particularly history books. And he could do anything— from expert carpentering, to motor repair, to butchering a beef or hog, to curing a ham and making sausage, to dryland farming, to custom combining, to trading cattle.

He emancipated himself by running away from home when he was sixteen. On motorcycles—my dad had traded a horse for his—he and a friend, Shorty McIntyre, went north, working in the broomcorn harvest, among other things, and on a free day in Colorado, even wheeling up the narrow switchback road to the snow-capped summit of Pike's Peak. From age sixteen on, Daddy was able to live by his wits. He was seldom forced to "work for the other fellow," as he put it, and never had to go on welfare, even in hardest times, though he was not overly judgmental about those who did.

During most of my boyhood, Daddy made us a living, and particularly in the later years, a decent one, too, as a cow buyer. Every weekday afternoon, he bought cattle at a local sales-ring auction—in nearby Duncan on Monday, Lawton on Tuesday, Walters on Wednesday, Temple on Thursday, and Waurika on Friday. Every weekday and Saturday morning, he and about five or six other regular Walters cow buyers—including such close friends as gravel-voiced Stud Yoakley, clean and starched Bill Moon, and jolly, overall-bellied John Cofer—gathered early on the downtown Main Street corner in front of Collins Drug, "whittled and spit," traded stories for a while, then, alone or sometimes in two-man ad hoc partnerships, drove out in the country to try to buy—"worth," as they said, meaning worth the money—some local farmer's cattle directly.

A good many times, especially on a Saturday morning, Daddy took me with him on a buying trip to a local farm. I really liked that, and I marveled each time at the way he operated. He would look over a herd of cattle, bunched up in a cow lot or loose out in a pasture, then in his mind grade the individual animals (as stocker calves, say, or fat steers, or old cows, called "canners and cutters"), estimate the weight of each, multiply that by what he knew from the early-morning radio market report was that day's hundredweight price at the Oklahoma City stockyards for that class of animal, calculate and add the whole thing up, then make the farmer a beginning overall offer for the whole group. A haggling ritual would thereafter commence—Daddy called it "chiseling." Sometimes, he would get in his truck, as if to end negotiations and leave, even starting the motor, maybe even beginning slowly to move off, only to be stopped by the farmer's finally agreeing to my dad's last offer.

Once when we were driving away after he had bought a load of cattle like that, I said to him, critically, "You spent thirty minutes arguing, just to make ten bucks."

Daddy replied, "That's a damned sight easier than working for it!" Which reminds me of one time when my dad was drunk and undertook to give Kathryn and me some advice. "Always be nice to everybody, no matter who they are," he said. I remember thinking, *Now, that's a good sentiment.* Then he repeated himself. "Always be nice to everybody," he said, but this time adding, "because you never know when you might make a dime off of 'em." But that was whiskey talk; in reality, he wasn't nearly that cynical.

Daddy also sometimes took me along when he hauled a load of cattle to the stockyards at Oklahoma City. We'd load the cattle in his truck at night, then drive 120 miles northeast to Cow Town, as we called it, on the southwestern outskirts of the "the City." I soon knew by heart the twists and turns of the narrow highway we'd follow and the sequence of towns we'd pass through—Comanche, Duncan, Marlow, Rush Springs, Blanchard, Newcastle, Oklahoma City. I knew where we'd stop for gas, where we'd get hamburgers.

I was an inveterate whistler and a singer. Still am. I guess I got that from Ma Harris, but she whistled and sang only church hymns. I whistle or sing everything, all the time, often unconsciously and without realizing I am doing it until somebody mentions it to me. And I sometimes get started on one song that is stuck in my head at the time and just stay with it, over and over. I think my dad liked to have my company and maybe even liked my whistling and singing some. But on more than one trip to Oklahoma City with him, he suddenly turned to me, exasperated, and said something like, "By God, Fredie, if you have to sing, could you sing something *different* every now and then!" I would.

Hauling cattle, he and I would get to Cow Town around midnight. Daddy would pull into the line of trucks already waiting there in the middle of the brick Main Street. Then, in our turn, we would finally turn left and pull in, then back up to a chute and unload our cattle, consigning them to the stockyards sales agent he always used, Ralph O. Wright. Daddy and I would have a short night's sleep in a second-story hotel room. We would get up early the next morning for a good greasy breakfast at the Stockyards Café, and afterward, he would sometimes buy me and himself some new Levi's—the kind of pants he nearly always wore—at a Main Street western-wear store. Then we would head back home.

Daddy never kept any financial books. He had what we would now call a line-of-credit arrangement with the president of the little Walters National Bank. He wrote a check when he bought a load of cattle, and the bank would process the check like a short-term loan if there weren't sufficient funds in the account to cover it. Then, after Daddy sold the cattle, he deposited his sale check in the bank account. We lived on the difference between the purchase price and the sale price, if there was a profit—and my dad was good enough at what he did that there usually was a profit of some kind.

He regularly threw his check stubs, bank statements, sale slips, and deposit slips, all jumbled together in no order, into an old trunk. Then, at tax time, consulting these records very little if at all, he simply told his accountant at Waurika the amount of federal income tax he wanted to pay that year, and the accountant worked backward from that figure and filled out my dad's tax returns accordingly.

Years later, when I was taking a third-year law school course on taxation, I warned Daddy one weekend that he'd better change his ways, that the Internal Revenue Service could audit him, assess him for underpaid taxes, and make him prove them wrong. I didn't scare him in the least. But the next time I was home, I learned that he had indeed been called in for a federal tax audit and told to bring in all his records for the past four years.

He wasn't worried. "Hell, I'll just take that old trunk down there and dump all my check stubs and deposit slips on their desk and let *them* figure it out."

"You're in a lot of trouble," I said.

Back home again a few weeks later, I immediately asked about the tax audit. "It was a woman auditor," Daddy said. "I took her everything in my trunk, just like I said I would. She called me back in about a week. Turned out her own daddy was a cow buyer, too. She said, 'Mr. Harris, I can't make heads or tails out of your records, but I can tell that you haven't made much money.' I said, 'Hell, I could have told you that!'"

My dad was on that occasion confirmed again in his lifelong philosophy: Things are never as bad as you think they are. And for him, and the rest of us in the family, they usually never were—at least not until he came down with the highly aggressive lung cancer, from heavy smoking since childhood, that quickly killed him very soon after the cancer was detected. When he told me what he had and about the bad prognosis, I said—meaning it as a great compliment, and that's the way he took it—"Well, you've been a tough son of a bitch."

"Not tough enough for this," he said.

It was the only thing I ever knew about that he was not tough enough for.

2

—∞—

Growing Up Okie

WE MOVED INTO TOWN—INTO WALTERS—IN 1937, after being starved out of farming by the Great Depression, which drove a lot of other poor and busted Dust Bowl Okies to California. We stayed. Daddy rented a narrow glass-fronted one-story brick building on the strip of concrete highway at our little town's north-end "foot of the hill." There, he opened a grocery store, intending, I guess, to make us a living primarily by using his skills at buying livestock, butchering, and meat cutting, though we also sold all the other usual grocery products, too.

Our family lived in the back part of the one big room in that little grocery building, behind a makeshift wall of homemade quilts that Mama had hung over a galvanized clothes line, stretched from one side wall of the store to the other. I was going on seven and started the second grade when the Walters school opened its doors that fall (and enjoyed everything about school that year except the penmanship lessons). I went to Cub Scout meetings at the white two-story home of the county sheriff's son, about a block and half up the hill toward the main part of town and across the street west from the county courthouse.

But the Depression proved to be just as tough on the grocery business as on farming. Daddy sold groceries "on the credit." You had to in those days, if you were going to attract and keep customers. "Put it on my bill," the customer would say, after the bought groceries were sacked and the price for them was totaled up on a pad. And in those hard times, as weeks and months went by, Daddy was never able to collect on a lot of those bills.

He closed the door of Harris Grocery after a year and finally went full time into buying and selling cattle for a living. We moved to the second of what would be our twelve homes in Walters, the low-lying five-room frame Billings place on the east edge of town. We were to live there twice, as it turned out. There was a city water hydrant in our backyard, but no water line, or sewer line, in the house itself. No telephone or gas, either. No electricity, the first time we lived there.

The only heat in the house was from a cheap, thin-skinned woodstove in the dining room. Mama cooked on a coal-oil cookstove in the kitchen. Kathryn and I did our school lessons at night by the light of a coal-oil lamp. One of Kathryn's chores was to keep our lamp globes cleaned of soot. My own chores included carrying in stove wood and buckets of water, keeping the lamps and the cookstove tank filled with coal oil, and feeding and taking care of the livestock. The first time we lived at the Billings place, I slept nights on the divan in the front room, while Kathryn and Sue occupied one of the house's two bedrooms, the northwest one. The second time we lived at the Billings place, we not only had electricity by then, but Daddy walled in and insulated the house's small back porch so that I could have my own room.

We had a big floor-model cabinet radio, powered by a car battery. To get reception, we had to run two wires from it out the window, one up to a copper-wire antenna stretched on the roof, the other to a metal stake hammered into the outside dirt as a ground, and taking care of all this soon became my job, for this house as well as later homes of ours. Radio programs were great entertainment, especially for us kids, second only to the local picture shows. It was at this Billings place, the first time, that Kathryn, little Sue, and I, huddled all by ourselves around the radio one night (I don't know where Mama and Daddy were; they often left us with Kathryn more or less in charge) and had the living daylights scared out of us, worse than when Aunt Vera told us ghost stories, as we listened to Orson Welles' now famous *War of the Worlds* program. We half believed that aliens from Mars might at any moment show up at our back door.

At that Billings house, we had a large, mostly dirt yard that Mama had us sweep from time to time, in the southern way, to keep it neat. There was a dugout storm cellar—a dirt-floored, dank, and spidery place where Mama stored her jars of home-canned fruits and vegetables and where, when the clouds looked bad some nights and Daddy roused us out of bed, we'd run to, and hide out in, until the storm blew over. We had an out-house, a chicken house, a small tin-roofed barn with a big cow lot, a large and bountiful vegetable-garden plot that the whole family worked in and watered by hand under Daddy's close supervision, and a few acres of oat pasture. We had our own milk cow. We raised chickens for eggs and fryers, a hog and a calf for our own pork and beef.

Mama was always busy. In addition to keeping house; looking after us kids; cooking our meals; washing, hanging, and ironing our clothes (with our help); picking and canning fruits and vegetables for us; sewing all the girls' clothes (which she could expertly do, without a pattern, just by looking at a picture of a dress or blouse she wanted to replicate); and making our quilts, Mama also worked at outside jobs—from cleaning other people's houses (for twenty-five cents an hour, originally), to washing other people's clothes at a help-yourself laundry, to clerking at the Walters and Temple cattle-sale barns. She had only an eighth-grade education, but she was smart, and she taught herself some rudimentary accounting and how to handle sale slips and payments. And she was good at dealing with people.

My sisters and I thought Mama was quite pretty, especially when she dressed up, though she was self-conscious, I think, about being a little heavy sometimes and about her overly brown and sun-damaged arms and neck from having had to work in the sun so much. She laughed a lot, pale blue eyes sparkling. She had really close women friends. All her life, she had always worked hard and been her own boss. She had been able to sign checks on her father's bank account from the time she was a teenager until she married Daddy.

You could depend on Mama in a crisis. "I wait until afterwards to go to pieces," she used to say. She was often called upon to serve as a midwife (as she did, later, with our first two babies, both born at home, the second one tragically born dead). A number of girl babies in our county were named Alene after her. She was a feminist before her time. I was with her on more than one occasion when she would shame a man—a store owner, say—into gender fairness by saying something like, "You treat me like this because I'm a woman; it'd be different if you were dealing with my husband."

Mama was not demonstrably religious, but she did encourage us kids to go to church and Sunday school at the First Baptist Church. I do not remember her as much of a hugger, though my sisters and I never wondered whether she loved us. She would have gone hungry to be sure we had enough to eat—and maybe did in our earliest years, when cornbread, greens, beans, and milk were our frequent suppers.

I would bet that for the longest time, Mama and Daddy did not know for sure what to make of me. If I had been born in a hospital, they would probably have wondered whether I had been switched at birth for someone else's baby. I was a virtually insatiable reader. I loved school and whizzed through my classes with astonishing ease. Who *is* this boy?

Nobody had to tell me to go to work, either. I used to say that I sponged off my folks until I was five, and then I got embarrassed about that, straightened up, and went out and got a job. That was a joke, but it was pretty near the truth, too. Summers, until I was twelve, I worked all day, usually bare-headed and bare-backed, in the hay fields with Pa Harris and some or all of my uncles. Starting out riding the horse that powered the baler, I then moved on to "monkeying wires," and finally wound up in the later years driving a two-horse or two-mule buckrake, walking behind it all day to bring hay to the baler. In that last job, I learned to cuss real well and colorfully, which seemed pretty much like a requirement when you were dealing with a team of hard-mouthed horses or mules. I still remember the names of horses and mules I worked, like the big, gentle, slow-moving bay horse, Barney; the one-eyed sorrel, Sam, scared to death of barbed wire; and tough little Jude, a sorrel jenny with a knot on her side, just right for a stirrup, who could run like a racehorse.

After I turned twelve, I worked that summer and the next eight as a part of my dad's custom-combining crew, cutting wheat for hire, starting each late May in Oklahoma and winding up each late August in North Dakota. On the wheat harvest, I began as a tractor driver in the field and finally graduated to driving a grain truck on road and highway.

During each Walters school year, I worked at odd jobs, sometimes two or more at the same time: as a horse, pulling in harness an ultra heavy homemade motored lawnmower for a guy who cut lawns for a living; shining shoes at a local barbershop; sweeping floors, cleaning restrooms, and washing windows at a dry goods store; washing and cleaning used electrical motors in an appliance repair shop; and, of course, delivering newspapers. I got a job as a printer my senior year in high school. By the time I went off to college, I owned seven head of cattle of my own and, that year, raised twenty acres of my own farmed-on-the-shares wheat.

People have asked me when and how I decided to become a lawyer and a politician. I sometimes say that it is like the story of how a certain evangelical preacher got his vocation. The man, the story goes, was picking cotton one long and sweltering afternoon when, worn out, he suddenly dropped to his knees, raised his eyes toward heaven, and said, "Lord, these old rows're getting longer and longer, this old cotton sack's getting heavier and heavier, and that old sun's getting hotter and hotter, and Lord, I guess what I'm trying to say to you is that I think I feel the call to preach." You might say that I worked in the fields, and at a lot of other hard jobs, until I felt the call to go into law and politics.

One day when I was a sophomore at Walters High School and sitting in a required study hall, I decided to check through some shelved books, trying to find something to read to while away an otherwise idle and boring hour. I picked out a book on careers that described all the main occupations and professions. More or less by the process of elimination, I settled that day on law. I decided that I would be a lawyer, partly because I couldn't find anything else in the book that I wanted to be.

Other considerations soon led me in the same direction. I was acutely interested, together with a couple of close high school friends, in radio technology. Lying about my age, I had signed up and taken a pay-by-the-month correspondence course from the National Radio Institute. But, looking around Walters later, I saw that the only person working in that field was a repairman who was barely getting by in a little hole-in-the-wall shop. Not for me, I decided. By contrast, the few lawyers in Walters seemed to me to have amounted to something, though Ma Harris wasn't too high on that profession. She had always wanted me to be a preacher, and much later, when I was getting ready to go off to college and I told her my career choice, she let me know that she thought I was heading in exactly the wrong direction by deciding to be a "*lie*-yer." I respectfully told Ma that there was as great a need for lawyers as for preachers and that I saw no reason why I couldn't be both a good person and a good lawyer.

And I think that I understood early, too, that there could be some connection between the law profession and politics. Walters lawyers held elective office—county attorney, state representative. The speaker for our annual Future Farmers of America (FFA) father-son banquet had been the dynamic orator Robert S. Kerr. Kerr impressed me. He had started out as a lawyer, had lately completed a term as Oklahoma's governor, and was then a Democratic candidate for the United States Senate, a race he would win. I had no way of knowing, of course, that seventeen years after I saw Senator Kerr that time, I would myself be elected to his U.S. Senate seat, but to tell the truth, I don't think I would have ridiculed a prediction like that about my future, if someone had made it back then.

The summer before my senior year in high school, day after day riding around boring wheat fields on a tractor, I got to thinking about two things I wanted to do when I returned to school the following fall. A friend and classmate of mine, Dan Bigbee, had the preceding year won the FFA state oratorical contest, and he had also served as the president of the Walters High School student council, elected to that position in a schoolwide vote. Why couldn't *I* do both those things? No reason not.

Back home that fall, I did my own research and wrote a speech about the exploding world population and the resultant pressures on the food supply. I titled my speech "Can Our Earth Feed Its People?" With my set presentation, followed by an onstage strenuous question-and-answer session with judges, I won the state FFA oratorical contest, held at Oklahoma A&M. After that, I won the regional championship at Texas A&M. That earned me a trip to the national in Atlanta. The Walters Rotary Club put up the money for my dad to go there with me on the train, but I placed only second in the national. As a result of the whole process, though, I found that I had a great interest in, and some ability at dealing with, social problems, logical argument, public speaking, and thinking on my feet.

I appeared in a number of school plays at Walters, and I found that I liked that, too. I also really enjoyed, and profited from, a one-semester senior-year speech class I took from the dramatic and well-spoken Marguerite Mullins, who believed in me and was to become a friend and supporter, though she was the daughter of a local Republican lawyer and a Republican herself. Looking back on that class, I find it especially interesting that I was already disturbed by the prevalent discrimination against African Americans; as one required class exercise, I chose to recite Shylock's speech, from *The Merchant of Venice*, but changed "Jew" to "Negro": "Hath not a *Negro* . . . senses, affections, passions . . . ? If you prick us, do we not bleed?" (And, growing up in Oklahoma, it was only later that I became equally aware of, and disturbed by, discrimination against Jews). Where did my early sympathy for the plight of African Americans come from? I am not sure. I must have, unlike a lot of people I knew, including members of my own Mississippi-origin family, internalized the words I had memorized in school from Jefferson's Declaration of Independence and Lincoln's Gettysburg Address, both of which proclaimed that "all men are created equal." I know that I early took to heart the words of the kids' Christian hymn, "Red and yellow, black and white; they are precious in His sight."

In my last year in high school, I was, as I had planned, elected president of the student council. Among other things, this meant that I presided over each Wednesday's all-school assembly and introduced the speaker or program of the day. On those weekly occasions when the whole school was packed into the gym, it got to be a funny habit of the students to stand and cheer me almost interminably the minute I walked onto the stage. Strangely, I did not find this student behavior the least bit offensive.

I have to say also that figuring in the mix of my thinking as I was making my decision about the law as a profession, which I knew was somehow related to politics, was the fact that I'd had drummed into me in school and through Ma Harris's good old Baptist teachings that "Service to humanity is the best work of life," as the Jaycee Creed that I was later to memorize would put it. And even then, I think, I had a strong desire to somehow make a mark, so that I wouldn't wind up, as a country and western song was later to put it, "Just a line in the *Oklahoma City Times*."

I knew I would have to go to college, but how was I going to do that? Nobody in my immediate family had gone. There weren't many scholarships in those days; so it was clear to me that I would have to learn a trade of some kind, one that would pay well enough to allow me to work my way through undergraduate school and law school. I looked around Walters again, and printing was the only locally available trade I could see that would fit the requirement. I presented myself right away to the newspaper office in Walters, where in the back shop, they did job printing, things like wedding invitations and church bulletins, mostly on Saturdays, and put out two country weeklies, the *Temple Tribune* on Wednesday nights and the *Walters Herald* on Thursday nights.

I went to see the curmudgeonly editor, John Penn. "I want to learn to be a printer," I told him. "I'll work cheap until I do."

"You mean a reporter, like you've seen in the picture shows?" he asked, skeptical.

"No sir," I said. "I want to learn the printing trade."

He offered me a job at five dollars a week, as long as he could pay me in cash and would not have to withhold taxes or Social Security. I worked hard, learned fast, and became at least in my own mind a journeyman printer. Before long, I caught John Penn alone one night by the paper-stock shelves and hit him up for a raise.

"How much you asking for?" he wanted to know.

"Seven-fifty a week, I was thinking," I said.

"My God!" he said, "you've only been here three months, and you already want a fifty percent raise?"

I hadn't thought about it that way. But I was worth it by then. John Penn liked me and gave in after a little obligatory grumbling. Working for him that school year was the way I learned the skill that would eventually help pay my way to a law degree. I also began to make some extra money on the side, printing cards and announcements at home on a small printing press, together with ten cases of hand-set type, that I had bought for myself.

— ℛℛ— —ℛℛ— —ℛℛ—

I loved growing up in Walters, Oklahoma. My senior year in high school was especially satisfying. At the start of that year, my dad bought the only house in town that he ever owned (though when I left home, he did buy and move to a farm). My senior year in high school, Daddy also bought the only new car he ever owned. The house was a quite respectable, wide white-frame house, catty-corner from the football stadium. My dad quickly built on a bedroom in back for me, with its own outside entrance. The house was a great place to bring my friends; I particularly remember a large surprise birthday party held there when I turned seventeen, when by secret agreement, everybody's present was a pair of socks, and I, before I finally got the joke, kept saying, trying my best to sound sincere as I unwrapped each new gift, "Oh, more socks! Just what I needed." The new car Daddy bought was a gleaming black 1948 Plymouth four-door sedan. I drove it a lot—on dates around town, to Lawton to the movies, to out-of-town football games.

These two things were highly unusual in my young life: our own home in town; our own new car. I did not think about it at the time, but obviously I was the reason Daddy bought them both. He wanted me to have a good last year in high school.

And that's the way it turned out. Not just because of the home and car. Nor my being elected president of the student council, or winning the state FFA oratorical contest, or continuing to have really close friends and classmates with whom I would stay in touch for the rest of my life, or being chosen Best All-Around Boy the year I graduated, or learning the printing trade that would help put me through college and law school, or fixing on a profession and vocation—law and politics. There was more.

I met LaDonna Crawford.

She was exotic. (Well, as exotic as it got in those days in Walters, Oklahoma.) She was an attractive, well-dressed, tall, dark Comanche Indian girl with green eyes (inherited from her father, a white guy who was long out of the picture, as I was to learn). I quickly noticed LaDonna on the school grounds that Fall, her first year at Walters High, and I asked around about her. She was a junior, a year behind me. Raised by her maternal Comanche grandparents—the Tabbytites—with Comanche as her first language, she had grown up on a farm south of Walters and west of Temple, just across East Cache Creek from where I had once lived as a child, on the Pres Baten place. LaDonna and I had never met back then, of course, but she would later tell me, "It was probably you Harrises who were slipping in and stealing Papa's pecans," causing him to frequently patrol his woods with a shotgun. I never denied it.

Together with her aunt, who was in my twelfth-grade class, LaDonna had rented a walk-up apartment on the second floor of the red brick post office building, just across the street north of the Walters school. Two high school girls living on their own in town: that was pretty exotic itself. Their large one-room apartment was soon to become a sort of hangout for me, my daytime home away from home. My closest pal, Ernest Hoodenpyle, Jr., thought I'd come down with a bad case of "the sweet ass," as people said. He wasn't far wrong.

LaDonna later told me that, early that year, she had asked one of her classmates who the president of the student council was, and when the girl pointed me out, LaDonna said, "That skinny little guy?"

Skinny? Little? I would have preferred lean, wiry, or tough. But whatever, I was glad that she was attracted to me, even if it was my school position that first interested her, as she would later admit. One night, I drove out in the country in the new black Plymouth to the home of a Comanche Indian friend and classmate, Reeves Nahwooks, whose mostly family birthday party I'd heard LaDonna was attending. An admiring little kid I knew, Mickey Titchywy, came out to the car, and I sent him back in to ask LaDonna to come out. She later told me that inside, Mickey had rushed up to her in front of everybody and, breathless, said, "Fred R. Harris"—saying the whole formal name that I was by then using—"is outside and wants to see you!"

LaDonna came out. We talked briefly. She would not leave the party or let me wait and drive her home afterward, but we both felt, right then, that something was happening between us.

It was. We became inseparable. She was warm, open, guileless, and really smart in a native, and Native, kind of way, with great intuition about people and things. She liked to laugh, a quality that was very important to me. And she liked me, which was also very important to me. We soon wound up in a school play together and in a number of other school activities.

All my life, for some reason, I had always been greatly interested in things Indian, and now I became absorbed in learning Comanche history, customs, songs, and language. I spent a lot of time at LaDonna's grandparents' rural home. Her grandmother, Wick-kie, wore long braids and traditionally cut flowered-cloth dresses, with butterfly sleeves and, around the waist, a folded blanket—a *peetsqueena*, in Comanche—cinched with a leather belt. She was one of the most intelligent and genuinely good persons I have ever known. Though born in a tipi in Comanche chief Quanah Parker's front yard near Cache, Oklahoma, and raised traditionally, she had become a faithful Christian and regularly attended a local Comanche church, where all the services and songs were in her native language.

Wick-kie had a marvelous green thumb; she could grow anything and always had a wonderful flower and vegetable garden that she and the kids watered by hand. Years later, when LaDonna and I brought her to visit us for a few days in Washington, where she was a sensation, we took her to Mount Vernon; on a tour of Washington, D.C.'s great monuments and the capitol; to the U.S. Senate, where she met some of its more famous members and leaders; to the White House for a private tea with Lady Bird Johnson; and to the Hickory Hill home of our McLean, Virginia, neighbor and friend, Ethel Kennedy. Afterward, Wick-kie was interviewed for a feature article, with photo, by a *Washington Post* reporter, who asked her what had most impressed her so far about her visit to the nation's capital. Without hesitation, Wick-kie said, "All the flowers and green plants." As a matter of fact, that whole day, from Mount Vernon on, she'd surreptitiously snapped off cuttings of various plants she liked and tucked them away, wrapped in moist tissue, to take back home to much-drier Oklahoma.

Tabbytite, LaDonna's grandfather, could speak very few words of English, though he could understand English a little, and he could not read or write. He wore long braids and, in the Comanche way, regularly plucked all his facial hair—his naturally sparse whiskers, as well as his eyebrows, eyelashes, everything. He was not a Christian but an adherent of the peyote way and an eagle-medicine man. At the same time, he was an industrious and hardworking farmer who had owned the first automobile sold in our county. He herded his own cattle, on horseback, until he was into his nineties, when he finally had to leave the farm and move in with his daughter, LaDonna's mother, in Lawton.

Born in the wild, Tabbytite was a man who had literally lived "from arrows to atoms," but television proved to be a little too much for him. In his late years, he loved watching it at his daughter's home, all right, but he believed that people on television could see the viewers. So, he never watched his favorite programs without first dressing up in his best clothes, hair newly braided, the two braids nicely wrapped in red felt, and with a colorful scarf tied at his neck. The old man especially liked a Saturday morning children's program of that period, starring a Miss Francis, and he regularly, smartly answered the simple questions she sweetly put to her intended young listeners, questions such as, "Did you eat a good breakfast this morning?" And when the Cisco Kid and Pancho, at the end of their program, rode their horses right up to the screen, waved, and shouted, "Adios, amigos!" Tabbytite waved right back to them and called out, "Adios!"

LaDonna and I were living in Lawton when I first appeared on television as a candidate for the Oklahoma State Senate. That night, she and I drove back from a live telecast at the local station to LaDonna's mother's house in Lawton to find out how LaDonna's mother and grandmother thought I had done. LaDonna's mother met us at her front door to give me a quick, quiet warning. She said that Tabbytite and the two women had gotten into a fractious argument while watching me on television because the old man kept insisting that I could see them while I was on camera. LaDonna's mother told me that I should quickly prepare myself to set him straight.

Sure enough, LaDonna and I had hardly sat down at the kitchen table for some coffee with everyone when Tabbytite confronted me. "Fredie," he said, talking partly in Comanche, partly in English, "tell these crazy women you can see us when you're on television."

"No, Papa," I said, "it's just the same thing as when you take a picture with a Kodak camera, except that you see the picture right now." Pretty clever explanation, I thought.

But it didn't work. "No," Tabbytite said, disgusted, "it's not like that; we can *hear* you, too!"

That was the end of that. And the old man told the two women later, after LaDonna and I had gone home, "Fredie may know a lot of things, but he doesn't know much about television!"

Of course, that incident, and my becoming a lawyer and a candidate for public office, were eight years ahead in the future when I was still a senior at Walters High School. In the meantime, I had to figure out how I might go to college and law school.

3

—⟊—

Education of a Democrat

HOW EXACTLY DID A PERSON GO ABOUT attending college and becoming a lawyer? Toward the middle of my last high school year, I still did
not have a very good answer to that question. I couldn't ask my parents.
They wouldn't have known what to tell me. And, unfortunately, the Walters school system had no college-advisement or career counselors.

I talked personally with the school superintendent, Clarence Davis, to
get his advice. He was encouraging, but he told me that he was not well
informed about the study of law, since he had attended Oklahoma A&M,
while the state's public law school was located at the University of Oklahoma. He suggested that I go to see the local county attorney, Luther Eubanks, a recently returned World War II veteran whose office was in the
downtown county courthouse.

Red-faced, sandy-haired Luther Eubanks, a down-home friendly man
with a toothy smile and a country way of talking, had himself been a prod-
uct of the OU College of Law just before going off to serve in WWII. He
took a special interest in me from our first meeting. He not only told me
what I needed to know, but also offered to drive me personally up to Norman and help me get situated at OU. And a little ahead of the beginning
of fall classes, that is exactly what he did.

We left Walters one morning in Luther's old 1938 Plymouth. But soon
after we got started, he suggested that we deviate a little from our direct
route to Norman, to go through the town of Purcell and see Jim Nance,
whom Luther knew, the editor and publisher of the *Purcell Register* and the
current, and very powerful, Speaker of the Oklahoma House of Representatives. Luther was surprised when I told him that I had never met
Nance. "But he's your boss," Luther said, explaining that Nance had once

lived in Walters and was the present absentee owner of the *Walters Herald,* where I worked.

In Purcell, Nance welcomed us into his newspaper office, and Luther told him about me and our present mission. The Speaker immediately picked up the telephone on his desk and called George Cross, president of the University of Oklahoma. He told President Cross that he was sending him "an outstanding young man from Walters who works for me," who was coming to OU to get a law degree, and who needed a job as a printer. (During the six years I was at OU, any time I saw President Cross, he seldom failed to ask me how "our mutual friend," Jim Nance, was doing. I always answered, "Just fine," or something like that, though after that one brief encounter, I did not see Jim Nance again until many years later.) Speaker Nance next called Fayette Copeland, dean of the OU School of Journalism (and, as we found out later, so had President Cross), with the same message. When Luther and I got to Norman and went to see Dean Copeland, he wound up inviting me to stay in his own home for a week, before the university dormitories opened, and eventually helped me get a good-paying job as a printer on the *Oklahoma Daily,* the campus newspaper, after I first worked for a semester for lower pay in the Journalism School Library until the printing job opened up. (Years later, in 1997, the OU School of Journalism, at a banquet on campus, bestowed on me their Outstanding Alumnus award. I suspect they thought I was a journalism graduate, since I had been around the Journalism School so long in my printing and library jobs. But when I got around to raising this question, the announcement of the award had already been made, and school officials hurriedly, and a little unconvincingly, said that you did not actually have to be a journalism graduate to get the honor. So, I thought, *Who am I to look a gift award in the mouth?*)

Much, much later, after I'd become a U.S. senator, I caused President Lyndon Johnson to appoint Luther Eubanks as a federal district judge, as senators can do. Today, students sometimes ask me how one plans a career to become a federal district judge, and I am tempted to say, "Pick out some young person very early whom you think has a good chance to become a U.S. senator and help him or her like crazy." That worked pretty well for Luther Eubanks. And he made a very good federal judge, too, as I believed he would when I got him appointed.

〜〜 〜〜 〜〜

Although I had been selected Best All-Around Boy of my 1948 high school graduating class, I was not the class valedictorian. Not the class salutatorian either. Both those highest and next-highest high school class honors were based on grades. It seems strange, now, but it is the gospel truth that, up until the moment when the valedictorian and salutatorian selections were publicly announced, late in my senior year in high school, it had never once occurred to me that there was any importance attached to making excellent grades. Really. I had always made good grades, but largely without exerting myself and certainly without calling attention to the fact that schoolwork was easy for me. A kind of undercurrent culture in school held that making good grades was for girls and sissies.

I remember actually being puzzled, and a little resentful, when my stern and demanding teacher in a senior-year world-history course, Mrs. Lee Mershon, said to me once after handing back exams, "Fred, you should put more effort into your work for this class."

My defensive rejoinder was, "I made a ninety-three on the test."

"You could do better," Mrs. Mershon said, "and you could learn more, if you'd apply yourself more."

Another thing Mrs. Mershon told me on that occasion was, "Young man, you've got too many irons in the fire." She may have had a point there, too, but I didn't change on that—and never have. I was working as a printer, after school and on Saturdays; running my own home print shop; serving as president of the student council; making numerous out of town FFA speaking and livestock-judging trips; acting in plays; and farming some—as well as hunting squirrels and fishing the creeks and doing all the other fun things, and occasionally wild things, that kids do. I also went out for track, basketball, and football, but I was small and late developing, close to a year younger than most of my classmates, and I never got good at sports, though that didn't keep me from trying—or dreaming of being a star. I did earn two high school football letters, but as a result of only minimal playing time.

I would eventually see the wisdom in Mrs. Mershon's advice about applying myself more to my studies, but only after I entered the University of Oklahoma. As a direct result of that intensified later focus, I spent six of the very best and most satisfying and worthwhile years of my life at OU. A new world opened for me. I found my undergraduate classes engrossing, even exciting—English literature's jewels, including Shakespeare's tragedies and Thomas Hardy's *Return of the Native*; international relations; geology and botany; a great philosophy course called Education for Democracy; anthropology and archaeology, which especially fascinated me; history classes, particularly one on English and American Origins of the U.S. Constitution; Latin; and even algebra. I was like a hungry customer at a Furr's Cafeteria. And the effect of my attention to my classes showed up in my grades. Scared as I had been to start with, it actually came as something of a surprise to me that all my freshman-year grades (as well as, later, all my undergraduate grades) turned out to be A's, except for one B each semester. I was named to the dean's honor roll and selected for membership in the first-year honorary society Phi Eta Sigma.

I got very much involved in extracurricular activities, too. My freshman dorm counselor, a married Ph.D. student, recruited me into OU's oldest organization, the Congress Club, or more properly, the Congress Literary and Debating Society. The club was mostly made up of older, progressive-minded, activist but fun-loving and irreverent law students (and, unbeknownst to me, was already dying because nobody had bothered for three or four years to take in any new members). At my first meeting, I was among those who were required to draw a topic out of a hat and give an immediate extemporaneous five-minute speech on it. My topic, about which I knew virtually nothing, turned out to be "Compulsory Arbitration in Settling Labor Disputes." So shaky I could hardly stand, I somehow got up. I took my cue from the word "compulsory" and, drawing on my naturally populist and pro–New Deal background, spoke in opposition. That and the fact that I used the leftist-tinged word "bosses" several times in my speech, frankly because I was so nervous that the word "employers" wouldn't come to me, earned me the approval and applause of the mostly union-sympathizing Congress Club members. Their pity for me probably had something to do with this, too, I suspect. At any rate, several in that bunch of impressive law students soon more or less adopted me as a protégé. They got me involved in campus and state politics; for example, I became an extremely low-level volunteer in the successful campaign of U.S. Representative A. S. Mike Monroney for the U.S. Senate, a man whose colleague in the Senate I would eventually become. And these Congress Club law students were also to be lifelong friends and political supporters of mine.

But I was pretty lonely and homesick a good part of the time that first year at OU, despite the fact that I hitchhiked from Norman to Walters to see LaDonna Crawford nearly every other weekend. Finally, toward the end of my freshman year in college and her last year in high school, she and I decided it was time we got married. We went to tell my parents. My mother cried, and LaDonna's mother, who thought LaDonna could do better, did too. My dad got mad—actually more hurt than anything, I think, because, as he said to me that night, "Well, that's the end of your damn law school!" I disagreed, arguing that with both me and LaDonna working, I would have an even better chance than before of getting a law degree. I proved to be right about that.

LaDonna and I were both nineteen at the time. By law, she did not need parental approval for marriage. I did. My dad reluctantly, and sullenly, drove me in his pickup to the county clerk's office to sign for me so that I could get a license. We rode in silence, neither speaking a word to the other, until just before we arrived at the courthouse. As we got out, he said, "By God, don't you ever ask me for anything!"

My angry retort was just as unfair and unmeant: "When have I *ever*?"

I saved some money from my work in the wheat harvest that summer, and moving to Norman for fall classes, LaDonna and I found cheap University married housing in some former Navy prefabs with outdoor community toilets and showers. I continued in my job as a printer, and she soon found an office job with the OU Extension Division. We made ends meet, but just barely, especially when, before long, we had a wonderful blond Indian baby girl, Kathryn, to love and raise.

I worked in the wheat harvest again that next summer, and then applied for an OU tuition scholarship the following fall. Soon, I received a telephone call to say that I was one of five or six students under consideration for the Robert Dean Bass Memorial Scholarship. I hadn't applied for it, didn't know about it, but I was told that all OU student scholarship applicants were automatically considered for any scholarship for which they were eligible. The catch was that I, along with the other students being considered, had to submit to a personal interview by a committee of OU deans and departmental chairs. I agreed, and we set the date and time for my interview.

After hanging up the phone, I quickly grabbed a copy of the university catalog and with near-palsied hands found in it the reference to the Bass scholarship, established by his family to honor a young man who had tragically been killed in WWII. The good news—no, the *astounding* news—was that the Bass scholarship was OU's largest and was for $640!

All the money in the world, it seemed to me at the time, when OU's semester tuition was only $48. My heart pounded when I read the amount, but there was worrisome news in the catalog, too: the Bass scholarship's interview requirement, of course, and a statement that the scholarship was to be awarded to an outstanding third-year student in political science or economics "who believes in the free enterprise system." I did, and do, of course, but I somehow doubted that I could just simply affirm that fact to the interview committee and then expect them immediately to declare, "Here's the money, Son."

When, a few days later, I nervously entered the interview room at my appointed time, I found the forbidding-looking committee members to be the dean of the College of Law, the dean of the College of Arts and Sciences, and the chairs of the political science and economics departments. Earl Sneed, the law dean (whom I would later work for in law school as his administrative assistant) asked the first question: What did I think about socialized law? I had never heard of such a thing, but I figured I should be against anything socialized and said so. That seemed to work. But Dean Sneed's second question was harder: What did I think about the current Chrysler strike? I was hardly aware that there was one, but I was afraid to admit that. Instead, I stumbled through a rambling, noncommittal answer, saying "on the one hand" and "on the other hand" several times before I was miraculously saved by the kindly Arts and Sciences dean—bless his heart—who said something like, "I think what you're trying to say is that labor-management disputes cannot be judged in the abstract, but only on the issues involved in the particular dispute. Isn't that correct?"

"Exactly," I said, relieved and grateful to that man forever. Things went a little more smoothly after that. And I got the money. Hallelujah!

I was elected president of the large and active OU League of Young Democrats. In that capacity, I spoke out publicly against U.S. Senator Joseph McCarthy and his bullying, false, and sensationalist red baiting, thereby earning my first editorial denunciation by the *Daily Oklahoman*; the newspaper said that they were worried about America's future if I was any example of the country's young leaders. I conducted a much-publicized campus poll that backed President Harry Truman's firing of General Douglas MacArthur as our Korean War commander.

One day, Charles Ablard, a friend and classmate who was president of the campus League of Young Republicans, told me that he'd been fascinated by a visit he'd just made to the Oklahoma legislature and that he'd come up with an idea that would give him, and me, a reason to hang out a good deal at the state capitol: he, as a Republican, and I, as a Democrat, would cohost a bipartisan weekly broadcast, reporting on the state legislature, on OU's statewide radio station, WNAD. An OU vice president approved this strange, and for the university somewhat politically risky, proposal, as long as a designated political science professor approved our radio scripts in advance. As it turned out, Ablard and I never prepared any scripts, and the friendly professor let us get away with this. We personally visited the legislature one day each week, and that allowed us to write, and read on the air, one or two original news items, but mostly we clipped legislative-news articles from the newspapers and shamelessly took turns reading these on the air, virtually unchanged. Embarrassingly amateurish as we were as radio commentators, Ablard and I did in the process learn a lot about Oklahoma government and politics and about how the state legislature operated.

At the end of my undergraduate years, I made Phi Beta Kappa and was selected for Pe-Et, a society made up of the university's ten most out-standing senior men. Then I was on to law school.

But the summer before we entered, Charles Ablard had talked me into taking a battery of oral and written OU-developed aptitude tests to see if he and I were really fitted for law study and lawyering. He was in doubt about whether he should go to law school. I was not, but I agreed to go with him anyway—when he admitted that he had already signed me up. He wound up hating the hours-long tests. I actually enjoyed them. He would not go back to get the results. I did. Mine showed that I had, as the testers put it, both an A-plus aptitude for and an A-plus interest in law and the law profession.

For me, those assessments, or predictions, proved to be quite accurate. I loved law school, too—the mental discipline, the acquisition of greater skills in logical reasoning and verbal and written expression, the close stu-dent camaraderie, the brilliant and challenging professors.

It has been my observation that new law students often take a semester or two to "break the code"—to learn how to study law and write exams. That was not true for me. I was instantly ready, somehow having come to the study of law—maybe somewhat unfairly, I thought, partly by accident or from birth—with exactly the peculiar set of mental skills and prepara-

tion that guarantee law-school success. So, at the end of my very first semester in the OU College of Law, I fell into what turned out to be a three-
year practice of "teaching" exam-review sessions for each of our courses
for a small group of my closest classmates. Still, before first-semester
grades were posted, I was as nervous and apprehensive as everybody else,
then was literally dumbfounded when an upperclassman who worked in
the law-school office called me one night with the advance word that I had
scored the highest grades ever made by a first-year student at the OU College of Law, nothing lower than an A-minus. Good Lord!

But, as always, I was not just concentrating on my studies. I was a husband and father. I was involved in campus activities. I continued to work
long hours as a printer. And then I decided to launch into something completely different: a 1952 campaign for public office. Another first-year law
student, Cleeta John Rogers of Oklahoma City, who like me had recently
turned twenty-one, told me he was going to run for an open seat in the
Oklahoma House of Representatives and urged me to do the same in my
home county, Cotton County, for the seat that my old friend Luther Eubanks was by then vacating. My law school professors really frowned on
this. "The law is a jealous mistress," Dean Earl Sneed was fond of saying.
But I went ahead and did it anyway. Back home, my dad, though a little
puzzled by my plans, generously bought me without my asking a used
1946 Ford sedan, my first car, for use in the campaign.

My main opponent was a longtime county commissioner, Bart Nelson.
Some people thought that at seventy-two he was too old for the job. Others thought that I was too young. But I was becoming a good speaker,
while Nelson was an unpracticed one. I knew state issues and the state
legislature; he did not. I outworked him that summer, making a personal,
house-to-house campaign. A lot of people voiced the idea that "We ought
to give a young man a chance," and I played off that sentiment effectively
with my campaign slogan: "A young man with a future." Nelson, though,
was a likable, grandfatherly kind of man who had one way or another
helped hundreds of families while a commissioner, and the gratitude and
long friendship of so many of these voters proved to be a formidable asset
for him.

On primary-election night, I ran first, ahead of Nelson by fifty-six votes,
but a third, minor candidate got just barely enough votes to keep me from
winning a majority, so, under Oklahoma law, I was thrown into a runoff

primary, to take place two weeks later. Nelson proved better than I was at getting his voters to turn out again, and he won the nomination and election (since there was no Republican candidate) by seventy-four votes. Cleeta John Rogers, incidentally, was elected to his Oklahoma City seat.

Much later, famous Oklahoma country music singer Garth Brooks put out a hit song that in sentiment described how I felt about that loss years ago: "Thank God for Unanswered Prayers." I hated losing that Cotton County state representative race, but I eventually came to think that the loss was actually a blessing. I was really too young, too unprepared, to go to the legislature then. I might have made a mess of the job. For sure, election would have interrupted my law study. And, had I won, I would have felt obligated to go back to the little town of Walters to live and practice law, surely narrowing my future horizons. But it was a race worth running, I believe. My strong, and near-miss, Cotton County campaign that summer of 1952 was to be a key factor in my successful candidacy for the Oklahoma State Senate four years later, from a two-county district that included that old home county of mine.

So, it was back to law school for me, and by the end of my last year there, in 1954, I almost hated to graduate. For one thing, I was nearly rolling in money, at least by my standards then. With law-school scholarships, fellowships, and employment as the dean's administrative assistant, doing research and letter writing for him, I had finally been able to quit my printing job and permanently scrub the stubborn printers' ink from my fingers. I was the elected president of the OU Student Bar Association, an officer on the *Oklahoma Law Review,* the winner of every available law-school award and honor, and first in my class, with the highest three-year grade point average in the history of the school.

I had been granted special permission by the Oklahoma Supreme Court to take the bar examination early, in the middle of my last law-school year, because, as I told the court in my petition, I was a married father who needed to make a living, and a three-month delay after graduation for the regular bar exam would work an unnecessary hardship on me. So, I was already licensed to practice law months before I graduated. The future looked golden.

It was. But, before I began life as a lawyer, I took a short detour to take a full-time paid job in the campaign of former Oklahoma governor Roy J. Turner in his effort to defeat U.S. Senator Robert S. Kerr for reelection. I had admired Turner since my FFA days, when he regularly sponsored many FFA activities. A mutual friend got us together for that 1954 campaign, which pitted two wealthy oilmen against each other in an unprecedentedly high-spending contest. There was a common saying at the time, as the two candidates rather lavishly spread their money around the state, that for many Oklahomans, the campaign was "better than a cotton crop and twice as easy to pick." My main job was to put together a statewide young voter's organization for Turner, and I also toured the state to make street-corner and other public speeches in his behalf. I did my best, and I learned a lot, but alas, we did not win. Turner, running behind Kerr in the Democratic primary, nevertheless made the runoff, but realistically deeming it futile to continue, soon announced his withdrawal from the race. After a near-tearful good-bye to Governor Turner and other fast friends I had made in the campaign, I finally packed up and headed for the city of Lawton, in southwestern Oklahoma.

I had always wanted to be my own man, not to have to "work for the other fellow," as my dad liked to put it. So, instead of accepting offers from established law firms, I had earlier decided to go into law partnership with a classmate. He and I had made plans to open our own private practice in Lawton, which was between, and equidistant from, our two hometowns— twenty-two miles north of mine. But his air force reserve commission was called up at the last minute, and I wound up having to accept an earlier offer to become an associate in what was the best law firm in Lawton— Bledsoe, Niklas, and Chrisman. The firm's three partners made me promise in advance that I had no plans to run for public office. I told them honestly that, as a husband and father, I was focused only on making a living and being a success as a lawyer.

Local newspapers had for years been running OU news releases about the honors and awards I was winning. So, I had already built something of a good reputation in Lawton and the surrounding area before I began to practice law there. Good law business came to me almost at once. Right away, I began to earn some big fees, though of course the law firm did not share these fees with me. According to our deal, they paid me only a fixed salary, and a quite modest one at that.

Positions of civic leadership came to me right away, too. I became the legislative chair for the Lawton PTA; an active worker in efforts to bring new industry to Lawton; an advocate for racial integration of the schools;

the attorney for the Comanche Indian Tribe, helping them write their first governmental constitution; and an outspoken supporter of an Oklahoma constitutional amendment to allow women to serve on juries. As a result of these and other efforts, I began to appear on local television quite a bit. I was on television, too, as part of a local hearing before a state senate committee that was televised live for three days; the senior partner in my law firm, Charles Bledsoe, a great friend and mentor, and I represented a local farmer who had been unfairly, and crookedly, charged by the state highway patrol when his car was run into by a bootlegger that a local patrolman was in league with and trying to protect. Meanwhile, LaDonna was becoming quite active in local women's organizations, in Comanche Indian affairs, and as a civil rights advocate.

Then, in early 1956, it was suddenly announced that the incumbent state senator from our two-county district—Comanche County, of which Lawton was the county seat, and my old home county, Cotton County— would not be able to run for reelection because of a brain tumor, from which, sadly, he would later die. Several people who did not like either of the two announced candidates—the Lawton mayor and a local state representative—began to talk to me about becoming a candidate myself. Though personally intrigued by the prospect, I always demurred, citing my promise to my law firm not to run for office. Then, late one night at Charles Bledsoe's home, as he and I wound up preparation for a next-day court trial, he mentioned the widening talk about my possible state senate candidacy. I assured him that I had not forgotten my earlier commitment to him and the other partners in the firm and had been telling people so. Surprisingly, he said, "I personally think you'd be a great candidate and that you really ought to consider it."

"Okay, I will," I said—that quickly. Suddenly, I was running.

I soon drove down to Walters to see my old employer John Penn, editor of the *Walters Herald*. "John," I said, "I need you to write an editorial, urging me to run for the state senate."

"There's the typewriter, Fred," he said with a wry smile. "You can write it better than I can."

I sat down at an old Underwood upright and banged out a first-rate piece. "It is quite natural, we think, that so many Cotton County citizens hope that Fred R. Harris, Lawton attorney who grew up in these parts, gets into the race for state senator," it read. Next came some truly won-

derful words about me and my qualifications, followed by a strong conclusion: "Cotton County is proud of this young man and would no doubt
give him the utmost support in any political venture he should choose. . . .
We recommend him as the logical choice for the office of state senator."

John Penn ran the editorial, word for word, under his own name. When
it appeared, I took a copy of it to my friend Ned Shepler, editor and publisher of the big daily newspaper of the district, the *Lawton Constitution*.
"Ned," I said, "I need you to run a front-page news story about the *Walters Herald* endorsement of me." I told him I had written it. He did what I
asked: "Walters Paper Endorses Local Attorney for State Senate." The
story repeated all the good stuff from the earlier editorial. People in Lawton stopped on the street to congratulate me. It was great what the Walters paper had printed about me, they said. My response was, "I couldn't
have written it better, myself!"

I had earlier spoken out in support of a local machinist's union strike,
and once I was a candidate for the state senate, the state organization of that
union quickly endorsed me. The state AFL-CIO decided to stay neutral, and
that left me able to say at joint appearances of the candidates before union
locals that I was the only state senate candidate in the race with a labor
endorsement. That was a help. So was the strong support I had in Cotton
County, my home county, where I was well known and well organized as a
result of my earlier state representative race. In speeches, I emphasized—
more than was justified, probably—the experience I had gained as a result
of my OU radio program, reporting on the state legislature.

Somebody has said that the principal quality a successful candidate for
public office must have in order to risk public rejection and put up with a
lot of criticism is desire. I guess that's true. You find yourself willing to do
some strange things to win. During my state senate campaign, for example, I got word that a ranching family of brothers, the Glovers, who lived
near the little town of Richards Spur and were longtime friends of my dad,
were surprisingly talking against me. The guy who brought me this report
said that the Glovers almost laughably believed that I was a "dry" and, in
office, would try to close down all the beer joints in the state, including a
Lawton one owned by one of the brothers.

So, one really hot afternoon, I drove out to the ranch home of Jeff
Glover, the oldest and most influential of the clan. I found him near the
barn, getting ready to unload some hay from his old truck. When I shook

hands with him, his manner was quite cold, and I could tell that what I had heard about his opposition to me was true.

"I'm running for the state senate, Jim," I said.

"Yeah, I heard that."

"Somebody told me you were against me," I said. He didn't respond. "They told me that you thought I was a dry, that I'd try to shut your brother's beer joint down."

"Well, are you—a dry?" he asked, hostile.

"No, nothing like that," I said. "And state senators can't shut down beer joints, anyway," I said, "even if they want to, which I don't."

"You take a drink yourself?" he suddenly asked.

"I do."

"You want one now?"

"Sure," I said. That was far from the truth. My stomach was empty and had been aching for several days.

Glover opened the door of his truck, reached in under the seat, and brought out a half pint of whiskey. He handed the hot bottle to me. I unscrewed the lid and took a long swig, trying not to gag as the biting liquid scorched down my throat, then handed the bottle back to him.

Glover first took a drink himself, then stuck out his hand and said, "Put 'er there!" I'd won over him and all his family. I felt that the small sacrifice I'd made was worth it.

I wound up winning the 1956 Democratic nomination for the Oklahoma State Senate from Cotton and Comanche counties, tantamount to election—a year and a half out of law school and twenty-five years of age, as young as state law permitted. (I was the youngest member of the state senate when I went there and still the youngest when I left eight years later.)

Being a state senator was a part-time job and paid very little—two hundred a month when the senate was in session. (Back when I had first told my dad that I was going to run for the position and what it paid, after telling him what my probable campaign expenditures would be, he had said, "You mean you're going to spend ten thousand dollars for a job that pays only two hundred a month?" I said that I wasn't running for the money—and it wouldn't be my money, anyway, but would mostly come from contributions. "Well, why *are* you running, then?" he asked. Good question, I thought.)

So, I continued to practice law to make a living, soon going out on my own and founding my own firm (although the three partners of the firm where I had been working tried too late, and reluctantly, to get me to stay with them by offering me a somewhat limited partnership arrangement). The new law firm I formed and managed—Harris, Newcombe, Redman, and Doolin—was a general-practice firm. My three partners were all respected lawyers of impeccable integrity and solid legal ability. We handled just about everything except criminal cases, and we prospered from the first.

Most propitiously, State Senator Don Baldwin of Anadarko, whose district bordered mine on the north, called me up to congratulate me on my election and to invite me to ride with him to a presession gathering of Democratic senators. He and I somehow hit it off at once, though he was twenty-one years older than me—forty-six at the time, which I thought then was really old. A longtime leader in the senate and soon to be elected its president pro tempore, Baldwin before long unexpectedly asked me if I wanted to share a suite with him in the old downtown Oklahoma City Biltmore Hotel during that first session (and, as it turned out, all those to follow during my eight years in the state senate). I eagerly accepted, of course. He became my close friend and mentor and, to borrow the old *Reader's Digest* feature title, "My Most Unforgettable Character." LaDonna and I named our son, Byron Baldwin Harris, born the first year I was in the Oklahoma State Senate, after him.

Senator Baldwin impressed me with what he said when he was sworn in to head the senate that January 1957. Everybody already knew that he was independently well off, that he had made a lot of money in oil and in the real estate and insurance businesses, and that there was no question he was a clean politician. He made a point of telling senators that day, as well as all the lobbyists who were listening, that if corrupt money was ever connected with any issue considered by the senate while he was president pro tempore, he would surely know it, would personally expose that fact on the senate floor, and would see to it that the legislative effort involved was roundly defeated. Nobody doubted that he meant it, and his words proved effective. He wound up his remarks that day by telling senators, "I'll never forget you, and I'll never let you down." And he never did.

Baldwin encouraged me to take an early leadership role in the senate and named me always to preside over sessions of that body when he was otherwise occupied. He soon appointed me to chair a senate committee, under the auspices of which I sent LaDonna as my emissary to visit Oklahoma mental institutions and women's prisons and reform schools and report back to me.

The Biltmore Hotel suite that Baldwin and I shared was a favorite gathering place, and watering hole, for senators and others at the end of each day's session, particularly senators like Keith Cartwright of Durant, happy, handsome, and dapper, youngest of a prominent Oklahoma political family and a man who prided himself on authoring at least one highly controversial legislative reform measure each session. Important Oklahoma political figures, like Aubrey Kerr, brother of U.S. Senator Robert S. Kerr, visited our suite often. The governor of the state, Raymond Gary, showed up to have room-service breakfast with us one morning, as other luminaries did from time to time.

I found that the state senate was like a club. I studied its members, its rules, its customs, and how things worked. I also became, on issues, what some people called a "goo-goo," that is, a good-government, reform-minded senator, a supporter of a merit system for state employees, for example; author of the bill creating the Oklahoma Human Rights Commission and outlawing racial discrimination in state employment; a champion for teachers and education; an advocate for economic-development measures and programs; and the sponsor of the legislation that finally built the long-desired southwest turnpike between Lawton and Oklahoma City.

It was the turnpike bill that first gave me a lot of trouble and brought me a good deal of unexpected public notice. The existing and badly deteriorated state highway between Oklahoma City, the state capital, and Lawton, the state's third-largest city, was a dangerously narrow, winding ribbon of asphalt and occasional strips of cracked concrete, all frequently punctuated by cramped, death-trap bridges along its more than one-hundred-mile way. The route was not part of the new federal interstate highway system. So, a toll road, or turnpike, was the only real possibility for getting a first-rate highway built between the two cities. My predecessor in the state senate, Bill Logan, had unsuccessfully made that his principal legislative cause. It was the main project, too, of my hometown Lawton Chamber of Commerce and the longtime dream of my close friend and great supporter Ned Shepler, publisher of the *Lawton Constitu-*

tion. When I got Governor J. Howard Edmondson, who had voiced support for our turnpike, to appoint Shepler as a member of the Oklahoma Turnpike Authority, I thought the southwest turnpike was wonderfully well on its way to becoming a reality.

But I had not anticipated how far people would go, how brazen they might be, in satisfying their personal greed—engineers, bankers, bond underwriters, attorneys, even public officials. Turnpike Authority chief engineer Harry E. Bailey came up with a southwest turnpike authorization bill that Governor Edmondson backed and that would have permanently earmarked a portion of the gasoline tax for any future turnpike, which would have allowed additional turnpikes to be built, feasible or not, and, the way I saw it, would have allowed a number of people to make unconscionable sums of corrupt money. The bill's backers assumed that, being from Lawton and a southwest turnpike supporter, I would have no alternative but to go along with their measure, like it or not, but I couldn't do it. I opposed the bill in the state senate. I even went to the governor's mansion late one night and subtly threatened a grand jury investigation if the bill got passed. But Edmondson would not change his position.

Otis Sullivant, the venerable and typically cynical but well-informed political reporter for the *Daily Oklahoman*, soon learned of my opposition to Edmondson and Bailey's southwest turnpike bill, and he said to me one day, indicating that he thought my fight was futile, "Are you just going to butt your head against the wall?"

I tried to shame him. I said that surely, E. K. Gaylord, the elderly publisher of the *Oklahoman,* would not support the official turnpike bill if he understood what potential corruption it entailed. Sullivant said he would make me an appointment with Gaylord. "But don't go talk with him unless you're sure you're not going to fold."

I said I was not going to fold. A meeting was arranged, and I went to see Gaylord at his downtown office. He heard me out, then agreed to back me—and did. (Later, after my turnpike bill passed, I earned probably the only good editorial I ever got from the *Daily Oklahoman*: "State Senator Fred Harris, author of the 1956 and 1961 Turnpike Acts, which made the financing possible, remarked, 'It took a long time but our chickens finally hatched.' Oklahomans can be glad that he and other boosters never gave up.")

I took to the senate floor and in a long and well-prepared speech laid out in detail what I felt were the corrupt aspects of the Edmondson-Bailey official turnpike bill, winding up, a little overdramatically, with the words, "I love the idea of a southwest turnpike, but I love Oklahoma more." Having learned of the content of my speech in advance, or while I was giving it, a good portion of the members of the state house of representatives came across the capitol and crowded into the back of the senate chamber to hear me. When I finished speaking, senators unprecedentedly agreed without dissent to have the speech, which had been taped, transcribed and printed in full in the *Senate Journal,* something that had never been done before.

But back home, my friend Ned Shepler was naturally very worried by my opposition to the governor's turnpike bill. I sat down with Shepler that weekend and gave him what I thought were the sorry facts of the matter. He said, maybe correctly, "But, Fred, isn't there always a little corruption with any big public project?" I told him that he might be right, but in this case, having personally found out about the potential corruption involved, I did not intend to be a party to it. I also reassured Shepler. I told him, hoping and believing that I was right, that Governor Edmondson and Harry Bailey would not be able to pass their turnpike bill over my opposition to it, and that they would eventually have to come around to an alternative bill that I was then preparing, with strong safeguards of the public interest written into it. Our turnpike would still be built.

The governor called me that weekend and more or less summoned me to a Sunday afternoon meeting with him and other turnpike backers in a Skirvin Hotel suite in Oklahoma City. I knew he intended to put the squeeze on me, to force me to give in and support the official turnpike bill. I was right. At the meeting, I was alone in my opposition, but I held firm. "What if we just go ahead and pass the bill without you?" Governor Edmondson finally said, exasperated with me.

"Do it, if you can," I said. But he and I both knew he could not. He knew he would not be able to get sufficient votes in the senate to pass his bill with the senate's strongest advocate of the southwest turnpike—me—standing against it.

Everybody at the meeting table looked pretty glum. Then the governor finally asked me what kind of turnpike bill I *would* support. I had mine ready and passed copies of its details around. There was nothing for the governor and the others to do but reluctantly sign on to it. The bill passed.

The southwest turnpike was built, and, somewhat ironically, I thought, was soon thereafter officially named the Harry E. Bailey Turnpike. (The documents and papers related to this whole episode can be found among my papers at the Museum of the Great Plains, Lawton.)

I was a supporter of State Senator Keith Cartwright's highly controversial constitutional referendum for the repeal of Prohibition in Oklahoma, a measure that was equally and vehemently opposed by the state's preachers and its bootleggers. I earned the opposition of my hometown Baptist preacher by supporting the referendum, but it was worse for Cartwright; for his advocacy of the repeal measure, he was "churched," voted right out of his hometown Baptist Church in Durant, with the public vote of church members taking place while he and his family were sitting there in one of the front pews.

I also got involved in a hot side issue. Anticipating that repeal of Prohibition would be adopted, a major state senate backer of the measure, as well as an Oklahoma City banker and a prominent former state official, had already made a deal for a state wholesale liquor franchise from one of the country's biggest liquor companies, a franchise that would be worth millions. That offended my sense of right and wrong. I discovered that when repeal had been passed earlier in neighboring Kansas, the state legislature there had written into law an outright prohibition against wholesale liquor franchises. I called the Kansas Legislative Council and got the exact wording I needed; it provided that every manufacturer of alcoholic beverages be required to sell to any licensed Oklahoma liquor wholesaler or retailer without discrimination. No franchises.

I went to the floor to offer that wording as an amendment to the referendum when it came up, to ensure that if the amendment was agreed to and repeal was later voted by the people, the prohibition against wholesale liquor franchises would be written right into the Oklahoma Constitution. Senator Baldwin knew what I was doing and strongly approved it, but he warned me that the state senator with the franchise interest, a former Golden Gloves boxing champion, was likely to attack me physically on the senate floor. "You're trying to cut him off at the pockets, Fredie, and he's liable to try to bust your beak," Baldwin put it in his colorful way of speaking. Fistfights, I knew, were not unheard of in the Oklahoma State Senate's recent past. In fact, not long before, one senator had even fired a pistol at another; concealed behind a framed photograph near my own desk on the senate floor was a bullet hole in the plaster to prove it. Don Baldwin always said that if you expected to have any influence in the state senate, "You have to be able to cover all the ground you can stand on." So, I was prepared for whatever might happen.

But when I offered my amendment, the offending senator seemed to panic more than get mad. He could see what was coming as soon as I told the senate, "I know that no member of this body would seek personally to profit from the passage of this referendum, but here's the way for each of us to prove that: adopt my amendment!" The senate did, and over-whelmingly. The senator with the franchise interest slumped at his desk, looking sick.

But the hottest issue I ever got mixed up with involved the purchasing and contracting practices of the state's powerful elected county commis-sioners, three in each of Oklahoma's seventy-seven counties. Keith Cartwright, who chaired the senate Roads and Highways Committee when I was its vice chair, convinced me that a lot of local county commis-sioners were stealing. He said he knew that because once, for a time, he had made a living selling to them. Cartwright got me to go with him to North Carolina to study that state's system, where they had lately taken away county commissioner control over local road and highway money and lodged it in the appointed state highway commission. While we were in North Carolina, Cartwright decided to author a bill to do the same thing in Oklahoma. I admired his courage and agreed to coauthor the proposed legislation, though he warned me against doing so, pointing out, as I al-ready knew, how enormously influential county commissioners were and saying that mine, back home in my two counties, might well beat me for reelection if I stood up against them. I told him, sounding a little braver than I may have felt at the moment, "If you've got the guts to take these guys on, so do I."

Cartwright and I both knew that our takeover bill had virtually no chance of actual passage, but we thought that we could use it to spotlight the blatant corruption that tainted so much of county commissioner spending. And we thought that, at least as a fallback position, we could get legislation passed to tighten financial controls and otherwise reform county commissioner practices. That's pretty much the way things turned out. Our original bill did not pass, though we did pick up two senate coauthors (as well as a decent number of senate votes) and the support of Governor Edmondson. County commissioner reform legislation was later adopted in Oklahoma, and eventual investigations led to several county commissioners being sent to prison. But, sadly, of the four of us senators who sponsored the original funds-takeover bill—the Four Horsemen, we were called—only I survived the next election. "Don't cry for Keith, Fredie," Don Baldwin told me afterward, when I was expressing to him my sorrow at Cartwright's loss. "He done his damnedest, and he liked doing it. And just like old Joe Louis, any time you stay around long enough, somebody's gonna eventually knock you out."

Baldwin said these words in dead-on mimicry of the earlier-era movie figure and humorist W. C. Fields. It was that unmistakable whiny, nasal voice that Baldwin always strangely lapsed into when he'd had a glass or more of Ancient Age whiskey, cases of which he kept stacked in his Biltmore Hotel closet and which he said were regularly replenished from bootleg liquor confiscated by a local police chief. Somewhat doughy looking, but really quite strong, Baldwin had been a champion wrestler in his student days at Oklahoma A&M, and everybody knew that he'd still fight if pushed too hard, so nobody challenged him. But Baldwin had another, more playful side: he knew by heart all sorts of low-brow poems and parodies, what he called "bawdies," and on lots of evenings, in his cups in our suite, pausing every now and then for a frightening emphysemic coughing fit between drags on an ever-present Pall Mall cigarette, he'd trade a bawdy with State Senator Buck Dendy for a classic, like Hamlet's soliloquy or "Thanatopsis." My favorite Baldwin selection, delivered in his unmistakable W. C. Fields voice, was Edward Paramore's rather long piece about the Hermit of Shark Tooth Shoal, one of the best stanzas of which, as I remember it, was,

> So, he rowed her ashore with a broken oar
> And sold her to Dan McGrew
> For a husky dog and a good eggnog,
> As rascals are want to do.

After I had served in the state senate for six years, I wanted to run for governor. I had seen governors and former governors up close, and measuring myself against these men, I thought I could do at least as good a job as they had. I believed that I knew state government and state issues well.

I felt that the governor's office would give me a better opportunity than the state senate did to really move Oklahoma forward, particularly in regard to education and training, jobs, civil rights, and economic development.

Senator Baldwin clearly did not think I should run for governor, though he had a strong and habitual aversion to giving advice of any kind, or explaining himself. Whenever I asked him directly about what I should do, or should have done, in a particular situation or what he meant by something he had said, he would never answer me straight. One time, I successfully offered an amendment to an appropriations bill on the state senate floor to provide five thousand dollars for building new restrooms at the site of what I thought of as a popular Lawton civic event, the Sunrise Easter Pageant, held each year at the nearby Wichita Mountains Wildlife Refuge. Baldwin voted against my amendment without comment, but when we got back to our hotel suite, he said to me, "That was a bad thing you did today, Fredie."

"I don't know why you say that," I said, irritated. "You got your amendment adopted for money for the Anadarko Indian Exposition, and Ray Fine got his adopted for the Gore Watermelon Festival. What was wrong with my getting five thousand for the Easter Pageant?"

Baldwin looked at me sternly. "If you don't understand it, Fredie," he said, "there's no way I can explain it to you." Nothing more.

Only later, after I had gone to bed, did I finally figure it out. Oddly, I had never thought of the Lawton Easter Pageant as a religious event, though it quite obviously was. Baldwin apparently objected to my amendment, providing state money for the pageant, because he saw it as a violation of the U.S. Constitution's First Amendment prohibition against the establishment of religion. And he was right, of course.

Sometimes when I sought Baldwin's advice, he would answer me with a kind of riddle—and in his W. C. Fields voice if he was drinking. That's what happened when I tried to get him to say what he thought about my running for governor. His response on that occasion was from one of his regular bawdy recitations:

> A girly who
> Would promise to be true
> To you—
> She might be true to you

Or who knows who?
Do you?
It's hard to tell
The depth of the well
By the length of the handle on the pump.

But then he got more serious and said, "Young as you are, Fredie, you'd probably make us one of the best, if not *the* best, governor we ever had, but, afterwards, you'd be a has-been at thirty-four"—Oklahoma governors could not succeed themselves. Then he added, "Uncle Bob [U.S. Senator Robert S. Kerr] and old Macaroni [U.S. Senator Mike Monroney] won't be in office forever." He obviously meant that I should be patient and aim, eventually, for the U.S. Senate. I did not agree.

Baldwin told me one night that he had once been urged to run for Congress and could probably have won, but that he had wanted to wait until his life was more stable. I knew that his young first wife, the love of his life as he sadly put it, had been killed when she jumped out of his moving car as they were driving back from a dance. He told me that he'd put off running for Congress that time, too, until his life was more settled and he'd made a million dollars, which he was to do, in oil, but that opportunity to get elected to Congress passed Baldwin by, and it never came again so clearly.

So, I said to him when he obliquely tried to discourage me from running for governor in 1962, "I may miss the brass ring, but I'm damn sure going to grab for it when it comes around." And I'm sorry to say that I added an unfair touch: "Win or lose, I'm not going to wind up a bitter old man some day, wishing I'd gone for it." He changed the subject.

Others I talked with, though, like my close Lawton friends—publisher Ned Shepler, for example, and Realtor J. C. Kennedy—agreed with me that I should run for governor. So did LaDonna. Members of my law firm were willing to keep on working so that I could go on the road. And that kind of encouragement was all I needed.

4

—∞—

Campaigning Statewide

I WAS NOT, AS IT TURNED OUT, THE ONLY DEMOCRAT who thought he heard the voice of the people urging him to run for governor of Oklahoma in 1962. So did several others. Among these were the state's likable and popular lieutenant governor, George Nigh of McAlester, whom I had known almost since he was a twenty-one-year-old state representative; a good former governor, Raymond Gary of Madill; and, most formidable of all the Democrats that year, a millionaire developer and civic leader from Midwest City, W. P. Bill Atkinson.

Nothing daunted, though, I began to put together a state organization, concentrating on Oklahoma's more urban counties, where I thought I had the best chance of success, that is, of running well enough in the Democratic primary election to make it into the later top-two runoff. I leaned heavily on people I had known at the University of Oklahoma, particularly law-school graduates, including many of my classmates—and they came through for me.

The bulk of my first money for what was always an anemically funded campaign was raised by getting supporters to sign several small post-dated checks that could be deposited monthly as the campaign progressed. We packed the national guard armory in Lawton for a great kickoff rally. "Onward Oklahoma!" was the campaign's slogan.

I was not long into the governor's race before I was summoned for a meeting with U.S. Senator Robert S. Kerr, Oklahoma's powerful senior senator, whom *Time* magazine had just called the King of the Senate. I knew from Senator Baldwin and others that Kerr had been asking about me for some time, expressing an interest in me. Kerr did that with people he thought might be "comers," moving early to take them into his camp.

Now, the senator's political handyman, his Oklahoma eyes and ears, U.S. District Marshall Rex Hawks, a big man called Hawkeye, came to see me. His message: "The senator wants to look you over and get to know you better." Hawkeye told me when to show up at Kerr's corporate office in the towering Kerr-McGee Oil Company building in Oklahoma City.

So, a couple of days later, I appeared there as scheduled and was shown into the senator's expansive and elegant dark-wood office suite. He was a man in his sixties, even taller than he seemed in his pictures. Up out of his chair, he strode toward me in two or three huge steps, extending his large hand. His suit coat was off, revealing a blue-gray work shirt and black suspenders. An out-of-date flowered red tie hung around his neck. His shirt collar looked too large, his baggy gray trousers too loose at the waist. His face, with its high hairline and piercing eyes, was thinner than the round and jolly face the Wirephotos showed. He had recently lost a lot of weight. I learned later that he had just finished one of his intermittent hospital-stay weight-reducing regimes, during which he regularly crashed from more than 240 pounds to something like 215 pounds and after which, just as regularly, went back up again.

"What have you got on your mind, Fred?" Kerr asked when we were both seated, his voice measured and deep, an orator's voice. *He* had summoned *me*, but I was suddenly made a supplicant. He took off his black-rimmed glasses in one grand sweep, leaned back in his chair, and fixed me with an unnerving gaze.

"I came to talk to you about my campaign for governor," I began. I went on to say that I wanted to be governor because I wanted to change things, and I said how. He listened intently, expressionless.

When I had finished, he asked me why I had opposed the Edmondson turnpike bill in the state senate. I told him that I thought the measure had carried with it a big load of potential corruption. Senator Kerr gave no hint of his own opinion of the matter but then leaned over his desk and said, "Fred, they *tell* me you're honest. You are the only one who *knows* for sure whether or not you are honest, but I am impressed by what they tell me about you." He paused for a moment, then, eyeing me sternly, asked, "Are you sober?" I knew, of course, that Senator Kerr was a militant tee-totaler and a former president of the Oklahoma Baptist Convention.

"Yes, sir," I said. "I'll take a drink from time to time, but I have never found that to be either a personal or a political problem."

"That's what I like about you; at least you're truthful," he said. "But let me ask you something. Did you know that I had the nerve to have the president of the United States in my home and not serve him liquor?" President John F. Kennedy had recently visited Senator Kerr at his baronial estate at Poteau, in eastern Oklahoma, staying all night in the senator's ranch-style, limestone mansion.

I answered that I had read that in the newspapers.

"Can you think of any way that hurt me?" he asked.

I said I couldn't.

"Can you think of any way that helped me?"

"Yes, sir."

"Fred, do you know that there are people in this state who would continue to vote for me, even if I lost my mind, simply because I will not serve liquor in my home, even to the president of the United States?"

I said I was sure that was true.

Senator Kerr leaned back in his chair again and continued. "Fred, you could make a lot of hay with some of these Baptist preachers if you were willing to say, 'I do not drink; neither does my wife. We do not serve liquor in our home, and we will not serve it in the governor's mansion.'"

"Senator," I said, "I won't *tell* you I'll do that, because I don't believe I *will* do it."

He changed the subject. "Fred, are you humble?" he asked.

I sensed that this was a riddle question. Kerr staffers later told me that it was a favorite of the senator's and that he judged people by their answers, saying, "If a man tells you he's humble, that's a sure sign he's not."

"I think I am, Senator," I said, warily. "I have no trouble remembering where I came from, but I don't always show it—especially when I'm 'pitching' somebody like I'm 'pitching' you right now." I smiled. He did not. But I got the impression that I had made a passing grade.

Earlier, I had read a newspaper report of another example of how Senator Kerr felt about the concept of humility. Known and feared as a slashing debater in the U.S. Senate, Kerr was once engaged in a harsh exchange on the Senate floor with Republican Senator Homer Capehart, not known for being "eat up with brains," as the saying goes, when Capehart said to Kerr, "I have more humility than the senator from Oklahoma." Kerr's immediate rejoinder, paraphrasing Winston Churchill, was, "Mr. President,

I never knew of anyone who had more to be humble *about* than the senator from Indiana."

In my meeting with Senator Kerr in his corporate office, after a little more talk, Kerr finally stood up and extended his hand. The interview was over, but he held on to my hand for a moment, looking deeply into my eyes, and said, "Fred, if I could do it without it hurting you or without it hurting me, I would like to see you governor."

I thanked him heartily and left, elated by these words, and I was outside the Kerr-McGee building and two blocks down the street before I began to analyze those words. What had Senator Kerr actually said? "Fred, if I could do it without it hurting you or without it hurting me, I would like to see you governor." I realized then that his ingenious use of the English language had actually carried with it no real commitment. And I later came to believe that, in fact, Senator Kerr quietly aided the rival candidacy of Bill Atkinson, who turned out to be the winner in the Democratic primary as well as in the runoff for governor.

I did not make it into the Democratic runoff, which pitted Atkinson and former governor Gary against each other. I was out of the race, but I had run a strong and notable primary campaign, built the beginnings of a good statewide organization, learned Oklahoma much better, and made something of a statewide name for myself.

I did not take sides in the runoff campaign, thereby earning the gratitude of Raymond Gary (and this would later prove important for me), but, of course, I endorsed Bill Atkinson as soon as he had won the runoff election and was declared the Democratic nominee. I made several general election campaign appearances in Atkinson's behalf, and I saw a good deal more of Senator Kerr in the process. At one Democratic-unity rally, in Oklahoma City, I witnessed another example of Kerr's ingenious use of the English language, as well as his biting wit. Just earlier, there had been a press flap and a lot of criticism of him as a result of reports that in an otherwise reasoned U.S. Senate speech attacking the federal government's tight-money and high-interest-rates policy, Kerr had said that the sitting president of the United States, Dwight Eisenhower, had "no brains."

Kerr denied it. "I never charged that President Eisenhower had no brains. I said he had no *fiscal* brains."

Senators can "edit and correct" the *Congressional Record,* which supposedly reports daily every word spoken—and many that are not—in Senate sessions. Most people have said to themselves, an hour or two after an occasion that called for an apt repartee, "I wish I'd thought to say such and such." Senators can do so, retroactively, and the printed *Congressional Record* will prove it. News reporters said that Senator Kerr, after his Senate speech, had doctored the *Record* to add the word "fiscal" to his reference to Eisenhower's brains. Kerr countered this before the Oklahoma City crowd.

He admitted that he had spoken of the president's brains in a derogatory way and that he had been out of bounds in so doing. His words were soaked with contrition, but as he spoke, there was the beginning of that well-known flicker of a smile around his otherwise riveting eyes. He swept off his glasses and paused for effect to let the audience know that we should get ready; something hilarious was coming.

"Our Republican brethren and their friends in the metropolitan press have undertaken to admonish me for having spoken critically, in any manner, concerning the brains of a man whom the people in their infinite wisdom have seen fit to elevate to the highest office it is within their power to bestow," Senator Kerr said. "And the Republicans are right, and I was wrong, as I now publicly confess."

Senator Kerr always spoke like that. And he always paused, almost interminably, for effect. He had the kind of stage presence and control of an audience that allowed him to indulge in galvanizing silences, frequently and at length, during any speech. At those times, he would pull off his glasses, straighten himself up to his full height, and gaze upon his hushed audience, almost daring a wet baby to whimper or a consumptive to cough. He would play out the last measured moments of such an expectant silence before finally delivering the stunning words that completed the thought and brought forth a bursting crescendo of laughter, or applause, or both. Now he did that before the Oklahoma City crowd.

"Yes, my Oklahoma friends, I was wrong and they were right," he boomed. "It is in the Christian way, which I learned in the Baptist church, that each of us should seek to profit through the admonitions of our fellows, and I have done so in this instance, as I freely admit.

"The Republicans have reminded me that, during all the long days of Franklin Roosevelt's presidency, they never, *never*—however vexed they felt themselves to be—uttered a single word in criticism of Franklin Roosevelt's crippled legs. Roosevelt, they rightly remind us, suffered from a physical affliction, not of his own making and not within his own power to correct. Those crippled legs, they say, were out of bounds to partisan comment—and they are right.

"I now see, my friends, by the same reasoning concerning what is, and what is not, a proper subject for political criticism, that I should never have made a comment of any kind concerning President Eisenhower's brains—because he cannot *help* it."

Crescendo.

I learned that Senator Kerr was very much aware that I had supported former governor Roy J. Turner against him in 1954. The matter came up when he and I were being flown to a meeting by his son-in-law in Kerr's sleek twin turboprop Beechcraft Baron; somehow the subject of our conversation turned to his Oklahoma colleague in the U.S. Senate, Mike Monroney. Kerr revealed that he, Kerr, had supported his earlier Senate colleague, Elmer Thomas, in the election in which Monroney beat Thomas for reelection. "I was serving with Elmer, and I believe in loyalty," Kerr said. Then he added something, using as he sometimes did, despite being a strong Baptist, an expletive for emphasis: "And Fred, if you're not loyal, you're not worth a shit!" I agreed.

"Mike never forgave me; he supported Roy Turner against me," Kerr continued. He paused, then pointedly added, "And so did you."

"I've learned you better since then, Senator," I said. Kerr changed the subject, and nothing more was said on that topic. He and I became friends in the last year of his life. We had some fairly intimate talks. Another day, for example, while we were flying into Lawton together for an appearance by him, I asked Kerr how he had become so powerful in the Senate. He answered me at once.

"First, I threw in right away with the southerners in opposition to repealing the filibuster rule," he said. He went on to assert that his motivation for so doing involved considerably more than just a personal desire for power: "Oklahomans vested me with one of their two Senate seats, one of only ninety-six in that body when I came there, and I did not propose to start off by voting to diminish the power of that position to serve the interests of Oklahoma.

"Second," he continued, "I soon came to run three Senate committees at the same time. I became chairman of the Space Committee in my own right when Lyndon Johnson became vice president. I ran the Public Works Committee because its actual chairman, Senator Dennis Chavez of New Mexico, was incapacitated or in the hospital most of the time. I ran the Finance Committee because its chairman, Senator Harry Byrd of Virginia, was senile."

I knew that there was something else, too: Senator Kerr had some kind of natural instinct for power—how to get it and how to use it. Burl Hays, the senator's administrative assistant, who later served me in the same capacity for a time, told me of one such example of Kerr's use of power. When Kerr, Hays said, wanted President Kennedy to appoint Kerr's long-time friend and key supporter Luther Bohanon as a federal district judge in Oklahoma City, after a committee of the American Bar Association found Bohanon "not qualified," the president and the attorney general, Robert Kennedy, the president's brother, refused to do so.

Negotiations between Kerr and the president concerning the appointment reached a standoff. Kerr would not withdraw his recommendation of Bohanon; the president would not send the name to the Senate for confirmation. To formally end the matter, Robert Kennedy dispatched his deputy, Nicholas Katzenbach, for a private meeting with Kerr in Kerr's Senate office. Burl Hays sat in on that meeting.

"Let me get right to the point, Senator," Katzenbach told Kerr. "The attorney general has sent me to tell you in person that under no circumstances will Luther Bohanon be appointed a federal district judge."

Kerr was not used to being spoken to in that way. He swept off his black-frame glasses and leaned across his desk, glaring at Katzenbach, then said, "You go back and tell the attorney general that if Luther Bohanon is not appointed federal district judge, there won't be any *fucking* federal district judge!"

And there wasn't. That is, until before long, President Kennedy wanted the Senate Finance Committee, which Kerr dominated, to agree to and the Senate to pass the Reciprocal Trade Act. Kennedy and Kerr then made a deal: the president appointed Luther Bohanon, and the Finance Committee and the Senate approved the Reciprocal Trade Act. (I happen to think that Luther Bohanon made a very good federal judge, too, as it turned out.)

Democrat Bill Atkinson lost the November 1962 general election for governor to a Republican farmer and former state legislator, Henry Bellmon.

That loss, interestingly, caused a lot of Democrats who hadn't supported me for the job, but who'd been favorably impressed by me and my primary campaign, to begin almost at once to talk to me about my running for governor again four years later. A number of influential people said that had I been the Democratic nominee, in place of Atkinson, we would have won. I was not so sure that was true, but I liked hearing it. And I did know that an underfunded and relatively unknown candidate for statewide office, as I had been, often had to run twice in order to build up to an ultimate victory. My hardworking law partners and my wife encouraged me to keep thinking about the next gubernatorial race, four years in the future. And I had reason to believe that next time, I would have the active help of Senator Kerr and his powerful organization.

On New Year's Day 1963, my wife and I excitedly gathered some friends in our Lawton home to watch that year's Orange Bowl spectacular, pitting our beloved Oklahoma Sooner football team against the powerhouse Crimson Tide of Alabama, led by quarterback Joe Willie Namath. On the television screen, we saw that President John Kennedy, a great sports fan and an admirer of famed and enormously popular OU football coach Bud Wilkinson, was personally in attendance in the packed stadium. So was Oklahoma's governor, J. Howard Edmondson, seated below the president and closer to the playing field.

Edmondson was winding up four years as the youngest governor in Oklahoma's history, and by law he could not succeed himself. He had been elected in 1958 at the age of thirty-three, and in a few days was scheduled to turn over the job to Oklahoma's first Republican governor, Henry Bellmon. Edmondson was a meteoric Oklahoma figure. He had been a crusading and photogenic Tulsa County prosecutor, but he had not been well known elsewhere in Oklahoma when he had first announced his candidacy for governor. At first, he had been way back in a large field of much better-known candidates.

To my mind, he advocated all the right things: repeal of Prohibition; a merit system in place of the spoils system for state employees; and central purchasing for all departments of the state government, which were then often buying wastefully and sometimes on the basis of favoritism. But I did not at first think that Edmondson had a chance. He seemed too young and inexperienced, and he was too little known. In the last few weeks of the campaign, his television ads changed all that. He won the race for chief executive of the state through an unprecedented and highly effective "prairie fire" television blitz.

I had used television advertising extensively in getting elected to the state senate, but nobody before Edmondson had ever conducted a *statewide* television campaign in Oklahoma. He was the first, and his campaign was a novelty. Most Oklahomans knew little, if anything, for example, about such things as television makeup or cue cards.

Once, in the early days of that 1958 gubernatorial contest, one of the other candidates for governor, Jim Rinehart, my friend and state senate colleague and an impressive old-timer in that body, came to Lawton on a campaign swing. I paid a courtesy call on him at his hotel room following his scheduled speech. A number of his local supporters were having a beer with him, and Rinehart was entertaining them.

"Now, you take this redheaded kid, Edmondson," he said in his habitually throaty voice. "I keep hearing that the women like his looks on television. But I'm going to tell you something that you're not going to believe. That kid reads every word that he says on television from big cards that somebody holds up in front of him." There were some murmurs of disbelief when Rinehart said this.

"It's the truth," he continued. "And I'll tell you something else that's worse. They put makeup on him before he goes on TV." Most of Rinehart's listeners seemed shocked to hear this.

"They sure do. A boy that works at WKY-TV told me himself."

It was a choice morsel of gossip, repeated often by Rinehart's supporters, but to no avail. Nothing, it turned out, could offset Edmondson's superb voice and dynamic television manner, selling the kind of government reform Oklahomans were hungry for.

I made speeches for Edmondson and introduced him when he came to my area, and after he had been swept into office, he asked for my advice when the two of us met privately in a Lawton hotel room. Humility does not come easy to a thirty-three-year-old governor elected by a landslide, and I made so bold as to caution him about that. I also told him that I was sure that if he was smart enough to be elected governor, he was surely smart enough to figure out how to be governor.

But Edmondson, once in office, got off to a bad start. He first announced that he would not live in the governor's mansion until it had been totally redecorated. He was roundly criticized for that, as he was for spending a lot of state money to refurbish and modernize his office suite in the capitol. He refused to court the old bulls of the state senate, a number of whom, like my friend Senator Don Baldwin, started out willing, if asked, to help the governor with much of his program.

Too, Edmondson soon let himself become the darling of the country-club set and the contractors. His friends stood to profit greatly from the building of the southwest turnpike, for example, and he and I got cross-wise on that. He picked up an image as a playboy and was portrayed nationally in this light in *Time* magazine. He had gained enough enemies by pushing good reforms and programs. He did not need any more.

After it was too late, he decided to try to build some bridges back to the state legislature, but even this was mishandled. He sent one of his least attractive and most flamboyant aides, an individual widely suspected of being a person of questionable ethics, to see Senator Baldwin in our hotel suite.

"The governor wanted me to come and ask your advice about what he should do to establish better relations with the state senate," the aide told Baldwin on this occasion.

"Well, he must not be *too* worried," Baldwin said. "I'm fairly available, and I'd be quite willing to talk to him in person."

The aide explained that the governor was very busy but promised to repeat word for word to the governor any advice that Senator Baldwin cared to give.

"That boy must do like it says in the Bible," Baldwin said at last.

"Sir?" the aide asked, puzzled.

"He must be born again!"

By New Year's Day 1963, Edmondson and I had become totally estranged. We'd had harsh words in private, and we'd disagreed strongly in public. We were no longer friends.

That was the situation when it was suddenly announced at halftime during that OU-Alabama Orange Bowl game that U.S. Senator Robert S. Kerr of Oklahoma had just died of a massive heart attack. This was very sad and shocking news. Kerr had seemed indestructible, and maybe had even felt that way.. His brother, Aubrey Kerr—Uncle Aub, Don Baldwin called him—later told me that the senator had made no recent will and that his estate was a mess, adding, "Bob was always lecturing the rest of us about getting our business in order, but he thought that he, himself, was too powerful to die."

But Senator Kerr did die. Oklahoma lost one of its greats, a leader whose water and Arkansas River navigation projects alone had changed the face, and future, of the state. I lost both a friend and, I thought, a supporter. I knew that in the last months of his life he had spoken warmly about me to members of his family and to some of his closest friends.

All over Oklahoma, and at the Orange Bowl game itself, people began at once to speculate about the political effect of Senator Kerr's death. The Orange Bowl television commentators pointed out that the resulting Senate vacancy would have to be filled by gubernatorial appointment until the next general election, and the television cameras focused on Governor Edmondson as he left his seat at the game, after getting the news of Kerr's death, and climbed up the stadium steps to confer with President Kennedy. Nobody doubted what the two of them were talking about.

In Lawton, J. C. Kennedy, my close friend and neighbor, whom I had helped get appointed to the state highway commission, called me immediately. He said that he and Ned Shepler were going to send a telegram to the governor, urging him to appoint himself to the Senate, to take Kerr's place. J. C. Kennedy asked me if I wanted to sign the telegram with him and Shepler.

I said I did not. I said that I thought Oklahomans would not like the idea of the governor resigning his office nine days before his term expired and having his friend, Lieutenant Governor George Nigh, who would then become governor, appoint Edmondson to the Senate seat. I said I did not think Edmondson would subsequently be able to gain election in his own right. (I was later to learn that a lot of governors through the years had been unable to resist the temptation to so appoint themselves to the Senate, but that only one, A. B. "Happy" Chandler of Kentucky, had ever been successful when later coming up for election.)

"Who then?" J. C. Kennedy asked me. I suggested the possibility that Howard Edmondson might appoint his older brother, Ed Edmondson, then an impressive member of the U.S. House of Representatives from Oklahoma, to fill the Kerr vacancy. "Ed'd make a better senator, and he might be able to win the next election on his own," I said. I also mentioned that one of Senator Kerr's sons would probably be interested in the appointment, but J. C. Kennedy told me that he and Shepler were neverthe-less going ahead with their planned telegram to Governor Edmondson, and they did.

Senator Baldwin also called me to talk about the sad news of Kerr's death. "They're already fighting over Uncle Bob's garments before they lay him in his coffin," Baldwin said. It was true. Few politically minded Oklahomans could pay much attention to the second half of the OU-Alabama game, which Oklahoma ultimately lost, for speculating about who would be Senator Kerr's successor. My own eyes, though, continued to be on the next gubernatorial race.

5

—⚞—

The Making of a United States Senator

NOT REALLY NEEDING MUCH encouragement from J. C. Kennedy, Ned Shepler, or anyone else for that matter, Governor Howard Edmondson resigned his office nine days before the end of his term and had himself appointed by Lieutenant Governor George Nigh, now governor, to the Senate seat left vacant by the death of Senator Robert S. Kerr.

Senator Kerr's family—Grace Kerr, the senator's warm and, like her name, gracious widow, as well as his talented three sons and a daughter—were furious. Edmondson had paid no attention to them, they felt, in making his decision. All around the state, the so-called Kerr people, who formed a close-knit and powerful network, were equally upset and highly antagonistic to Edmondson.

Despite the self-serving way he got the position, though, as the year 1963 got under way, Howard Edmondson was in fact the "sitting senator," the incumbent, and he began at once, of course, to campaign to keep the job, trying to win in the 1964 election the right to what would then be the remaining two years of Senator Kerr's unexpired term. But before Edmondson was able to establish his legitimacy in the public's mind as Senator Kerr's successor, Kerr's eldest son, Robert S. Kerr, Jr., announced that he would run against Edmondson for the Democratic nomination.

The race was on, and it dominated political talk in the state capitol when I went back there in early January for what would be my last session as a state senator. That talk got hotter when it soon turned out that Edmondson would have other opponents,—opponents just as tough, maybe tougher, than young Bob Kerr.

The old-guard, rural, and antireform forces in Oklahoma bitterly opposed Edmondson, as did the drys, those who had been against the repeal

of Prohibition, which Edmondson (and I) had backed. This large, amal-
gamated group began to coalesce around the likely candidacy of former
governor Raymond Gary, who, like Senator Kerr, had once been the president of the Oklahoma Baptist Convention. And Gary was obviously beginning to gear up for a campaign, renewing contact with his loyal
supporters in each of the state's counties.

He had started out as a country schoolteacher, had been elected a
county superintendent of schools in his home county in southern Oklahoma, then had been elected state senator, and finally, governor. Gary
was an expert on public finance and a fiscal conservative. I had served
in the state senate during his last two years in office, and I liked him personally. I admired his courage in steadfastly implementing the 1954 U.S.
Supreme Court decision on school integration at a time when neighboring Arkansas governor Orville Faubus, for example, was calling out his
state's national guard to block it. But Gary and I had disagreed on a
number of other issues. He was more rural in outlook, I more urban. He
was more a part of the old order, I a member of what some called the
good-government crowd.

Gary liked me because after I had lost in the 1962 Democratic gubernatorial primary, in which he was also a candidate (for a second, noncon-
secutive term), I had refused to endorse Bill Atkinson, his runoff
opponent, and had remained neutral during the runoff primary (which
Gary lost). Gary and Edmondson, as well as their people, hated each
other, and there was bad blood, too—over some prior business dealings,
I heard—between Raymond Gary and the Kerrs.

Politically, Howard Edmondson had virtually no support in the rural
areas and small towns, and Raymond Gary was very weak in the cities.
Somewhere in between was Robert S. Kerr, Jr. Young Kerr was as tall as his
father and looked a great deal like him. He was the beneficiary of the almost automatic support of the Kerr people, but it was already being said
that he was "no Bob Kerr," not his father. For one thing, he was not a
speaker, and his painfully halting platform appearances were inevitably
being compared unfavorably with the masterful performances of the late
senator. For another thing, young Kerr was remarkably shy and did not
relish shaking hands with herds of people and asking for their votes. He
had never liked politics, which he had regarded as his father's business,
not his. And this attitude showed.

Still, I decided to support Kerr, Jr. I personally liked Raymond Gary
better, despite the fact that he held decidedly less progressive views on the
issues than I did, but he seemed to many people to be a candidate of a past
era, not modern, and I thought that even if he could win the Democratic
nomination for the Senate, he would lose to the Republican candidate in
the general election. Gary could not ultimately win. That's what I thought,
especially as it began to look increasingly likely that the highly acclaimed
University of Oklahoma football coach Bud Wilkinson would soon become the Republican's Senate candidate.

You can't understand Wilkinson's tremendous appeal as a political candidate unless you've been to Oklahoma and inhaled the kind of crazy love
and half-wild fanaticism for Sooner football that's everywhere in the air.
An OU alum and, in 1963, the vice president of the OU Alumni Association, I was pretty much that kind of Sooner fan myself. I think the intensity of Oklahoma's OU football support grew partly out of our suffering
from a kind of group inferiority complex because of our collective sad,
hardscrabble, Dust Bowl and Depression, *Grapes of Wrath* past—until
Coach Wilkinson and his nationally winning Big Red football boys came
along and gave us something to cheer about and at last to feel proud of.
OU president George Cross was only half joking, I imagine, when about
this time he was quoted in the newspapers as saying, "We want to build
a university that the football team can be proud of."

For some years, it had been rumored that Oklahoma Democratic leaders, including Senator Kerr, had from time to time importuned Wilkinson,
who had registered to vote as a Democrat upon coming to Oklahoma from
Minnesota, to get into politics and run for state office. Wilkinson had always declined. In early 1963, though, word began to leak out that he had
finally given in—but to the Republicans! He was going to quit coaching, re-
sign as national chief of President Kennedy's physical-fitness program,
change his voting registration from Democratic to Republican, and change
his name legally to Charles B. Bud Wilkinson so that the voters would
know, when they saw his name on the ballot, that he was indeed the leg-
endary Bud, the good-looking, tall coach with the boyish winning smile
and the well-watched Xs-and-Os television program who had caused so
many people to hold their heads up high as Oklahomans.

As the 1963 state legislative session ground along, speculation grew
around the state capitol that young Bob Kerr would never actually file as

a candidate for the Senate, that he had been pushed into reluctant political activity by his mother and the rest of the family. Even Aubrey Kerr said to me privately, "The boy will never go." He added this pointed statement, "You'd better hold yourself ready, Fred; the people may have to send in a substitute."

Of course, this was a flattering idea for me but not a serious one at first, although a number of other people soon began to speak to me along the same lines. I felt certain that Robert S. Kerr, Jr., *would* run for the Senate. More important, my mind was still on running for governor again, and I thought that I was much better prepared to be governor than I was to be a senator.

It was true that the office of chief executive had been a graveyard for most of the Oklahoma politicians who had held it, but I had told Senator Baldwin back in 1962, with youthful confidence, that this was not an immutable rule. I admitted that I might like to be a senator eventually, but I felt that I ought to work up to it. I said, too, that a person like me, with no big name and no money, could never be elected to the Senate without first having served as governor. It did not occur to me then that a good but unsuccessful *campaign* for governor might be foundation enough.

In the early spring of 1963, Senator Baldwin was one of those telling me to give some thought to the possibility that I might have to run for Senator Kerr's seat: "Young Bob's liable to pull up lame in the backstretch, Fredie, and they may put the saddle on you." Don Baldwin would prove to be right.

Late one afternoon, that spring of 1963, when I arrived back at my Oklahoma City hotel suite after the state senate had adjourned for the day, I got my first word that Bob Kerr, Jr., had indeed just announced his withdrawal from the U.S. Senate race.

That news was passed on to me by LaDonna and a young Lawton lawyer, Bill Sexton, who had been the first person to urge me to run for the state senate and who ever since had been one of my most loyal volunteers. The two of them, waiting for me at the hotel to go out together to some political function, had heard about the Kerr withdrawal over the telephone. I couldn't quite believe that the report was real—I hadn't yet seen the afternoon newspapers—but LaDonna, Sexton, and I nevertheless began to speculate among ourselves about what impact young Kerr's withdrawal would have on the U.S. Senate race—not for me, since my mind was on the next gubernatorial race, but for the remaining Senate candidates: Edmondson, Gary, and Wilkinson.

Then there was a call for me on the room phone from Robert McCandless, a first-year OU law student, who thought of himself as close to the staff and family of the late Senator Kerr. Bob McCandless said that he was on his way to the hotel, that he was bringing his brother Bill, an Oklahoma City furniture retailer, and that they wanted to talk with me at once, downstairs in the hotel's private club bar. The brothers had grown up in Hobart, Oklahoma, not far from Lawton. I had met Bob McCandless a couple of years earlier when he was traveling around southwest Oklahoma for Senator Kerr, for whom he was then working in Washington as an intern. Bill McCandless I knew from my earlier gubernatorial race as a smart and solid businessman and a progressive Democrat.

As I left the hotel suite to go meet with the McCandlesses, LaDonna's last words to me were, "Now, don't let them talk you into running for the Senate."

"Don't worry," I said. "I'm running for *governor*."

But not more than thirty minutes later, I was back upstairs, saying to LaDonna and Sexton as I burst into the suite, "Okay, get ready; we're running for the Senate!"

Bob McCandless, though not presuming to speak for the Kerrs and professing no definite inside information about their thinking, laid out for me what he thought of as the inevitability of their endorsement of me for Senator Kerr's seat, now that young Bob Kerr was out of the race. I immediately saw that his reasoning and judgment were correct. And Bill McCandless made me believe that I belonged in the Senate and showed me how, building on my earlier race for governor, I could get elected.

My decision to switch gears and become a candidate for the Senate was a typically quick one for me, almost instantaneous, but no less soundly reasoned and considered for being rapidly made. I have never been one to dither. I have always gone with my instincts, and most of the time they have proved to be good. LaDonna and Sexton heard me out briefly, saw the possibilities the same way I had so quickly come to see them, then immediately signed on with my decision, but back home at Lawton that evening, my main political supporters, Ned Shepler and J. C. Kennedy, did not. They thought the evidence that I would have the support of the Kerr people if I ran for Kerr's seat was pretty flimsy, though they did not know just how flimsy. Further, since they had been named to state offices by Howard Edmondson and had been among those who had urged Edmondson to have himself appointed to the Senate, they felt they had to stay with him, to support him in the coming election. I could understand that. After all, I had agreed with Senator Kerr when he had said, "Fred, if you're not loyal, you're not worth a shit!" But I was nevertheless disappointed in Shepler and Kennedy.

Still, I was not for a moment personally deterred. I started at once to get organized, and I quickly let it be known to press and politicians, though without a formal announcement, that I was definitely going to be a candidate for the Senate. I quickly met with Bob Kerr, Jr., and Dean A. McGee, Senator Kerr's brilliant geologist partner in the Kerr-McGee Oil Company. Sure enough, I was pleased that they pledged me their full support, as I knew they would nearly have to do, given their bitter feelings against Howard Edmondson and their apparently longtime antagonism toward Raymond Gary. Not trusting my own political acumen, young Kerr and Dean McGee tried to make me agree, as a condition for getting their help, that I would hire an old-time political operative, H. C. "Coach" McNeil, as my campaign manager. I thought this was both ironic and bad advice. McNeil had managed Roy J. Turner's unsuccessful 1954 campaign to unseat Senator Kerr, so I knew, and liked, the Coach personally, since I had worked for him in that campaign. But I told Bob Kerr, Jr., and Dean McGee that I could not agree to have McNeil manage my Senate campaign because I did not think he was sufficiently conversant with modern campaign techniques and because I thought the campaign manager ought to be a person doing it voluntarily for love of the cause, rather than money. Young Kerr and McGee backed down, And I soon recruited Bill McCandless to chair my Senate campaign effort.

Sometime later, I met Grace Kerr when I was in Poteau, where she lived most of the time and, oddly, ran a local restaurant that featured on its menu her own wonderful homemade pies. She was delightfully warm, and she immediately expressed her support for me, whole hog. Before long, I found that the senator's youngest son, Bill Kerr, then an OU law student, was also unreservedly for me. Bill proved to be smart and unassuming, and totally reliable. I was to find his campaign advice good, and he turned out to be vital in helping me raise additional campaign money from time to time, when I most needed it.

I opened a campaign headquarters in the Biltmore Hotel in Oklahoma City. Early on, most valuably, the Kerr family assigned three high-level Kerr Senate staffers, who had been kept on a family payroll since the senator's death, to my campaign full time—Burl Hays, the senator's meticulously organized administrative assistant; Margie Banner, his solicitous and wonderfully efficient personal secretary; and Bill Reynolds, his legislative assistant. Hays and Banner switched their loyalties to me without losing a step and enlisted in the cause totally from the first moment we met. I soon had to send Reynolds back, though. He was too conservative for me, and he seemed to second-guess everything we did, nearly always expressing his opinion that "this is not the way Senator Kerr would have done it."

My first Senate campaign money came from a three-thousand-dollar personal loan I obtained from my bank in Lawton. We raised another sixteen thousand dollars from three dinners, at which the price was twenty-five dollars a couple, payable at the rate of five dollars a month. That was enough to get us going. There was talk from the first that the Kerr family was going to bankroll me completely. I did not discourage such talk, because it helped me gain standing as a serious candidate, and I did get substantial financial help from them, though not nearly so much as I had hoped for, nor anywhere close to what most people believed I was getting.

In campaign fund-raising, like everything else, nothing succeeds like success. A good campaign makes it possible to raise the necessary money, but money cannot save a bad campaign. As my Senate campaign picked up steam, and stature, we were always somehow able to raise the money we needed, though we had to work like crazy at it. Of course, later, after I became the Democratic nominee, fund-raising became somewhat easier, and I was able to pick up some money in a larger chunks, from the AFL-CIO, the Senate Democratic Campaign Committee, the Oklahoma Democratic Party, and other sources. Surprisingly, Howard Edmondson himself, whom I had just beat for the Democratic nomination, showed up at my hotel suite one day to deliver a five-thousand-dollar contribution sent, he said, by the chair of the Senate Finance Committee, Russell Long, senator from Louisiana. Campaign-finance reporting requirements in those days were quite minimal, so I never knew the total my campaign wound up raising and spending. I figure that first and last—for the primary, the runoff, and then the general election—that amount totaled something like $750,000, a huge sum at the time and far more than I would have ever imagined possible when I first announced as a candidate.

The first newspaper poll, taken quite early, showed that among the Democratic candidates, Edmondson and Gary each had the support of about one-third of those who expressed an opinion, and I had only about 14 percent. That might have seemed at first glance a discouraging result for me, but you had to consider the large undecided percentage reported in the poll and, more important, that while about 90 percent of those polled said they knew Edmondson and Gary and still only about a third of respondents supported each of them, less than half of those polled said they knew me. That meant, my campaign advisers and I thought, that I had a better chance to pick up the undecided Democrats, if I could just become as well known as the other two candidates. That is what we set out to do.

Nearly a year and a half before the general election, I embarked on the most personal statewide campaign Oklahoma had ever seen—or ever would see. I had read extensively about the fairly recent Senate campaign in Indiana in which a relative unknown, Democrat Birch Bayh, whose wife, Marvella, was from Oklahoma, had defeated a longtime Republican incumbent, Homer Capehart, by outworking him—by starting more than a year ahead of the election and running an intensive hand-to-hand campaign. I knew that was what I had to do, too.

A few years before, I had been on the same conference program in Oklahoma with an exceptionally articulate OU communications professor and head of OU's Southwest Center for Human Relations Studies, William R. Carmack. On that occasion, I had absorbed into my bloodstream his fascinating discussion about persuasion and the "two-step flow of communications," and I soon adapted what Carmack said for politics and my own use: what a good campaign should primarily try to do, through person-to-person contact, is to discover, or create, "opinion leaders"—those willing to say, for example, "I know Fred Harris personally; he's the best person in this race; I'm for him; and he's going to win"—and then reinforce these opinion leaders through advertising and by other means, so that they become active missionaries for the candidate and campaign.

So, in the spring of 1963, while also commencing a well-planned public relations effort, issuing a swirl of press releases on issues, and making a calendar-load of public speeches, I began a well-announced and months-long statewide effort to visit every single town in Oklahoma's seventy-seven counties. These trips into each county were advanced like a circus coming to town: news items in county newspapers and on radio, publicizing my local schedule and meetings; arranged coffees in people's homes or in local restaurants and other venues. In the smaller towns, I went into every store, met people and shook hands, and there and in the meetings, asked for, and very often got, on-the-spot commitments for my Senate campaign. Back at headquarters, after I had left a place, the staff immediately mailed personalized A letters from me to each person I'd met who'd made a definite commitment to me and personalized B letters to those whom I'd found friendly and receptive but needing more cultivation. Then we stayed in close touch with all these people.

By filing time, February 1964, I had compiled a very long list, indexed by name and town, of every person in the state whom I had met face-to-face, a great percentage of whom (starred in the list) had told me personally that they would support me for the U.S. Senate. We began to hold coffees in people's homes in the bigger cities, sometimes two or three a night, and every time, we added to our list of personal commitments. In each county, then, we would choose a supporter to host an organizational meeting there, sending out the invitations for the meeting from state headquarters, expecting, as nearly always happened, that the local meeting would wind up choosing the host as our county campaign chair. Nobody had ever put together so personal a political organization in Oklahoma. It was a largely subsurface, but enormously important and influential, campaign asset.

Then we had to buttress and reinforce this organization with an increasingly public effort, as well as appeal to the general voter, through more free media and the start of paid advertising. Running for the state senate, I had handled the media effort personally. Running for governor, I had hired a media firm that, as it unfortunately turned out, had little experience, or skill, in campaigns and whose work for me proved less than satisfactory. Now, in the Senate race, I had achieved enough stature as a major candidate that media firms were willing to audition to get my campaign account. I interviewed some of the best-known companies, but their ideas seemed old hat to me. Then I found a small media agency headed by a young guy named Ross Cummings, whom I had known of when we were both at OU. Back then, Cummings had caused the OU regents to kill the campus humor magazine, the *Wagon Wheel*, after he, as editor, devoted a whole issue of that university publication—as it turned out, its last issue—to photographs of a well-known professional stripper, Lily Christine, the Cat Girl, in provocative poses in the stacks of the staid old Bizzell Library and in other hallowed OU halls, mostly wearing nothing more than a very short OU football jersey. Cummings was clearly and appealingly nonconformist.

I interviewed him and instantly hired him. He was unconventional and smart, and he personally believed in me—three qualifications I was looking for. And he was full of ideas about how to get me elected to the Senate. Some of those ideas were terrific, some less so, but what a campaign needs is ideas, and Ross had plenty of them. His billboards, with my face on them so big that you could see my pores; his radio ads, with a succinct message and a background country and western jingle that he devised from an old Irish air and that little kids began to sing to me wherever I appeared; newspaper ads in which a photographed scene, with minimal accompanying words, told the whole story; and one-minute television commercials, filmed on site like newscasts, with me doing stand-up all eventually helped to make me a household name, and face, throughout Oklahoma.

For each of the three election contests—the Democratic primary, the Democratic runoff, and the general election—we came up with a different theme, or slogan. And each of our stage themes not only had a positive aspect, emphasizing my own qualifications for the Senate, but carried with it, too, an implied, and unfavorable, comparison with the opponent. Our Democratic primary-election theme, when the three-way contest was between Edmondson, Gary, and me, was "WIN" which we spelled out as standing for "Win In November." The positive idea behind the theme was that I was the Democrat who could beat Wilkinson in the November general election, with the implied corollary message being that neither Edmondson nor Gary could do so.

That primary-election theme was especially aimed at Raymond Gary. I knew that many of his own friends feared that Gary might seem a little too out-of-date and maybe a little too countrified for the national scene. Over and over, people said to me something on the order of, "I like Raymond, but I'm afraid he can't win in November." Our primary-election campaign made the most of that feeling, pretty general in the state, and we were able to do so while saying only good things about Gary and without unduly alienating him and his supporters. We knew we would need them if we were able to nose out Gary in the primary and make it into a two-way runoff with Edmondson.

It worked. In the first primary, Howard Edmondson ran first but got far less than a majority of the vote. I ran a close second. Raymond Gary ran third and was eliminated. Mutual friends, like Senator Baldwin, arranged a quick meeting between me and Gary. I flew down to Madill, Oklahoma, to see him, but I was surprised when I walked into the motel room where we met to find that Gary was accompanied by one of his key supporters, wealthy lawyer Reuell Little, and that Gary, sitting silently at first, let Little start the talking. I was even more shocked at what Little had to say. He declared that Gary would support me if I would agree, right then, to have the president appoint Little as a federal district judge, after I was elected to the Senate.

"Mr. Little, they'd send me to the penitentiary if I made a promise like that," I said. "I can't do it." And I added that, anyway, the next federal judge vacancy in Oklahoma, under a rotation system worked out between Senator Kerr and Senator Mike Monroney, would be filled on Monroney's recommendation, not mine.

Raymond Gary quickly spoke up then, as if Little's and my exchange had not occurred. He readily agreed to help me in the runoff, three weeks away, and that day he issued a public statement endorsing me. In every county, our campaign chairs were instructed to call the local Gary people immediately and bring them actively into our campaign. I was on the telephone constantly for a couple of days, making personal calls to Gary's most important state leaders, inviting them in. Gary leaders and supporters joined us in droves. Several editors of small daily newspapers that had supported Gary in the primary actually moved into my campaign headquarters to help with the press in our runoff campaign.

For the ensuing runoff's two-way matchup against the incumbent senator, Howard Edmondson, our theme was "Hard Work Is the Difference." I had built up a strong reputation for hard work and effectiveness in the state senate. An article in the *Tulsa Tribune* had said, "Work, work, work—easily the busiest member of the Legislature is Senator Fred Harris of Lawton." Jim Monroe of the Associated Press had written that, as a state senator, I had "graduated from being a 'comer' to a leader at the state capitol" and "a man to be reckoned with" in the legislature. United Press International reporter Harry Culver had written about me that "Unlike Edmondson, he has exhibited an unusual knack for getting legislation passed." We made much of these write-ups, of state capitol news reporters having named me the "busiest and hardest working member of the Oklahoma Legislature." My image as a worker was enhanced, too, by the fact that nobody in Oklahoma had ever seen a harder working statewide political *candidate* than I was.

We did not need to mention the negative corollary of our runoff theme as it applied to Edmondson. Everybody was already talking about the fact that Edmondson was not known as a hard worker. Far from it. Everybody already remembered well a highly publicized incident, even written up in *Time* magazine, when driving a car in the wee hours of the morning in Chicago in the company of a local television weather girl, Edmondson had been stopped by Chicago police, whom he had then tried to intimidate by aggressively declaring to them that they should know he was the governor of Oklahoma—thus making the story bigger. And there had been a more recent but equally well-publicized incident when Edmondson attended a boisterous outdoor Robert Kennedy party in Washington at which a guest had been pushed or had fallen, fully clothed, into the swimming pool, perhaps unfairly helping to give Edmondson a frivolous party image that did not sit well with a lot of Oklahomans.

The pivotal factor, though, in my ultimately successful runoff campaign against Edmondson proved to be a televised debate between the two of us that was broadcast throughout the state. Edmondson had wanted the debate because he was a consummate debater. I had wanted it because I believed the "Nixon-Kennedy effect" would work to my advantage. Edmondson was a little older and better known than I was. He enjoyed a deserved reputation as an excellent speaker and was very much at home on television. I felt that if I could just hold my own, just come off with a draw or a near draw, the televised debate would be helpful to my campaign. And that's the way it turned out. After the debate, even though it was not clear that I had bested Edmondson, I no longer seemed too young and inexperienced to voters who might earlier have thought otherwise. Their opinion of me changed, much as many people's opinion of John Kennedy changed for the better after his 1960-campaign televised debate with Richard Nixon.

On runoff election day, I beat Howard Edmondson in seventy-six out of the seventy-seven Oklahoma counties, even carrying Edmondson's home county, Muskogee. I was the Democratic nominee for the Senate. Next up: Bud Wilkinson.

Back at filing time, friends had asked me, "How can you ever hope to be as well known as Wilkinson?" My answer had been that if I could beat two former governors in the Democratic primaries, one of them the incumbent senator, while Wilkinson was coasting along with little primary opposition, I would be as well known as he by the time of the general election campaign, and, too, all the excitement and momentum would have developed in my campaign, not his. That was about the way it worked out.

Our main general-election goal was to spotlight the contrast between me and Wilkinson. I was experienced; he was inexperienced. I was a progressive on the issues; he was highly conservative, we knew, though the voters did not. I was a Democrat, supporting Lyndon Johnson in that year's presidential election; he was a Republican who backed Barry Goldwater, though he was trying to play down his party affiliation and Goldwater support. But how was I to make this contrast between me and Wilkinson known without causing a great backlash of voter resentment against me for seeming to attack such a popular, almost sacrosanct, Oklahoma figure?

First off, as our central campaign theme, we adopted "Prepared for the Job," which, of course, carried with it a corollary negative implication about Wilkinson's inexperience in politics and government compared with my nearly eight years' experience in the Oklahoma State Senate. The theme—repeated in all our advertising and in numerous small-newspaper editorials, as well as in a large newspaper advertisement spontaneously developed and paid for by a long list of OU faculty members who signed their names to the ad—was aimed at giving Oklahomans the freedom to continue to love Wilkinson for his work as OU's football coach, but to support me to be their U.S. senator.

Our campaign used a little humor, too, to help get the inexperience point across and at the same time highlight Wilkinson's decided conservatism. One example of this use of humor grew out of the publicized fact that Wilkinson had been giving set speeches that included a discussion of the question "Why Rome fell." He more or less told rotary clubs and chambers of commerce, for example, that Rome fell because the ancient

Romans became too dependent on welfare and gave up their freedom for security. And he indicated that something like the same thing was happening in America.

When I opened the fall campaign at a huge and enthusiastic rally in Oklahoma City, a kickoff we had delayed as long as possible so as to shorten the period during which we would have to buy costly television time, I started off by saying, "We are a little late in getting this campaign under way because I found that I was poorly prepared to discuss what apparently turned out to be the principal issue in the campaign: Why Rome fell.

"I've had to study up on that question," I said, "and what I've discovered is that the main reason Rome fell was that the Romans became so carried away with sports that they decided to let the gladiators help run the government."

Not very good history, maybe, but no worse than Wilkinson's. And it helped us get our point across.

LaDonna was an enormous asset in my campaign. We traveled a lot together. She was nearly always with me, though she made many campaign appearances on her own, too. Her growing advocacy for American Indians and women and her increasing interest in mental health made her an appealing figure and, at the same time, helped broaden the attractiveness of my campaign. But, strangely, about halfway through the campaign, in a special face-to-face meeting that he asked for, Bob Kerr, Jr., told me that he thought too much attention was being focused on LaDonna. This was at a time when in a lot of areas in Oklahoma, particularly in the southern portion of the state, many women took little active part in politics; some people still thought that such political activism by women wasn't proper. I rejected young Kerr's advice out of hand. Aside from both growing up in Cotton County, Oklahoma, getting married when we were only nineteen years old, both working to get me through the University of Oklahoma, LaDonna and I "tracked well," as they say in Oklahoma. Our ideas were the same because we had formed them together. We were each other's best friend. I thought young Kerr was flat wrong about LaDonna on two counts. Her active presence in my campaign was good politics, and we liked being with each other; it made the campaign more fun.

But we knew we were in a tough campaign against Wilkinson and that the stars would have to align just right for me to win. They did. Three principal factors were to figure heavily in that victory by twenty-two thousand votes: Wilkinson's decision to bring U.S. Senator Strom Thurmond of South Carolina to the state; President Johnson's national landslide win over Senator Barry Goldwater in the presidential election, held simultaneously that November 1964; and a televised debate between Wilkinson and me.

During the lull after the primary, I made news by going to Atlantic City as an Oklahoma delegate to my first Democratic National Convention. I was scheduled on the program to present a portion of the proposed party platform and was separately interviewed on CBS television by Mike Wallace. I afterward made news by going to Washington as the Democratic Party's nominee for the Senate from Oklahoma. I attended a kind of school for Democratic congressional candidates and took a publicity picture with President Lyndon Johnson. Back home, all the Democratic leaders in Oklahoma, like U.S. Senator Mike Monroney, warmly endorsed me, of course, and campaigned for me. The active support of U.S. Representative Carl Albert of Oklahoma, a longtime hero of mine and, before long, to become Speaker of the House, was especially pleasing and helpful to me. "I have long considered Fred Harris one of the coming leaders of Oklahoma," Albert's formal statement read. "He combines ability, drive and political judgment to an extent I have seldom seen. He will be elected to the U.S. Senate and will stride rapidly to a position of leadership in the U.S. Senate and the Democratic Party." Lady Bird Johnson came to Oklahoma, primarily to campaign for me, as did her husband's vice-presidential running mate, Senator Hubert Humphrey of Minnesota.

Meanwhile, Wilkinson had been tight lipped about the presidential campaign, not emphasizing that he was, in fact, a Republican, and a very conservative one at that. It had long been apparent to everyone that to beat Wilkinson, I would, among other things, have to get at least 90 percent of the African American vote. All the state's recognized black leaders supported me; LaDonna and I had been active in civil rights causes, and I had pushed through the state legislature a measure to create the Oklahoma Human Rights Commission and ban discrimination in state employment. But Wilkinson sent a really outstanding young man, Prentice Gautt, the famed first African American to play football at the University of Oklahoma, to black communities all over the state to show OU game films and urge a vote for his former coach. This, as well as Wilkinson's general fame and popularity, had some effect. The first poll we saw showed that 40 percent of African American respondents supported Wilkinson, and 50 percent supported me, with 10 percent undecided. It would clearly be disastrous for my campaign if those percentages held.

But we did not know what to do about it. Wilkinson was expressing no opinion on civil rights issues. Then, luckily, he helped solve the problem for us: he brought the U.S. Senate's most rabid opponent of civil rights legislation, the right-wing, racist, bomb-'em-back-into-the-stone-age Republican U.S. Senator Strom Thurmond of South Carolina to the state to campaign for him. We could not believe it. And Wilkinson booked Thurmond only for appearances in Little Dixie, Oklahoma's southeastern counties where the race issue was the hottest. Oklahoma progressives, black and white, raised a well-reported fuss about all this. Before long, polls showed us beating Wilkinson eighty–twenty among African Americans (and the split would later get even better for me after a televised debate with Wilkinson).

My campaign got an extra benefit from Senator Thurmond's Oklahoma visit to campaign for Wilkinson because Thurmond wound up scaring the daylights out of even a lot of conservative white voters with his jingoist speeches, advocating the escalation of the American war effort in Vietnam. This was at a time when President Johnson, particularly as compared with Barry Goldwater, was seeming to promise not to follow such a course.

In that fall 1964 campaign, somebody said I was hanging on President Lyndon Johnson like a cheap suit, and that was pretty much true. He was a neighboring Texan. He talked our language. He was highly popular in Oklahoma, and in winning that year, he carried our state, as well as the nation, overwhelmingly. For the first time since Harry Truman's upset victory over Thomas Dewey in 1948, a majority of Oklahomans were to give their votes to a Democratic candidate for president.

At statehood in 1907, Oklahoma had started out, and was for a long time thereafter, a strongly populist Democratic state, but with the rise of big oil, the decline of organized labor, and the increasing influence and rightward slant of the metropolitan newspapers, the state's voting began to grow more and more conservative. Many Oklahomans who were nominal registered members of the party came to be "Yes, but" Democrats— "Yes, I'm a Democrat, but I can't vote for Adlai Stevenson" or "Yes, I'm a

Democrat, but I can't stand John Kennedy." And the conservative voices in Oklahoma had reached their shrillest pitch in 1960, in opposition to the election of Kennedy.

I had met the senator from Massachusetts when he came to speak at an Oklahoma City Democratic fund-raising luncheon in 1957, the year after he had narrowly missed becoming the Democratic nominee for vice president, to run with Adlai Stevenson. I was among a dozen or so people who were invited up to Kennedy's hotel room after the luncheon to have a more intimate chat with him while he munched on a club sandwich. I was much impressed by his youthful dynamism and winning self-assurance, but I have to say that, at the time, I did not believe he was ready to win the next Democratic nomination for president. And, in fact, he was not my choice when he was later nominated at the 1960 convention. Neither was I then for Lyndon Johnson, whom most Oklahoma delegates supported that year. My heart still belonged to Adlai Stevenson—the losing 1952 and 1956 Democratic presidential nominee. LaDonna and I were not delegates to the 1960 convention, but back home in Lawton, in front of the television set, we kept pulling for the small band of die-hard "Madly for Adlai" Stevensonian delegates at the convention, led by people like Senator Mike Monroney, Eleanor Roosevelt, and others. But, alas, the convention vote soon showed that the Adlai Stevenson era in the party was over. John Kennedy became the 1960 nominee, and Lyndon Johnson his running mate. LaDonna and I enthusiastically joined up.

But in Lawton, Oklahoma, it was hell supporting Kennedy against Nixon. We organized teas to try to make our viewpoint more socially acceptable. We sent delegations to tell the local Baptist preacher that if he continued to denounce Kennedy from his Sunday pulpit, we would pass out campaign leaflets in front of his church, but we couldn't quite sell Kennedy in Oklahoma in 1960, though we were personally thrilled by his national victory. We were soon caught up by his memorable inaugural words and by the grace and style of his ensuing presidency.

Like most Americans, I can remember exactly where I was when I heard the shocking news of President Kennedy's assassination, in the middle of my campaign to win the Democratic nomination for the Senate. I was eating lunch in the Biltmore Hotel in Oklahoma City with some members of my campaign staff. Some man stopped by our table and asked if we had heard that the president had just been shot in Dallas. My first reaction was that this guy was about to tell another sick Kennedy joke; I had already encountered more than enough of them on the campaign trail. But, of course, his report was sadly true, and it knocked the props out from under us. I temporarily suspended my Senate campaign, even though the primary was to be held in about six months. Depressed and numb, I went home to Lawton and, like everyone else, spent long tearful days in front of a television set, mourning America's terribly shocking and tragic loss.

Then Lyndon Johnson rallied the nation—and me. Vietnam and its problems seemed small and far away. Johnson's conservative opposition was scattered and disorganized in the face of his "Let us continue" call. And as a presidential candidate in 1964, Johnson seemed even more appealing when compared to the Republican candidate, Senator Barry Goldwater of Arizona. I tied my Senate campaign to Johnson's. Our campaign bumper stickers told the whole story succinctly: "Harris/LBJ." That link helped me a lot.

— ·𝕞· — — ·𝕞· — — ·𝕞· —

I had not wanted to debate Bud Wilkinson, but I wound up glad I finally did. When I was in Washington after winning the Democratic nomination, Lawrence Spivak, the venerable moderator of the long-running NBC *Meet the Press* program, asked me to appear jointly on the national program with Bud Wilkinson, in a kind of campaign debate. I did not want to. I first hedged, then finally declined. I was worried about what I came to call the Salinger-Murphy effect. Pierre Salinger, who had been President Kennedy's press secretary, and George Murphy, the former film actor, were running against each other in 1964 for U.S. senator from California. They engaged in a televised debate, on Salinger's challenge. In the debate, Salinger, the more experienced of the two in politics and government, came across as a somewhat unappealing martinet. Murphy, who was not expected to excel in such a forum, nevertheless came across as a likable, nice guy. And Murphy ended up winning that election. I was afraid the same thing would happen if I agreed to debate Wilkinson, and I did not think I had to debate him to win.

So, I turned down Spivak and *Meet the Press* (though, later on, I was to appear on that Sunday program a number of times as a senator). I ignored Wilkinson at first, too, as he began increasingly stridently to demand that I debate him, face-to-face on Oklahoma television. Before long, my supporters were telephoning from all around the state, saying that they were losing the coffee shop arguments on the question; they did not know how to respond to the taunts that their candidate was afraid to debate Wilkinson. So I decided to challenge *him* to a debate—not the kind of joint appearance that he wanted, in which, as on *Meet the Press*, we would be questioned together by a panel, but a real debate, by college rules (though I had never been either a college or high school debater). I wanted each of us to have to stand on his own and make his own case.

In the debate, as planned, I took rapid-fire positions on numerous issues and then challenged Wilkinson to do the same. I stated my strong support for the Johnson-Humphrey ticket and challenged Wilkinson to say plainly whether or not he supported Barry Goldwater and William Miller. All this appeared to rattle Wilkinson. He showed his true ideological colors for the first time. He attacked what he called the "socialist" policies of the Democratic party, and in the process of all that, among other things, he alienated what little African American support he still had left. The debate, much as I had at first hated to go into it, proved to be a great plus for me.

When I rose before a great crowd of my near-delirious supporters, gathered for our victory party in the Oklahoma City Biltmore Hotel on election night, my mood was almost melancholy. I felt inadequate and somehow insincere in trying to thank everybody for their help. Thanks did not seem enough. I would wake up the next morning and fly to Washington to be sworn in as a senator immediately, since I had been elected to complete an unexpired term, but I knew that most of them would have to return to their everyday lives, perhaps never again to be caught up with such enthusiasm in a cause they thought so important and meaningful.

"I don't promise you that in the years ahead, you and I will always agree," I said at the conclusion of my remarks that night. "If I agreed with each of you 100 percent, I would either be dishonest or I'd be a fool. And I don't promise you that I'll always be right. I do promise you that I'll always be doing what I *think* is right, and you'll never have to wonder where I stand." Then I borrowed state senator Don Baldwin's old words: "I'll never forget you, and I'll never let you down." And I think I kept that promise.

LaDonna and I shook the last hands and said our last good-byes and thank yous and went back up to our hotel room, accompanied by my parents. My dad was dressed up in an unaccustomed suit, one of my old ones. Both he and Mama had campaigned for me untiringly and the best they knew how. Mama was ecstatic at the thought that her boy was about to become a member of the Senate of the United States. Daddy, partly to hide his true feelings, made a show of being a little less carried away by my election.

"Well, it's pretty nice," he said to an Associated Press reporter, "but I can't see that it will improve my credit at the bank any."

6

—∞—

Most of the Way with LBJ

LYNDON BAINES JOHNSON, TO MY MIND, knew the federal government better than any person who had ever occupied the Oval Office. He knew in his bones how the government worked. He knew how to make it work. As president, he was totally engrossed in the job, every day and all day. Most of the nights, too. He felt very deeply, I think, was centrally motivated by a sincere conviction that government ought to do better by poor people, Hispanics, and African Americans. He did the best he could for them, and others. And that was quite a lot indeed.

Shortly before I got to the capital as a senator, Johnson had been the most powerful and influential majority leader in U.S. Senate history. And the still-smoking memory of his near-legendary arm-twisting, cajoling, threatening leadership—the Johnson Treatment— swirled around in the Senate's high-ceilinged offices and halls when I arrived. He carried the skills he had honed in the Senate with him into the White House.

When I talked with him, he always appeared to know every detail of every bill, right down to, say, section 222d(1). He instinctively knew how to use people, too, like a carpenter knows how to use a hammer and nails. He knew how every senator and representative would vote on an issue, or could be influenced to vote, almost before they did. And he always seemed uncannily aware of what was going on almost everywhere in his government—sometimes, it seemed, right down to how much time a GS-3 clerk in Interior took off yesterday for a coffee break.

I found the president colorfully expressive, often laugh-out-loud witty, always engaged and engaging, and even surprisingly charming when he wanted to be, which was most of the time. It was easy for me to see how, all his life, he had drawn people to him magnetically, animating in them a personal loyalty that was both fierce and enduring.

But was Lyndon Johnson also cunning and devious? An overween-ingly ambitious and self-serving manipulator of people? Occasionally and embarrassingly somewhat gauche? Domineering and frequently harshly, and publicly, demeaning to those who served him or those he sensed were weaker than him? And, toward the end of his term in office, self-pitying and near paranoid?

"That was the real Lyndon Johnson." So said Horace Busby, his de-voted and loyal former staff member, when asked about such a man as de-scribed at much length and in great detail in Robert Caro's multivolume Lyndon Johnson biography. But, Busby quickly added at the time, there were simultaneously other, more attractive and appealing Lyndon John-sons, too, and they were just as real.

Busby was right, I think. Lyndon Johnson was a terribly complex human being, certainly the most complex one I ever knew, but he was also without doubt one of America's better presidents. Consider what he accomplished domestically: nation-transforming civil rights legislation and enforcement, strong and successful antipoverty efforts, the landmark Medicare program, previously long-stalled federal aid to education, and much more. Except for the Vietnam War—which, unfortunately, may be like the comic's rou-tine: "Except for *that*, Mrs. Lincoln, how did you like the play?"—Lyndon Johnson would be recognized as one of our great presidents.

My first talk with him was in a telephone conversation. He called me on the night I won the Democratic nomination for the U.S. Senate in 1964. Two things I find very interesting about that call. First, he recorded it, and, just as odd, kept the recording (as we now know he did with thousands of others, even telephone conversations with his wife). I have no actual memory of the 1964 Johnson telephone call, what he said or what I said, but I listened to it after a student of mine alerted me to the recording's ex-istence and availability. You can listen to it, too, by logging onto the LBJ Library website, going to the presidential tapes, then typing in my name. Why did Johnson record such a conversation, and others? Why did he re-tain the recordings? I have no idea.

The second thing I find interesting about my first telephone conversation with President Johnson is how familiarly I spoke with him, the president of the United States. He and I obviously struck up an immediate rapport. On the recording, the president can be heard congratulating me in a kind of weary drawl on my Democratic victory and wishing me success in the fall election against Bud Wilkinson. He asks what my general-election prospects look like to me. I answer easily and with optimistic confidence. I also assure him that in the Senate I plan to be a Johnson man. Then, in a kind of peculiar chattiness, I ask the president where he's calling me from, and he says from New York, that it would have been too late if he'd waited to call me from Air Force One on his way back to Washington.

In Washington I soon had a later face-to-face conversation with Johnson, in a meeting where I witnessed for the first time the harsher aspects of the famous Johnson Treatment—not of me, but of the man whose Senate colleague I was seeking to become, Oklahoma's senior U.S. senator, Mike Monroney. Senator Monroney went with me to the White House to meet the president. Johnson was waiting for us just inside the Oval Office door. I was struck by what a big and tall, powerful presence he was. He was well and expensively dressed, though his trouser legs seemed to me unfashionably loose and floppy, lopping over his shoes. His face was long and kind of beagle droopy, set off with a somewhat oversized nose and huge ears.

He shook hands with Monroney, then with me. "Fred," he said, bending over a little and locking eyes with me, "they tell me you've got what it takes; but you're in a hard race, aren't you?" I threw the ball right back to him: yes, I said, I was in a difficult campaign, but that if *he* would help me, I could win. The president said he would do what he could, adding, "Old Bob Kerr would never forgive us if we let a Republican take his seat."

A White House aide and a photographer were hovering nearby. "Let's take a picture," Johnson said to me. I agreed; in fact, a campaign photograph with him was what I had primarily come for. I followed as Johnson moved to his desk and sat. I took the chair temporarily pulled in to his right. The photographer began to click away. The president posed as he must have done thousands of times, gazing past my eyes, his face turned a little more toward the camera than it would have been if he had looked right at me. His eyes were slightly glazed, though he tried to appear as if he were listening to me intently. I looked directly at him, rather than a little to his left toward the covered wire-service Teletype machines and, just above them, three soundlessly flickering television sets, each tuned to one of the three national networks.

The photo session was quickly over. Johnson arose impatiently from his chair, not waiting for a "That's it" from the photographer. He took me toward the French doors in the east wall and pointed out to me the spike marks that he said President Dwight Eisenhower's golf shoes had left there in the floor's soft tile. He then motioned me and Senator Monroney to the two facing sofas in front of the fireplace, above which hung a painting of President Franklin Roosevelt wearing a navy dress cape. Monroney took the west sofa, I the east. Johnson sat down in his Kennedy-replica rocking chair, to the left of the sofa where I sat, a many-buttoned telephone at his right hand on a low table.

The president was finished with me. He quickly pulled his rocking chair a little toward Monroney and went to work. His first words were shockingly explosive. "Mike," he said, "when are you going to get that goddamn bill out of the Commerce Committee?" (I have no memory of what bill he was talking about.)

Monroney, a quiet and gentle man, visibly recoiled, then began a somewhat halting response. "There's some trouble with the chairman on that bill—"

The president cut him off. "I didn't ask you about the chairman! You're a member of the committee, and goddamnit, I want that bill out—now! Are you going to vote it out, or are you just gonna fool around with little shitty points until the Senate adjourns *sine die*?"

To tell the truth, Monroney said, he had some problems with the bill himself. The president forcefully countered, one by one, the questions Monroney then raised, almost before they were out of Monroney's mouth. Johnson was rough and overbearing. Monroney was courteous but held his ground. I felt sorry for Monroney, and I thought that I would never let anybody talk to me like that, not even the president of the United States. And I never did.

Later, I was to learn that the Johnson Treatment involved varying approaches for different people. The president seemed to have an intuitive feel for human nature and for what would work with whom. He was like an effective basketball coach, say, who knows which players he can motivate only by yelling at them and chewing them out publicly and which ones he needs to throw an arm around and talk to gently, mixing a little quiet criticism with a lot of warm encouragement.

In the Oval Office with Monroney and me that time, Johnson's manner changed abruptly as soon as he had made his point with Monroney. He leaned back in his rocking chair, and his expression became more pleasant.

"How's Mary Ellen?" he asked, almost sweetly. Mary Ellen was Monroney's wife. Mike said she was fine. "Tell her Bird and I enjoyed being over at y'all's house."

Monroney and I stood up when the president did. He ushered us to the door. "Good luck to you, Fred," he said to me. "You tell 'em down there that I'm gonna complete Bob Kerr's Arkansas River Navigation Project."

Later that fall, but before the general election, Johnson came to eastern Oklahoma for a big public ceremony to break ground for a reservoir, the Kaw Dam, that was part of the Arkansas River project, a multibillion-dollar U.S. Army Corps of Engineers system of lakes, locks, and canals designed for floating freight barges from the Port of New Orleans all the way up the Mississippi, then up the Arkansas nearly to Tulsa, then sending them back down in reverse. Johnson's visit was an official one, not a campaign trip, so I was not seated on the speaker's platform at the hugely attended Oklahoma presidential appearance.

Both Bud Wilkinson and I were present. The two of us, and our respective supporters, worked the sun-baked crowd at the dam groundbreaking, and our campaign placards were much in evidence. Mine, like my bumper stickers, read "Harris/LBJ." A couple of former Kerr staffers told me, only half jokingly, that the president probably would not appreciate his name being listed last.

After the ceremony, I had planned to hurry back to Oklahoma City by private plane, to work that crowd, too, when the president spoke there later, but at the last minute, although my name was not on the Secret Service manifest, a member of the staff of Carl Albert, then the majority leader of the House, pushed me onto the president's jet-powered helicopter along with members of the Oklahoma congressional delegation.

I was a little afraid the President would ask me to leave before takeoff, and indeed he did not seem overly pleased by my presence; at that time, the press was full of commentary to the effect that Johnson was avoiding getting involved in close congressional races and thus maybe reducing what otherwise looked like an overwhelming majority vote for him over the Republican presidential nominee, Senator Barry Goldwater of Arizona. Goldwater was way down in the polls. He was portrayed in Democratic television commercials as an irresponsible advocate of a super-hawk line on Vietnam and the scrapping of America's Social Security system.

As the presidential helicopter's rotors began to turn more rapidly, Johnson sat down in the telephone-equipped command seat, his back to the pilots. I took a seat just across the pull-up table from him. For a while after we took off, Johnson, paying no attention to me, addressed himself to Carl Albert and the members of the Oklahoma congressional delegation about Senator Kerr's and his own efforts to develop the water resources of the country.

But I was a good listener, and the president, like most of us are, was drawn to a good listener. So more and more, he began to speak directly to me. He reminisced about his close association with Senator Kerr. Then he began to tell of Kerr's reaction at the Los Angeles Democratic convention in 1960 upon first learning that John Kennedy had offered Johnson the vice-presidential nomination.

"I had just talked with Jack Kennedy on the phone, and Bobby Kennedy had just left my room, trying to get me to withdraw my name," the president said. I had read every report about this episode, particularly about Johnson's bitter encounter with Robert Kennedy on that occasion, and I listened with consuming interest to the president's side of the story.

"Old Bob Kerr came busting into my hotel room," the president said. "Sam Rayburn and I were talking, and Kerr charged in like a mad bull." Johnson, a superb mimic, then *became* Senator Kerr: "Lyndon, I hope you're not thinking about running with that liberal Irish boy from Boston. If you are, I feel like taking my thirty-thirty rifle and shooting you right between the eyes!"

The president paused and reached down beside his chair to pick up his white Stetson hat. He turned down the front of the brim, farmer style, and put it on. And he became Sam Rayburn: "Bob, you're in a campaign of your own down there in Oklahoma, aren't you?"

Now, the president acted out both parts, first becoming Bob Kerr again: "Yes, I am."

Rayburn: "It could be a tough one, couldn't it?"

Kerr: "It could be."

Rayburn: "Could be tougher to run with Kennedy at the head of the ticket?"

Kerr: "It will be."

Rayburn: "Now, wouldn't it be better for you to have a neighbor like Lyndon on the ticket?"

The president took the hat off and chuckled. He was Kerr again: "Lyndon, if you *don't* take that vice-presidential nomination, I'm gonna take my thirty-thirty rifle and shoot you right between the eyes!'" We all joined in the president's laughter.

When the presidential helicopter arrived at the Oklahoma City fairgrounds, President Johnson put on his Stetson hat and was the first down the steps toward the greeting party. The day was bright and clear. A band was playing a spirited march, and countless thousands had gathered on the first day of the state fair to see the highly popular president from neighboring Texas.

A motorcade had been arranged for the short ride to the bunting-draped speakers' platform. The president got into the first car, the rest of us scrambling into the cars behind him, but when we were still a hundred yards away from the stand, the caravan came to a sudden halt. The president got out to walk the remaining distance and mingle with the crowd, "pressing the flesh."

I moved up near him as masses of people began to converge around him and reach out frantically to shake his hand. The Secret Service cleared a lane for him. But suddenly, Johnson veered through the crowd to his left, toward a line of saddle horses held there by their proud riding-club owners. He stopped in front of a nervous palomino and asked the western-clad man holding the reins, "Pretty good horse, is he?"

"A little skittish today, Mr. President," the man said. Without warning, Johnson took the reins from the horse owner and swung up and into the saddle.

"God almighty!" a Secret Service man next to me muttered, "he's getting on the damn thing!" And indeed he was. The horse shied sideways a little, but the president gathered up the reins and got firm control. Then he galloped the horse off about thirty yards, wheeled, and galloped back. The crowd went wild.

After dismounting, Johnson moved briskly to the speaker's platform. I stopped short of it. Candidates like me were not allowed there. I stood off to one side as the president launched into a major statement on the Vietnam War. For me, as for most of those in the Oklahoma crowd on that sunny fall day in 1964, Vietnam was a million miles away and little on our minds. Still, we applauded and cheered when the president said that many people were demanding that he "go north" in Vietnam, but that he did not intend to yield to such demands for widening the war. "I'm not gonna send American boys to do what Asian boys ought to do for themselves," he declared, words that would come back to haunt Johnson—and the country. I have always wondered whether he knew when he uttered them that he would soon escalate enormously America's involvement in that tragic and mistaken conflict.

As soon as the president's fairgrounds speech was finished, he was scheduled to make an appearance at a small, closed Democratic fund-raising reception in a room under the nearby grandstand. Press and public were barred from the affair, but a friend of mine on the arrangements committee got me into it. Incredibly, the friend also waved in Ross Cummings, my advertising man, as well as Cummings's two-member sound and camera crew. Ross Cummings was intent on filming President Johnson personally endorsing my candidacy.

The president arrived. Somebody handed him a scotch and soda. Sipping his drink, he began to circle the room, shaking hands, and presently got around to me. Ross Cummings and his sound and camera crew quickly moved in. Johnson glared at my advertising man like he was a bill collector, then looked around for a rescuing aide, but none was at hand. I could imagine someone catching hell later on, in the privacy of Air Force One: "Goddamnit, I said no pictures with candidates!" But Ross Cummings was on a mission. He held the microphone out toward the president's face. The camera noticeably began to whir. Other people moved aside, out of the picture. "Mr. President," Cummings said in a reporter's voice, "would you say a few words about Fred Harris?"

Johnson was obviously seething, but he was also obviously conscious that the camera was already filming away. He handed his drink off to someone. His face softened. He turned to me and shook my hand again, then squared back up toward the camera. "I need Fred Harris in Washington," he said. "Send me Fred Harris, and together, we'll charge hell with a bucket of water. We'll tack the coonskin on the barn door, and old Fred'll bring home the bacon."

Perfect! Even with all those mixed images. Ross Cummings immediately released the text of the president's remarks to the Oklahoma press, waiting outside. And, through our campaign commercials, that presidential sound-on film endorsement of my Senate candidacy soon became as familiar to Oklahoma television viewers as the popular program *Gunsmoke*.

Lyndon Johnson was elected that fall by a landslide. I won in Oklahoma more narrowly. I sat in the stands behind him on that cold day in

January 1965 when he took the oath of office in his own right and
launched a new "hundred days" attack on ignorance, racism, ill health,
and poverty, such an attack as had not been seen since the first hundred
days of Franklin Roosevelt.

By that inauguration day, LaDonna and I had already been singled out
for special attention and preference by the president and the president's
friends, from aides like Jack Valenti and Bill Moyers, to capital insiders
like Clark Clifford, to Washington hostesses like Perle Mesta. LaDonna
and I were fresh and colorful, a new young senator, thirty-four years old,
and his attractive Indian wife. There were preinaugural parties and inaugural balls. There were small dances and even smaller dinners. We were
in Washington. Lyndon Johnson liked us, and people knew it.

As the ensuing months lengthened into years, LaDonna and I were to
spend a great deal of time at the White House, at formal receptions, dinners,
and dances, of course, but also at intimate private dinners in the White
House's small second-floor family dining room, as well as in the little basement theater where we watched first-run movies with the president (who
nearly always went to sleep soon after the opening credits).

At first in the early days, Johnson did not quite know what to say to me.
He would fall back on conversation about the old days with Senator Kerr.
But he and I soon began to get better acquainted. We literally talked the
same language, and I truly became a Johnson man, as I had promised, an
open and avid supporter of the president's efforts to remold America in
the short time allotted to him.

In the Senate, I became a member of the Finance Committee, which
has jurisdiction over trade (and taxes and Social Security). The president
asked me to be the principal author of a bill amending the Reciprocal
Trade Act. I agreed, provided Johnson would help educate me on the
complex issues involved. Over a couple of weeks' time, he sent me, one
by one, government trade officials as my special teachers in little private
sessions I set up for myself and held in a room I arranged for in the capitol. Though at the last, Johnson decided for various reasons not to proceed with the bill, I wound up as something of an expert on the subject
of international trade. Another time, the president had all the Democratic members of the Finance Committee down to the White House to
discuss the enactment of a system of public financing for presidential
campaigns. We all agreed to support such a bill. It passed the Senate,

and Johnson signed it. But, before the new law could go into effect, Senator Robert Kennedy, fearing that it would give Johnson unfair advantage in Johnson's upcoming reelection campaign, led a successful effort that very same session to repeal the law. The Congress unfortunately did not get back around to adopting such a public-financing system for presidential campaigns until 1974.

Lyndon Johnson had come a long way from the hill country of Texas. I once heard Senator Richard Russell of Georgia say that disapprovingly. This was in the capitol's private senators-only dining room. I came in there one noon and sat down with Russell and senators Herman Talmadge, also of Georgia, and Lister Hill of Alabama. The three were already deep in conversation. Senator Russell, who had once been Lyndon Johnson's mentor in the Senate, was expressing bitter displeasure with the more liberal line Johnson had taken since he had become president. "I told Lyndon in 1960 to look out for that Americans for Democratic Action and labor crowd," Russell said, "but he'd no more than got to the [1960 Democratic] convention in Los Angeles before he'd thrown in with them."

"He found out where the buttah was," Senator Talmadge said, in the Georgia molasses accent that he and Russell shared.

Courtly Senator Lister Hill joined in to tease Russell a little. "But, like I said, Dick," Senator Hill said, "you can't complain now. That's your boy, Dick. You raised him, Dick. You made him what he is."

"Yes," Russell responded, shaking his head in obvious sadness, "but as we say in Georgia, that boy riz above his raisin'."

Johnson had grown, and my thought at the time was, *Thank God for that!*

And thank God for Lady Bird Johnson, too. Averell Harriman, whom I saw and dined with often in Washington and stayed with in his Manhattan home, had been a valued adviser to a number of presidents. He once told me that Lady Bird Johnson was the greatest first lady he had ever known, and he had known all of them since Edith Wilson. In my opinion, Harriman was right. Lady Bird Johnson did not come across as well on television as she might have; her east Texas accent was a little too strong for some people, maybe. Photographs did not do her justice either. In person, though, she was a petite, attractive, smartly dressed, highly intelligent, gracious, well-spoken, and warmly engaging woman. Harriman even rated her above Eleanor Roosevelt because, he said, Lady Bird Johnson had a much closer relationship with her husband than Mrs. Roosevelt did. Lady Bird Johnson loved Lyndon Johnson, advised him wisely, put up with him, and helped to humanize him.

—∞— —∞— —∞—

President Johnson more than once asked me to suggest Oklahomans for presidential appointments. "It seems like the only recommendations I ever get around here are for Yale and Harvard boys," he complained. The first person I recommended to him was Bill McCandless, the businessman who'd headed my Senate campaign. I asked the president to name Mc-Candless to head the Washington-based Ozarks Regional Development Commission (for the Oklahoma-Arkansas-Missouri region), created by legislation I'd just gotten passed through Congress, but the proposed appointment was still hanging fire when I had to go off to Germany for a conference on NATO. Representative Ed Edmondson told me not to worry; he advised me to go on to Germany and call the president from there. "The effectiveness of a call to the president is in direct proportion to the distance from the White House," Edmondson said.

He turned out to be right. I called the president as soon as I had checked in at my Wiesbaden hotel (and the resulting conversation is another recorded Johnson telephone conversation that you can listen to today). Surprisingly, the president came on the line at once, and he sounded worried. I told him I was calling about McCandless. He did not quite understand, so I spelled McCandless's name and told him I wanted McCandless appointed to the Ozarks Regional Development Commission post. The president agreed at once and said for me to come by the White House to finalize things when I got back to Washington.

When I did get back and went to see him, Johnson told me that I had given him quite a start with my telephone call from Germany. "[Secretary of State] Dean Rusk was here in the office when they told me you were calling," the president said. "I said, 'My God, Dean, get on the extension with me; old Fred's got over there and got in some kind of trouble.'" I couldn't help but laugh, imagining good and loyal "mine not to reason why" Dean Rusk, sitting there listening in and taking notes as I carefully spelled out "m-c-capital-c-a-n-d-l-e-s-s."

Time magazine once reported that I was the only person in Washington who could have breakfast with President Lyndon Johnson, lunch with Vice President Hubert Humphrey, and dinner with Senator Robert

A 1941 photograph of my sisters, cousin, and me (age 11), all dressed up in our best clothes, taken on the west side of the Billings place, one of the homes where my family lived on the edge of Walters, Oklahoma. Left to right: my older sister, Kathryn; our cousin Mary Harper; me; my younger sister Loretta Sue; and my youngest sister, Irene. (Harris Collection)

My dad and me with three of his brothers, who were like brothers to me, at a family reunion at Sultan Park in Walters, Oklahoma, in the summer of 1960. Left to right: me, by then a member of the Oklahoma State Senate; Dick Harris; my dad, Fred B. Harris; Ralph Harris; and A. C. Harris. (Harris Collection)

Standing in front of Hubert Humphrey's vice-presidential campaign plane in Tulsa in fall 1964. Left to right: Jed Johnson, Jr., elected U.S. Representative from Oklahoma that year; me, Democratic nominee for the U.S. Senate from Oklahoma; U.S. Senator A. S. Mike Monroney from Oklahoma; my wife LaDonna Harris; U.S. Representative from Oklahoma Carl Albert, then House majority leader (and later Speaker); and unidentified aide. (Harris Collection)

Just outside the U.S. Senate chamber, July 1965, four Democratic freshman U.S. senators who sat together that year on the Senate's back row. Left to right: Walter Mondale of Minnesota, Joseph Tydings of Maryland, me, and Robert Kennedy of New York. (Harris Collection)

A photograph snapped when my campaign media advertising man, Ross Cummings, had just sort of tricked President Lyndon B. Johnson into endorsing me on camera as the Oklahoma Democratic candidate for the U.S. Senate. Taken at the state fairgrounds, Oklahoma City, September 1964. (Don Stoderl)

News photograph taken at the final working session of the members of the President's National Advisory Commission on Civil Disorders (Kerner Commission), U.S. Senate conference room, March 1968. Front row, left to right: unidentified staff member; David Ginsburg, commission executive director; Governor Otto Kerner of Illinois, commission chair; New York City mayor John Lindsay, commission vice chair; me; NAACP executive director Roy Wilkins; United Steelworkers president I. W. Abel. Second row, left to right: Atlanta police chief Herbert Jenkins, Democratic U.S. Representative James C. Corman of California, Republican U.S. Senator Edward W. Brooke of Massachusetts, Kentucky businesswoman and political figure Katherine G. Peden, Litton Industries president Charles "Tex" Thornton, and Republican U.S. Representative William M. McCulloch of Ohio. (*Washington Post*)

Vice President Hubert Humphrey and me in conversation in his ceremonial office, just off the floor of the U.S. Senate, spring 1968. Soon after this photograph was taken, I agreed to become the national cochair, with Senator Walter Mondale of Minnesota, of Humphrey's campaign for president. (Harris Collection)

Managers of the Hubert Humphrey for President campaign at the Democratic National Convention in Chicago, July 1968. Left to right: Lawrence O'Brien, Senator Walter Mondale of Minnesota, and me. (Harris Collection)

Taking the gavel after my election as national chair of the Democratic Party at the January 1969 meeting of the Democratic National Committee, Mayflower Hotel, Washington, D.C. Left to right: outgoing chair Lawrence O'Brien, me, former vice president Hubert Humphrey, and former national democratic chair John Bailey. (Mel Chamowitz)

Senator George McGovern of South Dakota and me at a press conference in February 1969 when, as national chair of the Democratic Party, I announced my appointment of McGovern to head the party's reform commission. (Harris Collection)

On the campaign trail, Fred Harris for President—1976. Left to right: young family friend Alexis Gover, my wife LaDonna Harris, our daughter Laura Harris, and me. (Harris Collection)

An unidentified aide looks on as I talk with President Bill Clinton, Albuquerque, fall 1998, when I was state chair of the New Mexico Democratic Party. (Leroy Sanchez)

With my wife Margaret Elliston in the Colorado mountains, near Carbondale, for snowshoeing, winter 2004. (Dayton Voorhees)

Kennedy. It was true that LaDonna and I were close friends with all three, and each of the three, of course, knew it.

But there was bad blood between Lyndon Johnson and Robert Kennedy, going back a long way, at least to the 1960 convention in Los Angeles. Johnson's anger had first been ignited when Robert Kennedy had tried to block the choice of Johnson as John Kennedy's running mate. Robert Kennedy resented the adverse stories the Johnson people had circulated at that convention about John Kennedy's health problems. Each man believed that the other paid money to secure convention delegate votes. And Johnson had, more lately, turned aside Senator Kennedy's desire to be his running mate in 1964.

Robert Kennedy never chided me about my friendship with Johnson, although he and his effervescent wife, Ethel, did tease me about it from time to time. Indeed, Kennedy once agreed to support me for a leadership position in the Senate precisely because I got along with Johnson and could therefore serve as a go-between with him.

Johnson never said anything directly to me, either, about my friendship with Robert Kennedy, but he let me know he did not like it. One time, of several, when LaDonna and I were weekend guests of Robert and Ethel Kennedy at their Hyannis Port home, the president called me there. LaDonna and I were having dinner with Robert and Ethel; Jacqueline Kennedy, John Kennedy's widow; and Rose Kennedy, the Kennedy matriarch, when Ethel had to leave the table to answer the telephone in an adjoining room. She rushed right back, giggling. "It's President Johnson for you, Fred," she announced. "He's found you, and you're in big trouble now, kid." Half thinking it was a joke, I went to take the call. It was indeed President Johnson on the line. "How're you doing, Fred?" he asked. And after that bland opening, there followed nothing more than some amiable chitchat between us. Johnson clearly wanted nothing in particular except to let me know that he knew where I was.

And not long after that, Johnson found a way to give me the message a little more clearly. I was back in Oklahoma one weekend, when Dean McGee, president of the Kerr-McGee Oil Company, telephoned and said that he wanted to see me, that he had something very important to tell me. We met. "I was with the president the other day, and he said something about you," McGee told me, "and I'm sure he meant for me to pass it on to you. The president said he really liked you, but he could do a lot more for you if you weren't so close to those Kennedys."

The following Monday, I went to see the president at the White House. "What's on your mind, Fred?" he asked me after I was seated across the desk from him in the Oval Office.

"Dean McGee told me you thought I was too close to the Kennedys," I said. Johnson made no response, remaining totally expressionless, his eyes hooded. I went on. "Bob Kennedy is my close friend, and I'm his, as you know. And I'll tell you the same thing that I told Malvina Stephenson of the *Tulsa World*. She asked me, wasn't I getting too close to the Kennedys and didn't I know that they were trying to build a power base in the Senate? I said, 'So am I, Malvina!'" Reacting not at all to what I had just said, the president changed the subject.

My relationship with Lyndon Johnson first began to cool as a result of my work on the president's National Advisory Commission on Civil Disorders, which came to be called the Kerner Commission, and my close collaboration and friendship with another member of that commission, New York City mayor John Lindsay.

I had originated the idea of such a commission. Earlier, holding hearings in the Subcommittee on Government Research, which I chaired, on the need for a system of national social accounting, I had become increasingly alarmed and depressed about the endemic and intertwined problems of racism and poverty that continued to fester and grow in America. Little public attention, I felt, was being paid to the substandard conditions in which most African Americans lived. Then, in the terrible summer of 1967, the black sections of Newark, Detroit, and many other American cities exploded in awful riots and burnings. Much property was destroyed. Many people were killed—mostly African Americans, a large percentage of them innocent bystanders. Racial passions were inflamed. Numerous white people believed that a massive African American conspiracy was behind the riots. The black community, on the other hand, was irate about the overreaction of law-enforcement personnel and resentful of the unwillingness of public officials to focus on the underlying causes of the disorders. Nobody knew what would happen next.

On July 25, I introduced a quickly drawn resolution to establish a blue-ribbon citizens' commission on civil strife. I got my Senate seatmate, Wal-

ter Mondale of Minnesota, and a few other senators to cosponsor the resolution with me, and Mondale agreed to come to the Senate floor and join
me in speaking in support of the measure.

In my own Senate remarks, I described the recent riots in Newark, Detroit, Cambridge, Maryland, and elsewhere. I urged that a commission,
similar to the Warren Commission, which investigated the assassination
of John Kennedy, be created. I said that I had just discussed this idea with
Senate majority leader Mike Mansfield of Montana and that he had endorsed it. "Actions which have been recommended by some," I continued, "involving prohibitions against interstate movement of persons who
may agitate for riots, or which seek to find some common organized cause
for such riots, however well intentioned, in my judgment, do not go deep
enough, nor do they recognize the national-crisis nature of the situation."

My resolution called for the formation of a commission, with members
drawn from both Congress and the general public, to make urgent recommendations for the prevention of riots and the elimination of their
causes. The resolution declared that riots and civil strife in American cities
"constitute a domestic crisis which must be met and dealt with on an
emergency basis," that "lawlessness and violence cannot be tolerated or
condoned in the American society, founded on law," and that "equality
of social, economic and political opportunity is the foundation of American society, and must be made real, immediately, for all American
citizens."

Even while I was speaking on the Senate floor, it occurred to me that
President Johnson, without waiting for congressional action, could go
ahead and set up the kind of commission I was proposing. So, after
quickly conferring with Senator Mondale, I told the Senate, "The senator
from Minnesota and I will this afternoon dispatch a copy of the resolution
to the president, urging him, as I now do, pending adoption of the resolution in Congress, to proceed at once by executive order to create this
blue-ribbon commission and set it to its work."

That message and a copy of the resolution were delivered to the White
House that afternoon. I called presidential aide Douglas Cater and asked
him to see that they reached the president. I also asked Senator Mansfield
to bring up the subject at a meeting of congressional leaders with the
president that was scheduled for that evening. The next day, I began three
days of hearings on the resolution in my Subcommittee on Government

Research. With heavy news coverage, urban authority Daniel Patrick Moynihan, later a U.S. senator, and National Urban League executive director Whitney Young testified in favor of the resolution.

The White House scheduled a major presidential television address for the evening of July 27, 1967, and put out the word that in it, the president would announce the creation of just such a commission as I had been suggesting. My wife and I invited several of our friends to our McLean, Virginia, home for dinner that night, and after dinner, we gathered in our living room to watch the president's broadcast. About fifteen minutes before the president was scheduled to come on, our youngest daughter, Laura, then six, came running breathlessly into the living room to say: "It's President Johnson! He's right on the phone, and he said, 'Let me speak to your daddy.'"

I quickly left our excited guests to go to the kitchen to take the call on the wall telephone. "Yessir, Mr. President," I said, standing, barely resisting the urge to salute.

"Fred, I'm gonna appoint that commission you've been talking about," Johnson said. I told him I was glad to hear it, that I thought he was doing the right thing. "I hope you're gonna watch me on television," he continued, "because I'm gonna mention your name." I said that indeed I was, and that we had invited some friends over to watch, too. "I'm gonna put you on the damn thing," the president said.

"I appreciate that, Mr. President," I said. "I never expected it, but I'll do the best I can."

"Now, I don't want you to turn out like some of your colleagues. I appoint them to things, and they never show up."

"I don't know how good I'll be at it, but I'll be there and I'll work at it," I said.

"And another thing."

"Yessir?"

"I want you to remember that you're a Johnson man."

"I'm your friend, Mr. President, and I won't forget it."

"If you do, Fred," the president said, "I'll take out my pocketknife and cut your peter off. You're from Oklahoma; you understand that kind of talk, don't you?"

I said I did, hung up, and went back to join our guests. "What did he say? What did he say?" they asked. I reported that he had told me he was going to announce the creation of the commission and name me as a member of it. "What else did he say?" they asked. I said that, well, that was about all, except for a few private remarks I did not feel at liberty to repeat.

That night, the president did indeed announce the formation of the president's National Advisory Commission on Civil Disorders. He appointed Governor Otto Kerner of Illinois as chair and Mayor John Lindsay of New York City as vice chair. Other members of the commission, in addition to me, included U.S. Representative James C. Corman of Los Angeles, a liberal Democrat; U.S. Representative William M. McCulloch of Ohio, a conservative Republican and civil libertarian; I. W. Abel, president of the United Steelworkers; Atlanta police chief Herbert Jenkins; businessman Charles "Tex" Thornton of Litton Industries; and Katherine G. Peden, a Kentucky radio station owner and political figure. Two African Americans were also named—U.S. Senator Edward W. Brooke, a Republican of Massachusetts, and Roy Wilkins, executive director of the National Association for the Advancement of Colored People. About the riots, the president directed the commission to answer three questions: What happened? Why did it happen? What can be done to prevent it from happening again? "Let your search be free," he said. "As best you can, find the truth and express it in your report."

That is what we set out to do. We were sworn in a few days after the announcement at a ceremony in the White House Cabinet Room, in the presence of President Johnson and Vice President Humphrey. We began to meet, either in a room in the Executive Office Building, adjacent to the White House, or in a Senate room I arranged for in the capitol. Washington lawyer David Ginsburg, who served most valuably as our executive director, put together a first-rate staff, and we all went to work.

The commission sent out investigating groups of staff members, contracted for independent studies, interrogated government officials, and held extensive hearings. But first, we divided up into teams consisting of two or three commission members each and traveled the country personally, walking the streets where the riots had occurred and talking informally with local people.

Tall and handsome, urbane and sophisticated John Lindsay was the nationally famous Republican mayor of American's largest city. I was a Democrat who had grown up in the little town of Walters, Oklahoma, where no African Americans had ever lived. Nevertheless, there was an immediate bonding between us, and he and I joined up to travel the country in tandem. Lindsay and I shared the same sense of urgency about urban problems. We both felt deeply and cared deeply about the despair, frustration, and hostility that characterized black communities throughout the country. Our first trip together, to Cincinnati, was a searing experience for both of us.

Shortly after I returned from that trip, I went down to the White House with my Oklahoma colleague Senator Monroney to introduce to the president Jane Anne Jayroe, a fellow Oklahoman who had just been selected as Miss America for 1967. Johnson first welcomed Senator Monroney and Miss Jayroe into the Oval Office. Then he turned to me and said sarcastically, "I'm surprised to see you up, Fred."

"Sir?" I said.

"I'm surprised to see you up," the president repeated. "I heard old John Lindsay had you down and had his foot on your neck."

Before I could respond, the president turned from me, back to Miss Jayroe. They took a picture together. Then he walked us all out to see his dogs in their south-lawn kennel. Afterward, back in the Oval Office, the president said good-bye to Senator Monroney and Miss Jayroe, but he asked me to stay on for a minute. When the others had gone, we stepped back to his desk, where Johnson picked up a copy of that morning's *New York Times*. He turned to a column-long story on an interior page and said, "Now look at this shit, Fred. The *Times* says 'Lindsay announces release of poverty funds,' and, by God, you've got to read all the way down to the bottom of the damn page before you find out it's *my* program."

Before I could say anything, the president moved on to what seemed to be a different point, one about which he obviously felt very strongly. "We made a big mistake in the poverty program," he said. "We should have put everything through elected officials, instead of through these local committees that nobody ever elected to anything." That comment did not seem to fit with Johnson's earlier-expressed annoyance about John Lindsay's announcement in the *Times*. But the president had apparently switched subjects and was now worrying aloud about mounting criticism of his antipoverty program.

"When I was head of the National Youth Administration in Texas," Johnson went on, "there was one county where the local officials wouldn't sponsor the program. So I came up here and saw Roosevelt and tried to get him to approve my idea of having the local rotary club be the sponsor for the NYA in that county. But Roosevelt wouldn't do it; he wanted local elected officials in charge. That's where I made my mistake on the poverty program. We should have put it under local elected officials. That way, when some jake-leg preacher went south with the money, there'd be somebody else to blame. Now, it's just me."

Saying that, Johnson abruptly got back to the subject of the Kerner Commission: "Fred, have you seen the FBI reports on these riots?" I said I had not, but our investigators had seen them and reported on them to us and that the commission had interrogated FBI director J. Edgar Hoover. The president said I should see the FBI reports myself. He called in Marvin Watson, his chief aide, and told Watson to get the reports and show them to me the next morning.

"John Lindsay and I have just come back from Cincinnati, Mr. President," I said. "We both feel that this thing is much deeper than most people know, and that there's no conspiracy."

"Wait'll you see the FBI reports," the president said.

I searched for a way to make him better understand what we had found. I knew he admired Franklin Roosevelt. "It's just like in Roosevelt's time, Mr. President," I said. "Thirty percent of the people were unemployed then, and God knows what leaders and ideologies might have gained a following if Roosevelt hadn't taken away their audience. That's the way it is now in the black sections of the cities, only worse. Unemployment is sometimes as high as fifty percent. We've lost the Stokely Carmichaels and the Rap Browns [two young black activists]. They've been driven mad by the system, seeing people attacked and killed while trying to do the most system-oriented thing they could do—getting blacks registered to vote. But there are hundreds of Stokely Carmichaels and Rap Browns that you've never heard of, and they are far more effective in their local communities. We may have already lost them, too, but we've got to think about their audience. We've got to respond to their legitimate complaints."

"Look at the FBI reports," Johnson said.

The next morning, I did read the FBI reports in Marvin Watson's office. They tended to indicate, quite mistakenly, that "outside agitators" helped cause the riots. The reports amounted to the most sloppy mess of reporting I had ever seen, and I told Watson so.

John Lindsay and I continued to press ahead in the Kerner Commission meetings. One or the other of us made virtually every motion that was adopted by the commission, and somehow, word of that continued to get back to President Johnson. So one night, following a dinner in the family dining room at the White House, as several senators and I sat down in the drawing room for cigars and brandy, the president opened the conversation by looking across the room at me and saying, "Fred, tell us about your friend Lindsay's campaign for president."

This time, I made fun of his obvious concern that John Lindsay might run against him. "Mr. President, you ought to quit worrying so damned much about Lindsay," I said, and laughed. "Hell, old John ain't got time to be running for president; he's already got more than he can say grace over, just trying to make New York City work."

The president was not mollified.

In the almost daily meetings of the Kerner Commission, I more than once quoted as a standard for our actions something I had read that Lincoln said during the Civil War: "In times like the present, men should utter nothing for which they would not willingly be responsible through time and in eternity." The commission decided, right away, that there were no short-range solutions for the riots problem. We also decided to tell the bald truth—first, about what had happened, and, next, about why it happened. In our answer to Johnson's first question, we said straight out that there had been no conspiracy behind the riots and that there had been frequent cases of murderous overreaction by the police and the national guard in the cities where the riots had occurred. As for causes, we concluded that most people in America, black and white, felt economically and politically powerless, and an overlay of racism on that sense of powerlessness had produced, for blacks, an intolerable and explosive situation.

Once having decided upon truthful answers to the president's first two questions, we were already locked into our central conclusion—"America is moving toward two societies, one white, one black, separate and unequal"—as well as our final recommendations for deep and fundamental social, political, and economic changes to make things right and to prevent future upheavals: guaranteed jobs; a guaranteed minimum income for those unable to get jobs; fundamental reform of, and strong support for, health, education, and housing programs; and vigorous federal action to root out racism.

The Kerner Commission Report, running to nearly six hundred pages, was finally adopted unanimously after some tough internal fights. The commission planned extensive background briefings for the press on the report, prior to its official release date, scheduled for the day when we were to deliver the report to the president in a formal ceremony at the White House. But one of the commission members—in my opinion, Charles "Tex" Thornton, who had fought the rest of us on almost every significant point in the report—got the false word to President Johnson that our report condoned and would tend to encourage riots, and that we were critical of Johnson by finding that his programs were insufficient to meet the problems. I am sure the president never read our report himself, but the White House abruptly canceled the formal delivery ceremony, and Johnson rejected the commission's request to stay in existence for six months more so that we could lobby for approval of our recommendations. Then someone, apparently hoping to create confusion and lessen the report's impact, leaked a copy of its summary to the *Washington Post*. When we could not talk the *Post* out of breaking the story prematurely, we had to release the full text to the rest of the press at once. With reporters scrambling to write whatever they could as rapidly as they could, the published stories were generally quite superficial: "White Racism is Riot Cause, Commission Says." Most people never learned of our solid findings of fact and sound reasoning in favor of adequate solutions.

At his next news conference, President Johnson was critical of the report's findings and conclusions, even though, responding to what we knew he had heard, we had earlier sent him a seven-page, double-spaced index of favorable references in the report to his programs. In Washington and around the country, many other politicians' reactions were similar to Johnson's, though, like him, these people had not actually read the report. "We were poor when I was a kid, but we never rioted," was a typical comment. The only cabinet members who braved the president's wrath and said a kind word about the report were the secretary of health, education, and welfare, John Gardner, and the secretary of labor, Willard Wirtz. In a favorable speech, Wirtz capsulized the report in this observation: "What the commission has said can be summed up in the words of that great American philosopher Pogo: 'We have met the enemy, and he is us.'"

America made real progress in regard to race and poverty during the decade following the Kerner Report. Then, particularly with the advent of the Ronald Reagan and George H. W. Bush administrations, that progress stopped, and we began to go backward. Two years after the report came out, then twenty years after, and finally, thirty years after, I led new studies that updated the report and reiterated what still needed to be done. Progress on race and poverty began again during the administration of President Bill Clinton. But then we slipped backward once more when President George W. Bush took office. I have never given up pushing, though.

— ∙ — ∙ — ∙ —

All the time Lyndon Johnson was president, I could tell by his manner, when I went through a White House reception line, for example, how he regarded me at the moment. If he felt good toward me, he would hold up the line and continue to clasp my hand while chatting with me, though never about much of importance. Society reporters would take note, as Johnson knew they would, and there would be plenty of time for news photographs of us together. When I was not in favor, Johnson's eyes would be hooded and expressionless. I would get a quick handshake and a weary "How are you, Fred?" and be moved on. I received that treatment frequently while I was working on the Kerner Commission Report, and especially after it came out.

The situation grew worse when I teamed up with another of my Senate seatmates and my close friend Robert Kennedy against a Social Security bill that the president wanted passed. The bill proposed a Johnson-sponsored increase in Social Security benefits, but by the time it came to the Senate, the bill also contained tacked-on House provisions that were terribly repressive and punitive toward welfare mothers, recipients of Aid to Families with Dependent Children. Johnson opposed the welfare amendments, but he wanted Robert Kennedy and me to let them pass and put off fighting them until the next congressional session, in order to get his Social Security benefits increase enacted. Kennedy and I refused to step aside. The two of us fought the bill like mad dogs, as we used to say in the Oklahoma State Senate, even trying to mount a filibuster against the bill's passage, until adroit Senate maneuvering by Senator Russell Long of Louisiana finally beat us. President Johnson was deeply angered by my intransigence on that occasion, and he had an aide let me know it.

My relationship with President Johnson was further frayed when, pretty late in the day, in the spring of 1968, I began to move away from

Johnson's position on the Vietnam War. For too long, distracted somewhat by my burdensome work on the Kerner Commission, I had accepted at face value regular White House briefings on the conduct of the war—full-dress presentations by the president himself, the chair of the Joint Chiefs of Staff, the director of the Central Intelligence Agency, the secretary of state, and the secretary of defense. Being so authoritatively told over and over that America was winning the war made it easier for me to continue to go along with the premise that we should be fighting the war at all.

My change of mind on the war paralleled that of Clark Clifford, Johnson's secretary of defense, whose judgment and advice on other matters I had come to respect. Outside the government, before becoming secretary, Clifford had supported the war, but once he became officially responsible for its prosecution, he began to ask some fundamental questions about it, and the answers he received convinced him that the war was wrong, that we ought to get out.

At about the same time, after my duties on the Kerner Commission had ended, I began to ask some of the same questions. The answers I got were terribly disturbing. I left the ranks of those supporting the war, including all my colleagues in the Oklahoma congressional delegation. Johnson did not take kindly to my defection (nor to Clark Clifford's, as I would later learn).

Nevertheless, I agreed to a request from Secretary of Agriculture Orville Freeman that I chair a national presidential reelection group, called "Town and Country for Johnson and Humphrey," to make a special campaign appeal aimed at small towns and rural areas. I took this post, incidentally, at a time when my friend Robert Kennedy, despite his growing opposition to the Vietnam War, was still saying that he, too, supported President Johnson's reelection. And I should say that my strong personal friendship with Johnson's running mate, Vice President Hubert Humphrey, was an important element in my decision to join prominently in the president's reelection effort.

But Johnson's campaign rapidly came unraveled. Minnesota Senator Eugene McCarthy, recruited by peace activists as a Democratic challenger to Johnson, ran much closer to the president than was expected in the New Hampshire primary. And, soon after that, Senator Walter Mondale came back from a trip to Wisconsin and told me—and the president, I think— that the Johnson reelection campaign in that state was "going through the cellar." Still, Mondale and I were as shocked as everyone else when President Johnson suddenly declared at the very end of a special television address announcing a Vietnam partial bombing halt that he would not be a candidate for reelection. Johnson's decision to drop out of the race was, I am sure, partly the result of his realistic assessment of the bad shape his campaign was in, that he was likely to be humiliated in the renomination process. But I am equally sure that the president gave up running again partly because he became convinced that only by doing so was there a chance he could begin to bring an end to the horrible Vietnam War.

It never once occurred to me that Lyndon Johnson would decide against seeking reelection. I knew, from Senator Mondale and others, that Johnson's campaign was in a lot of trouble. Still, just minutes before President Johnson's television speech in which he withdrew from the race, I answered a question at an evening meeting in New Orleans that the possibility Johnson might forego a reelection bid was about as likely as his suddenly dropping dead. Hardly were these words out of my mouth before I was interrupted at the lectern by a messenger with a copy of the wire-service report of Johnson's withdrawal. My reputation in New Orleans as a wise prognosticator suffered some.

Senator Mondale was even more embarrassingly caught unawares than I was. He had agreed to watch Johnson's televised speech, expected to be on Vietnam alone, from the NBC television studios in Washington and then make instant commentary. Preparing, Mondale had secured an advance text of the president's speech. An unknowing White House aide told Mondale that the president himself would add a peroration to the speech, but nothing that would change its substance. So, Mondale was well prepared, he thought, to express his "spontaneous" on-air judgments about the president's Vietnam pronouncements. The speech ended, with the shocking withdrawal announcement, and the NBC studio camera opened at once on Mondale. He told me that he could hardly get his mouth to work right.

I saw President Johnson two or three times during the ensuing 1968 presidential campaign of Hubert Humphrey that, incidentally, I wound up cochairing with Walter Mondale. On each such occasion, the president summoned me to the White House, where just the two of us met alone, up in the family quarters—once, one morning, while he was still in his pajamas, just getting out of bed. Each time, Johnson gave me political advice, but it was advice heavily laced with sharp criticism of Humphrey and his campaign. Johnson clearly expected me to pass along to the vice president the criticism as well as the advice, which I sometimes did and sometimes did not. Humphrey ought to quit talking so much on so many different issues, Johnson told me in one of our meetings. He complained that the vice president had "diarrhea of the mouth." Humphrey should say "no" more to leftist "redhots," Johnson declared, adding, "If Hubert was a woman, he'd be pregnant all the time."

My candidate, Hubert Humphrey, did not get elected president that November of 1968. Richard Nixon did. And the following January, on the Saturday before Lyndon Johnson's last Tuesday in office, I went down to the White House to see the president and bid him farewell. We had a soda and talked for close to a leisurely hour while we heard aides outside the Oval Office feverishly packing and carting away files and crates filled with the president's papers and personal effects. Once, we were interrupted by a staff member who said that the secretary of the Interior, Stewart Udall, was outside and wanted to see the president about signing an order—for something like creating a new national park, I think. But Johnson would not see Udall. "Fred, everybody is wanting me to sign something at the last minute," the president told me after he had turned aside the Udall request. "They should have thought of it earlier. Hell, if I signed some of the things people have pushed at me, I'd go to the penitentiary. I'm just not gonna do it."

While we were talking, Johnson also told me that his main regret as president was that he had not been able to pick his own cabinet members at first. He said he envied incoming President Richard Nixon's freedom to do that. "But," Johnson added, in his characteristic and somewhat embarrassing style, "John Kennedy would have looked down from heaven and would never have forgiven me if I had turned his people out." Then he tacked on a comment which I thought made more sense: "I had to keep his cabinet in order to maintain some continuity."

Johnson repeated that same thought to me, about picking his own cabinet members, when I visited him at his Texas ranch in April 1969. I was still in the Senate and by then also chair of the Democratic National Committee. Johnson agreed to see me only on the condition that the meeting be kept secret; he did not want the press to write that he was trying to interfere in political or party affairs, he said. When I landed on his ranch's airstrip in a little private jet that morning, I was surprised to see Johnson himself out there to meet me, sitting alone in the driver's seat of a top-down yellow Lincoln convertible.

He and I spent most of the day together. First, he leisurely drove me around the ranch's back roads, through mesquite-grown pasture, all the time making running commentary like a tour guide. "Now, you see that deer there," he said once, "that's one that Prince Sihanouk sent me from Cambodia." He displayed detailed knowledge about nearly everything and everybody on his spread, as he had once done in regard to the federal government. He stopped the car as we passed a Hispanic boy. "Manuel," Johnson said to the boy, "are you still trying to sell that pony?" The boy said he was. "What are you wantin' for him?" When the boy named a figure, Johnson said, "Too much." He drove on, only to stop again soon, this time beside a ranch hand who was working on a grain drill. "Are you going to have enough pasture-mix seed to finish out the field?" Johnson asked the worker. The man said he didn't think so. "Finish the rest out with oats, then," Johnson told him. We drove around some more. Johnson showed me where he had gone to school and where he had grown up, along the Pedernales River.

Then we went to the main house. There, again like a tour guide, he walked me through it—and again with nearly nonstop commentary. "Now, this is Bird's bedroom," he said, as we entered one spacious, airy room with a king-sized bed. Lady Bird, we could see through some glass doors, was out in the yard by a swimming pool, apparently working on papers or correspondence. Johnson picked up some loose pages that were lying on her bed. "Now, look at this," he said to me, showing me one of the pages. It was dated, as I remember it, sometime in March 1967. "Bird's working on her diary," Johnson went on, "and it says right here that she is looking forward to a year from this day, when we can announce we will leave the White House." Indeed, I saw that the entry did state something like that. I was aware that this was a big point with Johnson; he wanted it known that he had voluntarily left the presidency, as long planned, that he had not been driven out. My guess, now, is that, feeling increasingly beleaguered and beaten down toward the end of his term in the White House, as the Vietnam War continued to go bad and public opinion concerning it turned more and more sour, the president more than once probably expressed a determination to quit, never really thinking that he actually would have to do so.

Johnson now put Lady Bird's diary pages back on her bed, and we passed on through that room to his own large bathroom, with its adjoining walk-in closet. At the sink, he said, "Look at this mirror. Have you ever seen anything like that? It magnifies everything and makes it easy to shave." He had me try the mirror. I found he was right and said so. We stepped into his walk-in closet. Along one wall, there was a long row of boots and shoes and a long rack of shirts and suits. Opposite, there stood a hat rack festooned with a great many neckties, all already tied and each tie looped onto one of the hat rack's numerous rungs. "Now, let me show you something," Johnson said. He took up one of the ties and, demonstrating as he talked, slid the knot of the tie up and down. "When you take off your tie, just leave it tied, and it'll be ready for the next time." A little embarrassed for Johnson by his special attention to such an unimportant subject, I tried to joke with him, saying that he probably left the ties knotted because he didn't know how to tie a tie. Johnson ignored my attempt at humor and went right on. "Saves a lot of trouble and time. But you've got to remember always to slip the knot back up after you take the tie off; otherwise, it'll leave a wrinkle."

Back in the large living room, we were served a late lunch—a cold beer and a sandwich—and Johnson's talk turned more serious. He said that he was selling all the personal assets he didn't need and borrowing all the money he could because he was sure that the new president, Richard Nixon, was going to bring on a recession. "I know the bankers that backed him, and the first sign of the coming recession is gonna be high interest rates," Johnson said. But he asked me not to quote him on this, because he hoped he would prove wrong, and he didn't want to cause a panic by anything he said. (High interest rates did come, incidentally, and with them, a recession.)

Johnson was clearly hurt and angry about his longtime adviser and former secretary of defense, Clark Clifford. Author Townsend Hoopes had just published a book in which he detailed how Clifford, a hawk before he had joined the Johnson cabinet, had been the main influence in causing the president's latter-day partial bombing halt in Vietnam, action that got peace talks going. But Johnson made a big point of denying to me that

Clifford had played such a key role in his decision. "Clark Clifford and one or two others have been running to the *Washington Post*, leaking like a sieve, saying they were the ones that changed my mind on the war," Johnson told me, and he obviously felt strongly, very strongly, about the subject. "Why, Clark Clifford didn't even know what I was going to say in that last television speech [announcing a partial bombing halt and saying that he would not seek reelection] until he heard me say it. [Aide] Tom Johnson and I were just going over the cabinet minutes today, working on my book, and it was Dean Rusk who made the motion for the bombing halt. Dean Rusk is the best man I ever had."

Nevertheless, somewhat inconsistently, the president later that day repeated what he had said to me on the Saturday before he went out of office, that he regretted most not having been able, at first, to name his own cabinet members. I thought that, in a reverse sort of way, Johnson was right. Had he been able to appoint Clifford earlier—Johnson's own man, speaking his own language—the Vietnam War might have been ended sooner.

The day at the ranch was a wonderful experience for me, and flying back to Washington, I wrote a kind of sentimental, too-gushy note to Johnson on Braniff stationery. I said that I liked him, that I thought he had been a good president, and that I was sorry he and I had disagreed from time to time.

I did not see Lyndon Johnson again until about a year before his death, when he came to Oklahoma as a special guest to help dedicate yet another reservoir that was part of Senator Kerr's Arkansas River Navigation Project. He was not really so old, but he seemed old, and a little weary, though relaxed. His gray hair was long in the back and wavy. He wore a built-in hearing aid in one earpiece of his glasses.

Lady Bird was with him. At a small, private luncheon outdoors, LaDonna and I engaged in a warm and light conversation with the two of them. "Luci [the younger Johnson daughter] has always been crazy about that dog, Yuki, and she's writing an article for *Ladies' Home Journal* about him," Johnson told LaDonna and me at one point. "She's babied that dog since he was born. Why, she even supervised his castration, but they cut that out of the *Journal* article."

Lady Bird, who had been engaged in another conversation, caught only some of the last few words of her husband's remarks and turned back toward him to say, "Hon, they cut that out of the story."

Johnson responded, with an air of loving indulgence, "Bird, if you'd get you a hearing aid like me, you'd know that's what I just got through saying."

A little later, Johnson said to my wife, "LaDonna, I miss having you to watch movies with me."

"That's a damn lie," I said. "You never saw a whole movie in your life; you always go to sleep."

"Well, I still do that," Johnson said. "But Bird's gone a lot; she's been more places in America than Miz Roosevelt, and she don't have as long a step as Miz Roosevelt did. So, I found this little Catholic priest in Stonewall, and I get him to come out and watch movies with me. The other night, we were watching *The Graduate,* and sure enough, I went to sleep. And I woke up just when that couple was cuttin' up. I punched this priest, and I said, 'Father, what do you think about that?' and he said, 'If they're doing that in Stonewall, I don't know about it.'"

I was really sad when I got the news of Lyndon Johnson's death. He had been wrong on the Vietnam War, but so had I during most of his term as president. There were a lot of rough edges in his makeup—some endearing, some fairly unattractive—but so it is with most of us. The main thing was that he grew to fill the office, and he showed genuine passion in his fight against racism, disease, ignorance, and poverty. He had, indeed, riz above his raisin'. And that's what made him one of our better presidents.

7

Hubert Humphrey, the Happy Warrior

HUBERT HORATIO HUMPHREY WAS THE MOST IMPORTANT and influential member of Congress in his, and my own, generation. I knew him as a pragmatic idealist, which is what you have to be if you want to be an effective legislator. I knew him as an innovator. His were the ideas, for example, that became the basis for the Peace Corps and the War on Poverty, and more often than not, he saw his ideas come to fruition. He was a passionate advocate—for such far-reaching proposals as a much needed Marshall Plan for the Cities and for the Humphrey-Hawkins bill, which would have made full employment a systematic and enforceable goal of the U.S. government.

He was a teacher. He was a preacher. I knew him as one of the best and most persuasive speakers I ever listened to, though he nearly always talked a little too long. In any one setting, to any one audience, he would give, as someone said, "*two* of the best speeches you ever heard." He would make you laugh. He would make you cry. He would make you care about the rotting cities, about the desperate lives of poor people, because *he* cared and could not keep from showing it if he tried.

There were down years in Humphrey's career, to be sure, the often humiliating years for him when he served as vice president under Lyndon Johnson and spoke out too forcefully for Johnson's Vietnam War. But unlike many people, he won for himself a second chance, a personal and political renewal. After losing in his presidential race in 1968, he was a professor for two years and then got himself elected again to the U.S. Senate from Minnesota. And there, the real Hubert Humphrey blossomed once more.

I knew him especially as a friend, fun to be with, to laugh a lot with. So did LaDonna. From our earliest days in Washington, LaDonna became a first-rate capitol tour guide for Oklahomans who came to visit, as well as for others from around the country, especially American Indian delegations. When Humphrey was in his ceremonial vice-presidential office just off the Senate floor, he always personally welcomed her and her guests there and spent more time with them than he should have.

"Fred, I'm sitting here with a good-looking woman [LaDonna]," he would frequently say to me on the telephone toward the end of a day's Senate session, "and we want you to go out with us and have some dinner." It was often like that. Humphrey would sweep LaDonna and me along with him when he was getting ready to leave the capitol. We might go down to his suite in the Executive Office Building, adjacent to the White House, for a drink and a little conversation. And as likely as not, we would wind up accompanying him during the balance of the evening, wherever else he was going. One time, for example, we went with him to meet some Minnesota constituents at the Georgetown Inn, had dinner, and stayed on dancing there until midnight. Humphrey loved to dance.

Another time, Humphrey asked us to come along when he dropped by for a moment at a prewedding party for one of his staff members, David Gartner. The affair turned out to be rather formal, and LaDonna and I were seated at the head table and introduced, along with Humphrey, as special guests. That night, after most of those attending had left, LaDonna, Humphrey, and I, with Gartner and some others, wound up around a piano, joining in familiar old sing-along songs.

Once, LaDonna and I went on an official trip with Vice President Humphrey to South Korea, and on the return journey we all stopped over in Alaska for a couple of days, to recover from jet lag and to give the vice president the opportunity to make a speech in behalf of the great old Alaska senator Ernest Gruening, who was up for reelection (and who, unfortunately, later lost). When the political duties were over, we flew to the little town of Seward and settled in at a nearby air force recreation camp. There, the next morning, we had wonderful luck at fishing in Resurrection Bay. That night, as we finished eating our catch for dinner and were preparing to head for our separate cabins, Humphrey got word that there was a wonderful old saloon in Seward, with a rinky-tink piano player, and that a few people were dancing there. Humphrey piled us all into our cars, and escorted by the somewhat disconcerted Secret Service men, who'd had little time to check out the place, we drove off into the night and descended upon the rustic bar, which, I'm sure, had not seen such activity since the gold rush.

At first, only four or five people were in the place, including three woman habitués old enough to have been frequenting it since the days of gold fever, but Humphrey immediately asked one of them to dance, then another, then the third. Word somehow spread through the town that the vice president of the United States was dancing at the local saloon, and soon the place was packed. Every woman who came in wanted to have a turn dancing with Humphrey, and he did his best to accommodate them all. It was a great night for Humphrey, and for the rest of us. And I am sure that Seward has never forgotten it.

Humphrey had come to Oklahoma to campaign for me in 1964, the year I was first elected to the U.S. Senate. I think that when he had left Washington to fly down to help me, and himself (he was a candidate, running with Lyndon Johnson, that same year), he probably did not really believe my race against Bud Wilkinson was winnable. But after we had spent the day together and he had seen me perform, seen the crowd's response to me and my campaign, he changed his mind. That late afternoon, after we put him on his plane at the Tulsa airport and prepared to turn and walk away, Humphrey suddenly appeared in the airplane's open door and bounded down the steps, just to say to me before taking off, "Fred, you're going to win this thing!" That spontaneous and reassuring gesture gave me a personal boost, just as his campaign appearances had given me a political one.

In that first encounter with Humphrey in Oklahoma in 1964, I saw a different person than I had expected to see. For one thing, his physical appearance was different. He was not at all dumpy and a little pudgy, as television and news photos often made him look. He was actually trim, well-dressed, and rather tall.

And he did not seem like a wild-eyed radical, as he had been called. Earlier, on the airplane with other Oklahoma delegates, going to Atlantic City in 1964 for my first Democratic National Convention, I and the others had been told that Lyndon Johnson's upcoming choice for running mate had come down to Humphrey and another Minnesota senator, Eugene McCarthy. Virtually that whole planeload of Oklahomans had expressed their support for McCarthy as the more down-to-earth, less radical of the two (perceptions that would be completely reversed, in

Oklahoma and in the country, by the time, just four years later, McCarthy became a presidential candidate against Johnson).

Once, after I was a senator and Humphrey was vice president, he and I and the House majority leader, Carl Albert, flew together somewhere on a small air force passenger jet. On the way, the three of us somehow got started telling about how poor we'd each been, growing up. Albert won the unspoken contest on that occasion: Humphrey and I soon conceded that he'd clearly been the poorest of us. (After Albert had finished the eighth grade at a rural school, he told us, his father had asked him to stay and work on the farm another year instead of moving into the town of McAlester so he could go to high school, promising, "I'll see that you get to go to high school, Carl, even if I have to sell the farm.") Still, Hubert Humphrey's own poor boy story was pretty impressive, too.

He grew up in the tough 1930s Dust Bowl and Depression poverty of a little town on the South Dakota plains. He knew what it was to see his father, a family druggist, powerless, broke, at the mercy of wholesalers and banks and economic conditions generally. As a young man, Humphrey had to drop out of school to help his father in the drugstore. And he stayed home out of loyalty far too long for his own good and his own career. Indeed, his sense of duty toward his father almost prevented him from finally marrying his wife, Muriel, when he did.

But Humphrey did get married, and a story about that, which Humphrey himself told me and which is also related in his autobiography, *The Education of a Public Man*, says a lot about him. When he and Muriel, just married, drove off on their honeymoon trip, Humphrey's sister, Frances Howard, rode with them for the first two hundred miles because good old Humphrey had agreed to drive her to a place where she could best catch a train back to Washington. I can't help but smile every time I think of those bashful newlyweds, riding along in the front seat of a borrowed Ford, too embarrassed to say much to each other, with Frances, who was as bubbly and talkative as Humphrey himself, sitting right there behind them, a daunting and dampening presence.

If Humphrey came to have too great a desire to be liked, perhaps it grew out of his decidedly second-class background, but I think some of his more important personal traits came from that background, too: deep compassion for less fortunate people; a strong conviction that inordinate economic power should be curtailed; an instinctive human warmth and friendliness; a resolution to take pleasure in all of life; a steadfast and joyful loyalty to friends; an enduring trust in himself and a faith in the improvability of the conditions of life; a Chautauqua-style speaker's ability to galvanize individuals and whole audiences; and a firm belief that determination and hard work always pay off and that virtue is, indeed, its own reward.

Humphrey told me that he came to the Senate in 1949 as something of a pariah. A popular former mayor of Minneapolis and the Democratic nominee for the U.S. Senate from Minnesota, he had been a delegate to the 1948 Democratic convention. There, he had refused to go along with an establishment-backed platform-committee compromise on civil rights. Instead, he had taken a really tough civil rights minority plank to the convention floor—and won.

He had courageously, and quite correctly, maintained that the Democratic Party stood for very little unless it stood for human equality. A majority of the delegates agreed. And that was the first time that the national Democratic Party had ever faced up to the North-South split in its ranks, the first time that it had ever taken a firm stand for African American civil rights. Deep South delegates walked out of the convention. Old-time party unity was in shambles.

Still, in the ensuing presidential election, with a Dixiecrat candidate, ex-Democrat Strom Thurmond of South Carolina, siphoning off some of what would have otherwise been a larger vote for the Republican candidate, Thomas Dewey, incumbent Harry Truman was elected president. Back home in Minnesota, Hubert Humphrey was elected to the U.S. Senate.

And nobody was ever prouder and happier to come to Washington than he was. Being a member of Congress had been Humphrey's lifelong dream, but, as he told me, he was in for a rude shock. The Senate was at that time a kind of southern "gentlemen's" club, he said. And there was very little acceptance among its courtly barons for the northern liberal who had caused the southern walkout at the Democratic convention.

Humphrey, who wanted more than anything else to be an effective senator and to belong, ran up against cold ostracism and cruel ridicule. He told me that one day, for example, as he walked down the center aisle of the Senate chamber and passed by the desk of Senator Richard Russell of Georgia, the chamber's patriarch and most powerful member, Russell said to a nearby colleague, purposely speaking loudly enough for

Humphrey to hear, "Why would anyone send a son of a bitch like that to the Senate?" On many evenings during Humphrey's first months in Washington, he told me, he drove home crying.

Perhaps Humphrey thereafter tried too hard to make the team. Perhaps he made too dependent an alliance with Russell's protégé, Lyndon Johnson, when the majority leader sought him out and made him his liaison with the growing number of liberal senators. But characteristically, Humphrey never changed his convictions, and he did not tailor his advocacy. He did, however, spend a lot of extra time in the senators' private dining room, cultivating Senate leaders. He learned that the personal amenities and courtesies were of almost as much consequence as was ideology to the southern senators. He found that contacts, friendships, helpfulness in little things were extremely important, and his alliance with Lyndon Johnson provided him with an entrée, an opportunity to take advantage of the gift he had for ingratiating himself with others, to employ to good effect his ebullience and his natural desire to be helpful.

Humphrey soon became a leader in the Senate, and after Johnson became president following the assassination of John Kennedy, it was natural for him to turn to Humphrey as his choice for a vice-presidential running mate. Before announcing that decision, however, Johnson flew Humphrey back to Washington from the 1964 Atlantic City Democratic National Convention for a kind of final audition in the Oval Office. The president had already made up his mind to go with Humphrey, but he did not tell Humphrey. He kept Humphrey off balance and on tenterhooks, wanting Humphrey to kiss the ring one more time. To confuse the press and for window dressing, Johnson brought two men back to Washington on that same plane—besides Humphrey, Senator Thomas Dodd of Connecticut. Dodd was a Roman Catholic, and Johnson wanted to signal to Catholic voters that a Catholic was among those whom he was seriously considering for a running mate, though he really was not. (Johnson's earlier floating of the name of Senator Eugene McCarthy, also a Catholic, was just for show, too—and McCarthy resented this deeply and never forgave the president for it).

In the Oval Office, still not telling Humphrey that he was the choice, Johnson first handed him a folder filled with papers and said, "Here, Hubert, this is your FBI file; go in the other room and look through it, then come back and let's talk." Humphrey said he was shocked by the reports,

mostly pretty flimsy stuff, that the FBI had accumulated on him, including a false claim that, in Chicago, I believe it was, Humphrey had once had
a prostitute up to his hotel room. He went back into the Oval Office white
with nervousness, shaken, but before he could offer explanations for what
he had seen in his file, the president interrupted dismissively, saying,
"Don't worry about it, Hubert; if you think that's bad, you ought to see
what they've got in *my* FBI file." And then the president abruptly told
Humphrey he wanted him to be his running mate.

After the Democratic convention and the Johnson-Humphrey nomi-
nations, the president brought Humphrey down to the LBJ ranch in Texas
for a strategy session and kickoff meeting. On this occasion, well covered
by the national press corps, Johnson had Humphrey dress up in some out-
sized cowboy boots, a western hat, and other western garb—looking out-
landish and awkward—and climb on a horse for a picture-taking ride
with the president. LBJ, no matter what his pose, was not in fact a particularly good horseman—at least that's what my dad, a real cowboy kind
of guy, told me after watching this episode on television. Johnson's personal mount that day was a specially trained Tennessee walking horse, as
easy to ride as a rocking chair, but he put Humphrey on a spirited, somewhat jumpy quarter horse, and apparently took a kind of mean delight in
the resulting discomfiture of his running mate. I could never imagine,
when Humphrey told me about this, why he would let the president do
him this way. And Humphrey was embarrassed about it, too, just as he
was when, at Johnson's insistence and though he was not a hunter, he had
to shoot two deer on that same trip to the LBJ ranch.

As vice president, Humphrey never stopped being Humphrey on do-
mestic issues. He closely followed the work of the president's National
Advisory Commission on Civil Disorders—the Kerner Commission—
and strongly supported our eventual findings and recommendations in
regard to race and poverty. He warmly supported the idea, which
LaDonna and I pushed, for the establishment of a Cabinet Committee on
Indian Affairs, and he became its hardworking and effective chair. But the
Vietnam War was another matter.

Humphrey was right at first on Vietnam, then wrong, and then wrong
too long. David Halberstam, news reporter and author of the classic book
on the Vietnam War *The Best and the Brightest*, once asked me in private
conversation whether I felt Humphrey ever really, personally, supported

the Johnson war policy. The implication of the question was that Humphrey only did so publicly, in order to stay in Johnson's good graces.

I told Halberstam that I never doubted that when Humphrey spoke in support of the war, he was saying exactly what he thought at the time. He said the same things to me privately. And I do not think Humphrey could ever have been a good liar; he was too transparent. Maybe some critics of the Vietnam War will think less of him because he supported the war out of conviction, rather than for political reasons; I am not offering a defense. But I am saying what I think is true: he did become convinced that the Johnson war policy was the correct one.

As is well known, though, Humphrey originally opposed the Vietnam War. He wrote a lengthy internal memorandum, now part of the public record, telling President Johnson why he believed his Vietnam policy was wrong and ought to be changed. That was the real Humphrey, the Humphrey who had stood up for a strong civil rights plank at the 1948 Democratic convention, the Humphrey with the strong and correct moral and human instincts.

But, truth to tell, I suppose you could say it was also the real Humphrey who was wounded and hurt when Johnson ostracized him for a time, denying him access to the White House and involvement in high-level decisions, after the president received Humphrey's critical Vietnam memo. It was the real Humphrey, too, who, when thereafter sent to Vietnam as Johnson's emissary, apparently took at face value the military and other briefings he received there—and came back a convert. And it was also the real Humphrey, a superb advocate, who began to couch his new support for the Vietnam war—support that was genuine, I felt, though perhaps complex and conditional—in fairly simple and persuasive public phrases of apparently unconditional approval. This was a bad time for our country and for the Vietnamese. It was a bad time for Humphrey, too.

Typically, Lyndon Johnson did not give his vice president the courtesy of any advance notice at all before suddenly renouncing reelection and throwing the ensuing presidential race wide open to all comers. Humphrey was on an official trip in Mexico at the time. He got the news that night, just like everyone else, and flew back to Washington at once. I got back there the same day, after speaking at a Tulane and Loyola conference in New Orleans the preceding night, the night of the surprising Johnson announcement.

Humphrey called me right away and invited me and LaDonna, just the two of us, to come to his apartment the following morning for a private breakfast with him and Muriel. Driving there, I warned my wife that it was not our place to urge Humphrey to run for president. He would have to make up his own mind. Our job, I said, was to help him look at the whole situation dispassionately and make the wisest decision for himself and the country. "I don't think it's right to advise or encourage him to run," I told LaDonna, "if we ourselves are not ready to pledge our full support—and we're not."

At breakfast and over coffee, the four of us spent a couple of hours talking things over. Humphrey said that some people, among them labor leader George Meany, president of the AFL-CIO, thought it imperative that he announce immediately. Humphrey had been told, too, that Mayor Richard Daley of Chicago would probably go over to Robert Kennedy unless Humphrey announced right away. I told him that in my opinion he had to resist those kinds of pressures, that if Mayor Daley was going to jump to Kennedy, nothing Humphrey did or said immediately would prevent it. I said that he ought to try to assess in some detail the kind of support, particularly financial support, that he could expect, and that he ought to decide to run only if he got concrete, almost contractual, assurances of sufficient support. The commitment that I made to Humphrey upon leaving that morning was that I would not come to any decision about supporting him or Senator Kennedy, who he knew was also my close friend, until Humphrey'd had plenty of time to decide upon his own course.

LaDonna was in tears by the time she and I got down the hall and into the apartment-building elevator. "It just all seemed too cold," she said. "I think he needed more warmth and reinforcement from us."

My response to her was, "But we owed him more, out of friendship, than blindly agreeing to his natural inclination to run."

"I know, and I understand that," LaDonna said. "You're right. But I'm not thinking about the decision or the campaign. I just wish there'd been some way we could've let him know how much we like him as a person, and that we're his friends, whatever he decides."

On the spot—that's where I was. Not many Americans have ever had to choose between two close friends running against each other for president of the United States. Robert Kennedy, too, had called me on the morning after Lyndon Johnson's renunciation announcement. He did not get me because I was on a plane at the time, coming back from New Orleans, and he left a message. I returned his call as soon as I could but could not reach him; he had gone to Pennsylvania to make a speech. I left word with Angie Novello, his secretary. Robert never called me back after that. I think that as a close friend, he had probably figured out what I was going to have to do and did not want to pressure me.

Following the breakfast meeting with Humphrey, I gathered my principal staff members and some close friends for a meeting in my office. What should I do? All but one of this group thought that I had to support Humphrey if he ran. Most thought that, as a practical matter, Humphrey as president would have a better chance of actually getting enacted the kinds of policies all three of us—he, I, and Kennedy—supported and believed in. I had reason to believe, too, that Humphrey would break with Johnson and set a different course in regard to the Vietnam War.

So, that is what I did: I decided to support Humphrey for president, for a number of reasons. Among them was the fact that in my mind I had already made a partial commitment to Humphrey when I had earlier signed on to head the national campaign organization "Town and Country for Johnson and Humphrey." Another factor in my decision to support Humphrey was my close friendship with Humphrey's fellow Minnesotan Senator Walter Mondale. He, Robert Kennedy, and I had been seatmates from our very first day in the Senate—Kennedy on my right, Mondale on my left. Beginning at the very bottom in seniority, the three of us started out being assigned to the Senate's back row. As we gained seniority, we moved forward, but only if we could do so as a unit. (After Robert Kennedy's death, Mondale and I would continue as seat-mates, only moving in the Senate together.) LaDonna and I and Fritz, as we called him, and Joan Mondale, as well as our children, were close. We once took a house together for a week at the Delaware beach, for example. We each helped out the other with meeting and entertaining constituents. We collaborated on legislation, such as his proposal for the creation of a national social-accounting system and mine that first advocated what became the Kerner Commission.

It was Mondale who got me actively involved in the Humphrey campaign—by degrees. He first caught me in the Senate cloakroom one day and asked me to join him as cochair of a Sheraton Park Hotel luncheon at which Humphrey would formally announce as a candidate. I agreed. The luncheon proved to be a great success, though it did have one sour effect. In it, Humphrey quoted a John Adams phrase that mentioned, among other things, a "politics of joy." Eugene McCarthy and others would soon unfairly use this Humphrey statement to try to show that Humphrey was insensitive to the dying in Vietnam, rat bites in the ghettoes, and the ravages of poverty in general.

Not long after the Humphrey formal announcement, Mondale, at Humphrey's direction, asked me to become national cochair with him of the whole Humphrey for President campaign. Again, I agreed. The two of us flew down to Key Largo, Florida, where Humphrey was vacationing with Dwayne Andreas, the native Minnesotan who headed the Archer Daniels Midland Company. On the way there, Mondale, who had been active in Humphrey campaigns since he was eighteen years old, told me that it was essential that we establish a clear understanding with Humphrey about whether he wanted us to run the campaign or just serve as figureheads. Mondale said that in the past, Humphrey campaigns had always tended to split up, to become hydra headed.

We met on Andreas's luxury boat, where Humphrey emphatically declared that, indeed, he wanted Mondale and me actually to run things. And we went back to Washington and set out to do so. Mondale and I divided the campaign-management functions between us. My realm included administrative oversight of the organization, as well as our effort to secure delegates. I brought in Robert McCandless, now a Washington attorney, and told him to read Theodore White's *The Making of the President in 1960* and set up a delegate operation like the one John Kennedy'd had in his nomination campaign. McCandless did that—and well. But the first weekly meeting Mondale and I had with the McCandless operation was a disaster. McCandless was still trying to learn his job. The Humphrey effort had hardly had time by then to shake down and was still having to depend a lot on people in the states who had been part of the old Johnson effort. McCandless brought a Johnson operative into that first strategy meeting to report on the situation in West Virginia. This guy matter of factly told us that we would have to follow through on his earlier promise to deliver forty-five thousand dollars in cash to a couple of West Virginia officeholders, adding almost casually that, by the way, both these men were under indictment by grand juries. Mondale exploded. He leaped out of his chair, shouting to the Johnson man, "Get out of this room! Out! Out!"

When the Johnson man was gone, Mondale turned to McCandless and, close to foaming at the mouth, said, with me in agreement, "I don't *ever* want to hear that kind of talk again." We never did. Some people involved in the Humphrey campaign came to call Mondale and me the Boy Scouts.

But sure enough, just as Mondale had feared, soon three separate, somewhat competitive Humphrey campaigns were in operation. There was the large official campaign that Mondale and I organized and directed. There was another, smaller campaign run by some of Humphrey's more conservative staff members, principally Bill Connell, as well as by certain leftover operatives from the Johnson campaign, including Richard Maguire (who had also been active in John Kennedy's campaigns). And there was still another campaign, a small and confusing effort run by old and loyal Minnesota friends of Humphrey's, including Secretary of Agriculture Orville Freeman, trucking magnate Robert Short, and attorney Max Kampelman, whom Mondale could not stand and would not let into our headquarters. (Mondale questioned Kampelman's ethics and once said to Humphrey in my presence, "If I ever see Kampelman in our headquarters again, I'm out of there.)

It was a mess. So, just prior to the 1968 Democratic convention in Chicago, Mondale and I agreed on a way to rationalize the organization. Lawrence O'Brien was brought in as the campaign czar. He was set up in an office immediately next to Humphrey's own, in the Executive Office Building, so that nobody could come between him and the candidate. This change resulted in marked improvement, though we were never able totally to integrate all the separate preconvention campaigns.

An item in the Periscope section of *Newsweek* (the source for which, my press secretary found out, was Robert Kennedy's great staff member Frank Mankiewisz) reported that Kennedy had in mind choosing me as his running mate if he got the presidential nomination. I did not give this much thought, though. For one thing, I figured that Humphrey, not Kennedy, was going to be the Democratic nominee. And regarding the vice-presidential nomination, I assumed that Humphrey would need to choose someone from a populous state, maybe someone from the Kennedy camp, perhaps a Catholic. But as the time of the Democratic

National Convention drew nearer, there was increased press speculation about my possibly being Humphrey's vice-presidential nominee. I found this embarrassing. I was worried that people might question my motives, might say that I was supporting Humphrey just because I wanted to be vice president.

So, one night at the Pierre Hotel in New York, after a campaign appearance I had made for Humphrey, LaDonna and I sat up late talking about all the speculation and concluded that I should remove myself from consideration. We made that decision in part, too, because we had seen what the office had done to Humphrey, under Johnson. We even called our daughter Kathryn, an active worker for Humphrey, in Washington and told her what we had decided. She agreed. I decided that the way to make my decision believable was to endorse another person for the vice-presidential nomination—Senator Edmund Muskie of Maine.

Back in Washington the next morning, LaDonna and I went directly from the airport to Humphrey's office to pose with him for pictures for a *Look* magazine article. As soon as the photographer left, Humphrey said to me, "Fred, I have not discussed the vice-presidential nomination with you before, but I want to now." I interrupted him. "LaDonna and I decided last night that I should take myself out of the running," I said. I told him that I really meant it and that I intended to underscore my decision by endorsing another person in an appearance I was scheduled for right away in Los Angeles on the late-night ABC *Joey Bishop Show.*

Before I could tell Humphrey the name of the person I planned to endorse, he stopped me. "Don't do that, Fred," he said. "I kept you on privately here to tell you that you are one of four people that I'm seriously considering for the vice-presidential nomination. Don't take yourself out of it." Then he went on: "I want to be sure that you understand that I'm making no commitment to you. And I'm not playing any games with you, as Johnson did with me in 1964. I am seriously considering you. Go on out to California for the Bishop show, and make as good an impression as you can. That will help you, and it will help me. And we'll see what happens."

My plan had ended almost before it had begun. And frankly, I now found myself a good deal more interested in the vice-presidential nomination than I had been before. I made the appearance on the *Joey Bishop Show,* to good reviews. Then I headed to the Democratic convention in Chicago. I knew from reliable insiders the identity of the four people

Humphrey had narrowed his choice down to: Governor Richard Hughes of New Jersey, former Peace Corps director Sargent Shriver, Senator Edmund Muskie, and me. There was also some peripheral and less serious consideration of Terry Sanford, a former governor of North Carolina. Then, immediately after the convention began, I learned that the list of those being seriously considered by Humphrey had been pared down by him to just two names—mine and Muskie's.

But first, the Vietnam War had to be dealt with. Lawrence O'Brien later wrote in his book *No Final Victories* that in July 1968, prior to the Democratic convention in Chicago, he met with Humphrey to discuss Vietnam. "Hubert read me a statement he said he would soon be making public. In it, he favored a bombing halt and a negotiated end to the war. It satisfied me, and I agreed to join his campaign through the Convention." Senator Mondale and I had also listened to and approved the same speech, which Humphrey told us had largely been written by Asian expert Edwin Reischauer.

Just before we had left Humphrey's office on that occasion, Senator Mondale asked the vice president whether he would have to clear the speech with President Johnson before delivering it. Humphrey told us that he would not have to clear it, because he would be making the statement as a presidential candidate, not as the incumbent vice president. He did say that he intended to inform Johnson of the general content of the speech.

Unfortunately, that speech was never given. O'Brien would later write, "About a week later, Humphrey visited Johnson at the ranch and on his return, he told me that the President had advised him of a major new development on Vietnam. Naturally, he said, he should not make any statement until after the President had made his announcement. He added that for security reasons he couldn't reveal the details, but he indicated that the President was about to take a step that would please the anti-war people. That was the last I heard of Humphrey's statement, and his position on Vietnam was to haunt us throughout the Convention and campaign."

I felt that I ought to do something, so in a press conference in Puerto Rico, where LaDonna and I had gone to visit Native Americans training for the Peace Corps, I announced my own support for an unconditional bombing halt, de-escalation, and a negotiated settlement to end U.S. involvement in Vietnam. My statement made more news elsewhere in the world, especially in Paris, the site of Vietnam peace talks, than it did in the United States. It did make news in Oklahoma, however; I was the only

member of the Oklahoma congressional delegation who was publicly opposed to the Johnson policy, a political problem for me.

Our ambassador in Paris, the venerable diplomat Averell Harriman,
later sent encouraging word to me through Bill Moyers, a former Johnson
aide, to the effect that my statement was on the right track and that I
should persist in my position in order to help move the Johnson administration in the right direction. But in the Humphrey campaign, there had
been no public effort, by the time of the Chicago convention, to differen-
tiate the vice president's views on Vietnam from those of President Johnson. "I believed . . . that to be elected Humphrey had to disassociate
himself from Johnson's Vietnam policy," O'Brien wrote. "Harris and Mondale agreed, but we were by no means a majority in the Humphrey circle
of advisors." That was true.

A part of my job at the convention, since O'Brien had taken over day-
to-day direction of the campaign itself, was to work with Washington attorney David Ginsburg on the platform. A strong peace plank was
drafted, using almost the exact words that Senator Edward Kennedy had
employed in a recent speech at Worcester, Massachusetts, calling for an
unconditional bombing halt, de-escalation, and a negotiated settlement.
Humphrey approved the plank, and O'Brien, Ginsburg, and I began the
task of selling it to key Democratic leaders.

The platform chair, Representative Hale Boggs of Louisiana, agreed to
this peace plank only after I "looked him in the eye," as he asked, and
swore that it was what Humphrey wanted. Ginsburg and I, with success,
then began to lobby other convention-delegation leaders. Governor John
Connally of Texas did not like the plank, but reluctantly agreed not to fight
it. Another conservative governor, Buford Ellington of Tennessee, said he
would go along. So did the others we were especially worried about. But
then some of President Johnson's people moved in. They blew up our
coalition in the platform committee and among delegates generally and
began to organize to oppose the Humphrey peace plank openly.

When that happened, late one night, David Ginsburg and Humphrey
staffer Bill Welch came and asked my advice about what we should do
next. "It's time for some moxie," I told them, using a word I had learned
from Robert Kennedy. I said that Humphrey should stand firm for the
peace plank. "If Johnson opposes it, that's his business," I said. "I believe
Johnson'll back down, but even if he doesn't, Humphrey will have done
the right thing, and he'll have made his break with Johnson."

After I said that, there was a rather long silence. David Ginsburg and Bill Welch sat there a moment, and then they asked me what my fallback advice was. I said I didn't have any. They left to discuss the situation with Humphrey.

Unfortunately, the Humphrey group decided upon a "compromise" peace plank, watering down the language that had previously been agreed upon. Bill Welch asked me to lead the effort on the convention floor for the adoption of the compromise plank. I refused. Instead, Senator Ed Muskie and Representative James O'Hara of Michigan took on the responsibility for pushing it through. The compromise plank was adopted by the convention, but at great cost. The divisions within the party were widened, and the day was delayed when Humphrey would have to break openly with the Johnson war policy.

I do believe that prior to the convention, Humphrey had begun to change his mind about the Vietnam War and was moving back toward something near his original position. And I do not believe he delayed saying so publicly out of fear of Johnson's wrath, or because of political considerations. My judgment is that Humphrey was told by senior administration officials, probably including the president himself, that peace in Vietnam was nearly at hand and that any statement by Humphrey criticizing existing U.S. policy would weaken and perhaps ruin the chances for negotiations to succeed, thereby causing a lot more young American soldiers to be killed.

On the night Humphrey received the Democratic nomination, he began more detailed and serious conversations with advisers and supporters about the choice of a running mate. Outside, there were demonstrations and violence in the streets and terrible misuse of force by the Chicago police. LaDonna had been invited to watch the balloting for the presidential nomination with Humphrey and some of his closest staff people in the Humphrey hotel suite, one floor up from mine. Our daughter Kathryn, our son, Byron, and I had intended to watch the balloting on television from my office at the convention center. Instead, we spent most of the evening looking at television reports of what was happening in the streets—and crying, all three of us.

Back at the hotel, much later, when the streets were finally quiet and our children had gone to bed, LaDonna and I received periodic reports from friends in the Humphrey suite about how the selection of a vice-presidential nominee was going. We heard that Humphrey had called in the mayor of Pittsburgh and the mayor of Philadelphia. One had voiced support for Muskie, the other for me. We were informed that labor leaders he had consulted had also been equally split in their recommendations. Lawrence O'Brien was for Muskie; Mondale was for me. Finally, a friend came to tell us that Humphrey had gone to bed at about four o'clock in the morning with the decision still not made.

Dead tired, I did not wake up the next morning until half past ten. Since I knew Humphrey had scheduled a press conference for ten o'clock to announce his choice of a running mate, I assumed that he had selected Muskie. I must say that I felt some relief at this point. I was heartsick about the violence and the insensitivity of Mayor Daley's police, as well as by too many of the Johnson people, who were in rigid control of the convention, toward the demonstrators. I was deeply disappointed that Humphrey had not stuck with his original peace-plank proposal.

But I had not lost interest in the vice-presidential nomination. That was rekindled when, in a little while, a report came from the Humphrey suite that no decision had yet been made and that the scheduled press conference had been postponed. Close friends began to gather in my hotel sitting room, to await the decision with me. Hour by hour, the discussion continued upstairs, and hour by hour, the press conference at which Humphrey was to announce his running mate was further delayed.

At one point, a young aide of mine came bursting into the room to announce, "It must be you! The Secret Service are here on this floor!" But it turned out that the two men he had seen were from hotel security. We resumed the vigil. Suddenly, the same young aide returned to say, "This time, I know the Secret Service are on this floor! I asked one to show me his identification." It was true, but it turned out that the Secret Service men had come only because Humphrey's wife, Muriel, was scheduled to attend a meeting on our floor.

At last, my phone rang. It was Humphrey, and he asked me to come to his suite. I left the hushed group of my family and well-wishers and speeded up the stairs. Humphrey greeted me at the door and took me through an anteroom, where a number of his staff people were waiting, and into a bedroom. Our conversation was very brief. He told me that he had narrowed the choice down to me and Muskie. We discussed the vice-presidential nomination, the office of the vice president, and the qualities and qualifications I might bring to the campaign and to the office itself. I frankly do not remember much of that conversation.

Humphrey then asked me to please wait, and he left the room. Soon, he came back again and talked to me some more, then left again. When next he returned, he put his hand on my shoulder and, with tears welling up in his eyes, said, "Fred, I'm going to have to choose the older man."

I said, "If that's your decision, I'll be glad to nominate Muskie."

"Would you really?" he asked. I said that I certainly would. He then asked me to accompany him to notify Senator Muskie of his decision. That is when I first realized that Muskie and I had, all the time, been in adjoining bedrooms and that Humphrey had been shuttling back and forth between us. Humphrey and I walked into the room where Muskie, facing away from us, was nervously leaning on a bureau. He turned. Humphrey then spoke what probably seemed to Muskie one of the longest sentences he had ever heard: "Ed, shake hands with the man . . . who is going to nominate you."

I congratulated Muskie, and he and I left the room immediately. He had to get ready for the press conference. I had to notify my friends and start working on my nominating speech. Ironically, a few minutes after I returned to my hotel room, a representative of the Secret Service rushed in breathlessly to ask whether I knew Senator Muskie's room number.

That night, I stood before the convention and made my nomination speech for Ed Muskie for vice president. I was proud to do so. I had served with him. He was a good and solid man, and I felt he would be an asset on the ticket. I am also proud that I took the occasion of that nominating speech to express publicly my strong disapproval of the conduct of the Chicago police in the streets.

I returned to Oklahoma. For several weeks after the convention, my participation in the campaign was slight. As a matter of fact, my heart had not been in it much since the assassination of Robert Kennedy, prior to the convention. Robert McCandless arranged for me to have a desk and secretary at the offices of the Democratic National Committee; technically, Senator Mondale and I were still the national cochairs of the Humphrey-Muskie campaign, although we had not had day-to-day administrative responsibility for it since Larry O'Brien had been brought in, prior to the convention. Following Humphrey's nomination, Mondale and I had been participants in a meeting in which Humphrey had talked O'Brien into becoming chair of the Democratic National Committee, and he continued to direct the campaign.

I made speeches and other appearances when asked, and I took part in the policy meetings. The campaign was obviously in deep trouble. For one thing, the administration of its several facets was still fragmented, despite O'Brien's overall responsibility. One group, under Orville Freeman, was responsible for scheduling and publicizing campaign events, while another group, under Robert McCandless, who reported directly to O'Brien, was responsible for the organization of support at various levels and for getting out the vote. Frequently, the local operatives of these two units did not communicate with each other. Fund-raising was going very poorly. And there was general despair, a feeling that the campaign was hopeless.

One of the few who did not think it was hopeless was Humphrey. His courage was heroic, and his efforts were Herculean. He kept going doggedly on, against all odds, and he almost pulled the thing out.

A turning point in the campaign was a nationally televised Humphrey speech on the Vietnam War. As soon as Humphrey had agreed to make this major policy address, O'Brien called to ask me to join the staff on the campaign airplane, so that I could help Humphrey write the speech and could use my influence to get him to embody in it a clear differentiation between his own Vietnam policy and Johnson's. This would be Humphrey's last chance to do so.

I flew to Los Angeles, met with Humphrey, and then went on with him and the traveling entourage of campaign staff and press people to Sacramento, San Francisco, Portland, Seattle, and finally, Salt Lake City. All along this route, the inner-circle debate between the supporters of the Vietnam War and those who opposed it grew hotter and hotter. At each stop, suggested drafts and redrafts of the Vietnam speech were sent by Teletype back and forth between the Humphrey entourage and the campaign headquarters in Washington. Before long, each side in the debate brought up reinforcements. Larry O'Brien joined the side I was on, the peace side, as did Humphrey staffer Bill Welch and former State Department official George Ball. Incredibly, the debate was still going on and still unresolved when a late-night meeting broke up in Salt Lake City on the very evening before the speech was scheduled to be taped. It was still going on the next morning and right up until thirty minutes before the speech had to be typed for the TelePrompTer.

I was frankly disappointed in the final version Humphrey decided upon. It did not go far enough to suit me. Also, the three most important paragraphs were mutually inconsistent. The first of these seemed to call for a bombing halt without preconditions, but the next paragraph stated that the "other side" ought to be willing to take certain steps first, and the third paragraph declared that if we stopped the bombing and the other side did not respond, the force we would then use would be greater than ever.

I sat in the studio as Humphrey taped the speech. Soon after the taping was finished, we moved to a next-door viewing room. Minutes later, the Salt Lake City station began to feed the tape to the network for immediate broadcasting, and at this point, Humphrey stepped outside the viewing room to make a telephone call. It is my impression that the call was to President Johnson. When Humphrey came back, his face was ashen. I imagine that the call had not been a very easy one to make, and my guess is that Johnson did not take very kindly to receiving Humphrey's report on the content of the speech after it was already being broadcast throughout the nation.

I rode back from the television studio to the hotel on the press bus so that I could gauge the reactions of reporters. I found the newspeople in disagreement about what the lede for the story should be. Some said Humphrey's speech was a mere rehash of his previous statements. Some said he had just restated the Johnson line. Some thought the speech was an unmistakable break with Johnson's war policy.

By the time we got back to the hotel, we already had the news that Senator Edward Kennedy had hailed the speech as a very good one and had said he was now willing to pledge his full-fledged support of the Humphrey candidacy. This, I'm sure, impressed the reporters. And Kennedy's statement started a flood of other endorsements from political figures who up until that time had been hanging back.

It was soon clear, too, that the Humphrey speech had come across to the television audience as a call for a change in the Vietnam War policy; viewers understood it to be a peace speech, as to a great extent it was. The Humphrey-Muskie campaign began to catch fire from that moment, and, incidentally, a last-minute tag line on the televised speech asking for money brought in twice as much in contributions as the broadcast had cost.

Soon, Humphrey was no longer campaigning alone. More and more politicians were willing to be seen with him. Experienced observers began to feel that the campaign might just possibly be successful. President Johnson and Governor John Connally of Texas put on a huge rally for Humphrey in Texas, bringing together all elements of the fractious Texas Democratic Party.

I flew out to Los Angeles to take part in a national telethon for Humphrey on the night before the election. An earlier campaign parade in downtown Los Angeles brought out one of the largest crowds ever seen for a candidate there. Thousands thronged the streets to cheer Humphrey. And a respected California poll, the Field poll, that day indicated that Humphrey had pulled even with Nixon in California.

Our campaign telethon could not have gone over better. Spirits were high. After the telethon, we all went to a party at the Beverly Hills home of former White House aides Lloyd and Ann Hand, who had erected a giant tent in their backyard. A wonderful crowd of friends and supporters, movie stars and political figures, attended. There was excellent food and music, and dancing continued until the early hours of the morning.

Finally, we went in a caravan to the airport and boarded the campaign plane for Minnesota. Immediately upon landing, Humphrey and Muriel went to vote. The rest of us checked in at the Leamington Hotel for a few hours of sleep.

On election night, as the returns began to come in, it was soon clear that the best Humphrey could expect was a no-majority deadlock in the Electoral College, which would leave the decision up to the U.S. House of Representatives. That prospect seemed no better to me than defeat. But defeat was what we got. And Humphrey's defeat was awfully sad for all of us who'd been involved in the campaign, especially so because we admired the way Humphrey had worked his heart out, never giving up during the days of abuse by peace demonstrators, of despair about the public-opinion polls, of humiliation when various public officials had at first declined to be seen with him.

"We were with him at the first, and we ought to go down and stand with him at the last," I told my tearful wife. She fixed her face, we joined Humphrey and Muriel, and together with Senator Mondale and other close friends and family members, we walked into the Leamington ballroom. It was tough for all of us to keep the tears out of our eyes. Humphrey made a good concession statement, and it was all over.

The plane ride back to Washington was much like an Irish wake. Humphrey stayed on in Minnesota. The rest of us flew back together, and almost everyone on board alternated between singing, laughing, and crying. At the airport, we shook hands and embraced, some of us never to see each other again, and most of us never again to be as close.

Humphrey was not the best possible candidate for president, but perfect candidates don't exist, or if they do, they don't run. I was proud to be associated with him. I could never understand the attitude of some liberals, during that campaign, who claimed it would make no real difference whether Humphrey or Richard Nixon was elected. They could not have been more wrong, as they were soon to see. And I was personally glad that I did not have to have Richard Nixon's election on my conscience.

I went back to Washington and the Senate. Lawrence O'Brien announced that he was stepping down as national chair of the Democratic Party. There was talk that I should take on that job, but I did not want to. I thought it would interfere too much with my Senate duties. Then I had lunch one day at the Monocle Restaurant, near the Senate, with columnists Rowland Evans and Robert Novak, whom I knew well and who had, back during the presidential campaign, coauthored a feature article for the *Atlantic Monthly* on me and Walter Mondale, calling us "establishment radicals." Evans and Novak, looking for a story, quizzed me hard about my interest in the Democratic Party chairmanship. I told them truthfully that I was not interested in it. We talked on. They mentioned how someone had said that I would be able to heal the terrible divisions in the party caused primarily by internal differences over the Vietnam War. And suddenly, even as the three of us talked and I continued to disclaim any interest in the party job, I simultaneously began to think seriously for the first time about the good that I could accomplish as party chair—knitting the party back together, reforming it and making it more democratic, developing it as a stronger voice on progressive issues, and putting it on record against the war. Without saying so to Evans and Novak, I changed my mind in mid-conversation with them.

When I left them, I went immediately to the Russell Building office of Senator Edward Kennedy of Massachusetts and asked him for, and received, his endorsement of my candidacy for party chair. I then called Hubert Humphrey, now the titular head of the party, and set up a luncheon with him for the next day; at it, I got his warm endorsement, too. I set up a small war room in the Mayflower Hotel in Washington and began the intensive election campaign that I knew would be required. By telephone or in person, I spoke with every single member of the Democratic National Committee, some of them a number of times, telling them of my plans for the party and soliciting their support. In the ensuing meeting of the National Committee, I was chosen to succeed O'Brien by unanimous vote.

It seemed like a dubious honor to some. One reporter likened my becoming chair of the Democratic Party to somebody parachuting onto the
Titanic, but I had been deeply troubled about not having done more earlier to help end the war in Vietnam. I had also felt awfully uncomfortable
before the 1968 election about finding myself joined, in support of the
same candidate, with opponents of what I believed was needed party reform. I wanted to have a chance to make amends and to help put the party
back together again as a vehicle for helping put the country itself back together again.

So, almost at the last minute, I had sought the job—and got it. Right
away, I appointed a Democratic Policy Council, which, as I wanted, took
a strong stand against the Vietnam War and placed the party squarely on
the progressive side of social, economic, and civil rights issues. I set up a
Democratic Party Reform Commission, soon called the McGovern Commission for Senator George McGovern, whom I named to head it, and I
made up the membership of the commission to ensure that it would recommend the reforms I thought were needed: changes to provide, for the
first time, full representation of women and minorities in party affairs and
complete transparency and fairness—democracy—in all party processes,
including the selection of delegates to the party's national conventions. At
the same time, I also set up and appointed another commission, which I
named U.S. Representative James O'Hara of Michigan to head, to reform
the party's archaic rules.

I found the worst part of my job as head of the Democratic Party was
trying to raise money. I could make no progress toward reducing the
party's debt, but in those terribly divisive times, it was no little accom-
plishment, I thought, just to keep the party on its feet—to pay the rent,
salaries, and phone bills—while we rehabilitated it. And I did bring in a
full-time direct-mail expert, previously with UNICEF, to start the party on
the small-givers program, which had the potential to become its main financial base.

Being head of the Democratic Party hurt me badly in Oklahoma. Too
many people resented my taking on a job other than the one to which they
had elected me. And my new, more partisan image was a handicap for me,
both at home and in the Senate. So, when I could—when I was sure the
party was locked into its new directions—following a successful fund-

raising function we held in Miami, I stepped out of the job. The once and
future chair Lawrence O'Brien stepped back into it again.

While the Democratic Party was achieving renewal, so was Humphrey.
He was reelected to the Senate from Minnesota two years after having
been defeated in the 1968 presidential election. He began to seem like the
old Humphrey of Senate days again. Then someone talked him into seeking the nomination for president in 1972. Perhaps no talking was necessary; it is hard to get rid of the presidential urge. I know.

Political careers are much dependent on the vagaries of fate, and in
Humphrey's case, fate always seemed to dictate bad timing. He should
not have run in 1972. He should have helped George McGovern, as I did
after I was for a brief time a candidate myself that year. Instead,
Humphrey not only ran in 1972 but let himself get talked into a bitter, last-
ditch, stop-McGovern effort at the Democratic convention in Miami
Beach, an effort that hindered the healing of Democratic lesions and
helped seal the doom of McGovern's general-election campaign against
Richard Nixon.

Some said Humphrey should have run in 1976. I don't know about that.
One reason he enjoyed such popularity and was the object of so much
laudatory comment in the press during the 1976 Democratic primaries
was precisely because he was *not* a candidate. Had he become one, I am
sure that many of his old critics would have begun to go to work on him
again.

In any event, we are all lucky that Humphrey had some additional
good and productive years in the Senate and on the national scene before
he finally succumbed, after a courageous and stoic fight, to the terrible
bladder cancer that eventually took his life.

We celebrated his great life in a wonderful memorial service in the
capitol rotunda. To my mind, Humphrey ranked right up there with the
all-time Senate greats. Franklin Roosevelt dubbed Al Smith the Happy
Warrior. I felt that title suited Humphrey even better. "Be of good cheer,"
he would always say in the face of adversity, and eyes twinkling, he
would call upon us all to continue to do "the Lord's work."

8

—∞—

Robert Kennedy—Moxie and Heart

"MR. PRESIDENT, A SMALL BOUQUET OF PINK ROSEBUDS, widow's lace, and fern now rests upon the lonely and vacant desk to my right," I said in the U.S. Senate on the sad morning of Thursday, June 5, 1968. "It bespeaks the melancholy nature of this day." Senator Robert Kennedy of New York had been killed in Los Angeles in the early hours of the previous morning.

He and I had been seatmates in the Senate since the day we had both arrived there, elected in the same year, 1964. No two members of the Senate had been closer friends than we became.

I had gone to sleep with the television still on, two nights before those Senate remarks, the night of the California Democratic presidential primary, which Robert Kennedy had won. Screams coming from the set, frantic voices, alarmed reporting—all this suddenly scared LaDonna and me awake. And we woke up to an incredible horror. Robert Kennedy had been shot—and killed.

LaDonna got up quickly and dressed. Ethel Kennedy, Robert Kennedy's wife, was with him in California. LaDonna knew that. She jumped in our car and hurried to the Kennedy house, around the nearby corner in the old McLean, Virginia, neighborhood where we lived, to see about the smaller Kennedy children whom she knew would have been left at home. To offer what little comfort she could.

I stayed immobilized, stricken, in front of the television set during the rest of those early morning hours, all that day, and for a good portion of the next night. I watched as the news video loop was replayed over and over—in the hotel ballroom, the victory speech; in the hotel kitchen, the fatal shot, the wrestling down of the assassin, the almost hysterical confusion; in a parking lot, the somber death announcement by Frank Mankiewisz. But it was not until I entered the Senate chamber on the following morning and saw that Robert Kennedy's desk, next to mine, had been cleared of all papers and the papers replaced with a small bouquet of flowers, that I finally fully realized he was dead.

I stood in the Senate and, after noting the vacant desk and flowers, said, "Senator Kennedy daily lived with enormous personal burdens of duty and moral commitment which caused him, with incomparable courage, to take upon himself the cloak of the alienated, the despised, and the dispossessed and to become their voice."

There would be no more of that by him. There would be no more action pictures of him on television. There would be no more of his sailing at Hyannis Port, or walking along a California beach with his cocker spaniel, Freckles. There would be no more of his coming down to dinner with wet hair after a quick swim. There would be no more of his shy toothy smile or quick wit. There would be no more of his righteous outrage, or his passionate "I don't think that's acceptable," or his committed "We can do better."

Except in memory.

—⁂— —⁂— —⁂—

I did not start out thinking that I would like Robert Kennedy. Our backgrounds were utterly different. He had grown up rich. I had not. And I say, only half jokingly, that in my populist Oklahoma family, we were naturally wary of rich people. My old Baptist grandmother, Ma Harris, often repeated to us these words from the Bible: "It is easier for a camel to go through the eye of a needle than for a rich man to enter into the kingdom of heaven." Rich people, she believed, were never happy and seldom good.

Too, I knew well that Robert Kennedy had once worked for the infamous Senator Joseph McCarthy of Wisconsin (on the staff of the Senate Permanent Investigating Subcommittee, which, after McCarthy was long gone, both Kennedy and I were to become members of). McCarthy was the demagogic, red-baiting senator whose irresponsible charges and threats had held whole segments of the country in paralyzing fear for far too long during the 1950s, before he was finally censured by the Senate and died in disgrace. At the time Kennedy worked for the senator, I was publicly denouncing McCarthy and his tactics, while I was campus president of the League of Young Democrats at the University of Oklahoma.

More lately, I had been put off, like so many other Oklahomans, by news stories I had read about seemingly frivolous, though fashionable, parties at Robert Kennedy's McLean home, Hickory Hill. Guests were sometimes pushed, or fell, into the swimming pool—once, as widely reported in Oklahoma, when Howard Edmondson, the man I would defeat for the Senate nomination, was in attendance.

My opinion of Robert Kennedy began to change the first time I saw him in person, when I went to Washington to a kind of school for Democratic congressional candidates. Robert Kennedy was one of the speakers, and it was his wry wit that got me. President Johnson, to kill off, without directly saying so, a nascent movement in the country to force him to name the attorney general Robert Kennedy as his 1964 running mate, had earlier cleverly announced that no one presently in the Johnson cabinet could be spared and, therefore, no cabinet member would be considered for the vice-presidential nomination. Alluding to that blanket disqualification when he spoke to our group of candidates, Robert Kennedy said, "I'm only sorry that I took so many good people over the side with me."

I softened more the next time I saw Robert Kennedy, at the 1964 Democratic convention in Atlantic City. I was terribly moved on that occasion by his tearful narration of a film about his dead brother, President John Kennedy. In that vast hall that night, we all saw Robert Kennedy, bereft and alone. There were tears in all our eyes, too, as he recited from Shakespeare's *Romeo and Juliet* (words that were wrenchingly sad but also, I thought at the time, evidencing a raw bitterness toward John Kennedy's successor, President Lyndon Johnson):

> And, when he shall die,
> Take him and cut him out in little stars,
> And he will make the face of heaven so fine,
> That all the world will be in love with night,
> And pay no worship to the garish sun.

I finally met Robert Kennedy personally on the very first morning after I was elected to the Senate, in November 1964. I had barely settled into my temporary Senate offices there when I got a telephone call from Majority Leader Mansfield, inviting me over to his capitol office for coffee. A little too full of myself, perhaps, while taking my first senators-preferred ride over to the capitol on the little subway train, I was thinking that the majority leader probably wanted to talk to me about my committee assignments and how I could be helpful to him in getting the Democratic program enacted. But, no, it turned out that this was to be a purely social get-together—and an auspicious one.

New York's new senator, Robert Kennedy, was there for coffee, too (as was the newly elected senator from New Mexico, Joseph Montoya). Senator Mansfield had his photographer take a picture of the four of us, then we sat down and drank coffee and talked a little. Robert Kennedy, who did not say much, was surprisingly shy and reticent, so unlike the image I'd had of him in my mind. His shyness was appealing.

The following January, 1965, when the Senate went into session, Robert Kennedy and I began to see each other quite regularly, not only because we were seatmates on the Senate floor, but also because we served together on the Governmental Affairs Committee, as it was then called, which Senator John McClellan of Arkansas chaired, as well as on three of its subcommittees: the Permanent Investigating Subcommittee, also chaired by McClellan; Senator Henry Jackson's Subcommittee on National Security and International Operations; and Senator Abraham Ribicoff's Subcommittee on Governmental Reorganization.

In Robert Kennedy, I saw right away great earnestness and commitment. He was fascinated with Indians, for one thing, and he spent a lot of time talking to LaDonna about that subject. But he was fascinated with everything. His curiosity about things, people, and issues was almost insatiable. When we first met, and as long as I knew him, he was, as I was, learning, growing, becoming. And he was always questioning—LaDonna about Indians, author Jack Newfield about young people, Jim Whitaker about climbing mountains, or Secretary of Defense Robert McNamara about the course of the Vietnam War.

Robert Kennedy learned a great deal from this relentless questioning, but it was partly a device, too. Reserved, he did not easily engage in chitchat; the questioning practice kept a conversation going without his having to say anything if he did not feel like it. I am sure many people went away from a meeting with him thinking they'd had a marvelous conversation, when actually they, under his prodding, had done all the talking.

But mainly, Kennedy was a relentless self-improver. In the Senate, he and I began now and then to hold little irregularly scheduled "skull-practice" luncheons, you might call them, in one or the other of our Senate offices, sessions featuring each time an appearance by some expert on a subject we both wanted to learn more about.

It was our wives, though, who first brought us together socially. Those two met at the first gathering of the year of what was then called the Senate Ladies Club, a meeting at which the first lady, as well as the wives of cabinet members, were traditionally present, too, as honored guests. When LaDonna and Ethel Kennedy were introduced to each other, Ethel, whose husband had been a cabinet member, surprisingly whispered to LaDonna, "Kid, stay with me; I hardly know any of these people."

Soon after that, LaDonna accepted Ethel Kennedy's invitation to lunch with her at Hickory Hill. Ethel had apparently told her children about LaDonna being a Comanche Indian, and Kerry Kennedy, then six or seven, stared at her in apparent wonderment all during the meal. Finally, Kerry could keep quiet no longer. "Mrs. Harris," she asked, "what's it like living in a tipi?"

LaDonna began, good-naturedly, to explain to the little Kennedy daughter that American Indians no longer lived in tipis, but Ethel interrupted. "Kid," she said to LaDonna, "don't disillusion her!"

LaDonna laughed and said, "But I don't want her to grow up in ignorance," and she then told Kerry that modern Indians lived and worked pretty much like everyone else, except that they had the special advantage of their unique history and culture. Nevertheless, later, down by the pool, Kerry came up to LaDonna again and asked, "Can you shoot a bow and arrow?" And the next time we saw Kerry, she was still fascinated by LaDonna's Indianness. She sweetly gave LaDonna a special crayon drawing she had made for her. It was crowded with tipis, horses, and figures of feathered Indians.

Robert Kennedy was like a movie-star celebrity, or as the present cliché goes, a "rock star," all the time I knew him, and he and Ethel could not go anywhere without being instantly besieged by fans and others of the star-struck public. Their social activities, then, necessarily centered largely on their own homes—in McLean and in Hyannis Port—with occasional small dinner parties, which LaDonna and I often attended, in the homes of one or another of their friends, people like humorist Art Buchwald, journalist Charles Bartlett, and columnists Rowland Evans and Joseph Kraft. The Kennedy residences had to be virtual country clubs, with equipment and facilities for all sorts of recreation and amusement, so that they could enjoy their leisure without having to go out in public. We regularly watched first-run movies with them, outdoors by the pool at Hickory Hill.

It was, of course, great fun to be with the Kennedys. And, wherever they were, there were also "sparkly people," as Ethel called them—from astronaut, and later U.S. senator, John Glenn, to singer Andy Williams, to decathlon winner Rafer Johnson, to author George Plimpton, to historian Arthur Schlesinger, Jr.

Ethel Kennedy did not mind asking friends for help. One weekend morning, she called me at home from her upstairs Hickory Hill bedroom, soon after her next-to-last child was born, by caesarean. "Bobby's not home," she said, "and I need you to get someone to come with you and carry me downstairs." I quickly recruited my friend and neighbor Bill Mc-Candless, and he and I hurried over to the house, then up to Ethel's bedroom. We sat her in a light but sturdy chair and, one of us on each side, gingerly carried her down the steps. All the time and all the way down, Ethel teased me about whether I was in good enough shape, had the physical strength, to keep from dropping her.

At times, Ethel seemed appealingly naïve, at times brilliantly and pointedly witty. A wonderful mother, cheerful in doing her duty, but sometimes almost whimsically scattered, she seemed, as someone once put it, a delightful cross between Mrs. Miniver and Mrs. Malaprop. She always said grace before a meal. One time, right after we all sat down for dinner, outside on the back terrace at Hickory Hill, she as usual asked us to bow our heads for prayer, but another guest, humorist Art Buchwald, who was Jewish, teasingly interrupted to ask, "Ethel, why don't you ever call on me to say the prayer?"

"But what God do you pray to?" Ethel asked Buchwald.

"Why, we pray to the same God you pray to," Buchwald answered, without hesitation. "After all, you know, He was ours before He was yours."

Robert Kennedy is still hard for people to categorize. "Ruthless" was the word his enemies most often used to describe him. "Determined" or "intense," I thought, would have been just as good, probably better. And, as I have indicated and as many people might be surprised to hear, "shy" and "vulnerable" fit Kennedy, too.

He was tough, no question, but he also had heart. He was a romantic, I think. He gave me a copy of his first book, *The Enemy Within* (about his

earlier racket-busting experiences on the staff of the McClellan Committee). He had dedicated the book to Ethel, with this additional cryptic message: "See Ruth 1:15–18." When I looked up that reference in the Bible, I
found it read (in the Revised Standard Version): "Entreat me not to leave
you or to return from following you; for where you go I will go, and
where you lodge I will lodge; your people shall be my people, and your
God my God."

Kennedy was a highly private person. For example, he did not particularly like being touched. One day, he and I were standing together in the
Senate when Senator Birch Bayh of Indiana came up to us. "What do you
say, Big Bob?" Senator Bayh said, tapping Robert on the chin with his fist,
locker-room fashion. Turning to me, Senator Bayh said, "How's it going,
Fred R.?" and punched me on the arm.

When Bayh had walked away to greet other senators in a similar manner, Kennedy said to me, "Can you stand that?"

"I hate it," I replied.

"So do I," Kennedy said. We looked across the chamber to where Senator Russell Long of Louisiana was almost hugging another senator as he
whispered in his ear; the two men stood so close together that their cheeks
ware actually touching. "If Russell Long did me that way, I'd say yes to
anything he asked, just to get away," Kennedy said.

When I first knew him, and for most of the time thereafter, Kennedy
was obviously damaged, still carrying around an almost unbearable sadness following the death of his brother. On the night Martin Luther King,
Jr., was assassinated, in the spring of 1968, LaDonna and I were attending
a Democratic fund-raising dinner in Washington. After the shocking announcement of Dr. King's tragic death was made, a callous and insensitive
master of ceremonies rose to say that the dinner would go on as planned,
almost as if nothing had happened. But Vice President Hubert Humphrey,
who was to be the principal speaker, intervened and rightly shut the event
down. LaDonna and I went home, where we found Byron and Laura huddled tearfully together in Laura's room. We tried to comfort them as best
we could. Then all of us watched on television as Robert Kennedy, in In-
dianapolis, left off campaigning for the presidency and went courageously and immediately to the black section of that city. To awful shock
and crying, Kennedy announced the terrible news to the African Ameri-

can crowd, and he called upon his own deep and personal past loss and anguish in trying to comfort them—to minister to them.

Kennedy recalled for the African American crowd how his own brother had been killed—and by a white man, he pointed out. He said that counterviolence and revenge were the wrong response, adding that, instead, "We can make an effort, as Martin Luther King did, to understand and to comprehend, and to replace that violence with an effort to understand, with compassion and with love." Then Kennedy quoted words from Aeschylus that had been, in his darkest days, a comfort to him: "Even in our sleep, pain which cannot forget falls drop by drop upon the heart until in our own despair, against our will, comes wisdom through the awful grace of God."

In the Senate, Kennedy benefited much from the work of an excellent staff, but I always had the feeling that when he became involved in an issue, he first made an almost instinctive emotional and moral commitment on his own, and then put his staff people to work to come up with the necessary facts and reasoning to support the position he had already taken.

That was the way it was when Kennedy and I first worked closely together in Senate subcommittee hearings on automobile safety, chaired by Senator Abraham Ribicoff of Connecticut. These were the hearings that made Ralph Nader famous. Ribicoff had known Nader, author of *Unsafe at Any Speed,* as an automobile safety advocate in their home state of Connecticut and decided to use him in the Washington hearings on the subject.

Then, in the course of the hearings, we discovered that General Motors had hired a private investigator, not only in an unsuccessful effort to dig up unfavorable information that might be used against Nader, but also apparently to hurt Nader's reputation by going around asking certain questions of his neighbors, like, "Do you think Ralph Nader, who's unmarried, is a homosexual?" and "Do you think Ralph Nader is anti-Semitic?" (Nader, who is not gay, is Lebanese American; Ribicoff was Jewish).

On our subcommittee, we were outraged. We subpoenaed some of the principal officers of General Motors to testify before us under oath. My careful questions, like those of a cross-examining lawyer, were designed to uncover the specific sordid particulars about what the corporation had done. Robert Kennedy's practice was to confront the witnesses with the overall fact of General Motors' wrongdoing in regard to Nader and force them to admit publicly, and on the record, their serious moral guilt. Before the hearings ended, the chair of the board had to come before our sub-committee and publicly apologize. (This led to a large legal cash settle-ment for Nader by the company, money he then used to launch his highly effective national consumer-advocate organization and activities.)

The same kind of moral force went into Robert Kennedy's questioning when we worked together in hearings covering racial discrimination in the building-trades unions, although in that instance we weren't able to secure as clear an admission of culpability. And this force was apparent during televised California hearings on migrant labor that I watched, hearings in which a local sheriff openly admitted to a regular practice of unjustifiably locking up Hispanic workers over weekends to keep them sober and out of trouble so that they would be sure to come to work on Monday mornings. "Sir," Kennedy caustically asked the official, "have you never heard of the Constitution of the United States?"

Robert Kennedy's intensity in his professional life found an outlet in his personal life through sports. And he was a little too competitive to suit me. I believe that sports—football, tennis, sailing, softball—all of which he loved, also provided Kennedy a way to satisfy his need to have people around him without having to make conversation with them when he didn't feel like it. He was never so intense in competition that he could not laugh about it, but he was never so carried away with laughter that he re-laxed his will to win.

Once, when LaDonna and I were guests of Robert and Ethel at Hyan-nis Port, she and I and columnist Mary McGrory politely but firmly re-fused even to try to water ski with the rest. "The only way to get along with the Kennedys is to admit in advance that you're an underachiever," Mary told us. It was all right with the Kennedys if you simply preferred to read a good book or to talk to each other rather than get involved in some strenuous athletic activity, but, as McGrory said, you had to make your position clear from the first.

Most of the time, though, we could not get out of taking part. One weekend afternoon in Hyannis Port, all of us, adults and kids, were di-vided up into two softball teams. I was the captain of one team, Robert of the other. He and I also served as the pitchers for our respective teams. Right up until the last inning, each of us slack pitched slow balls to the little kids like Kerry. But in the last half of the ninth, with the score tied, two people on base, and two out, Kerry Kennedy stepped up to bat for our team, and Robert pitched her three sizzling fast balls in rapid succession—and *struck her out!* The game ended in a tie.

That night, LaDonna and I and Ethel and Robert were joined for dinner at their house by Rose Kennedy and Jacqueline Kennedy. Over dessert, I jokingly told Rose Kennedy how ruthless her son had been in striking out his own daughter, and she remonstrated with her son in a similar teasing vein. His response, delivered in a tone of mock innocence, was, "Can I help it if Kerry is a sucker for a high, inside fast ball?"

I was glad to find that Robert Kennedy could temper his competitiveness with the understanding of friendship, unlike his brother Ted. The first time I sailed with Ted Kennedy, I knew right away that I would never be as close to him as I was to Robert. LaDonna and I were staying that weekend with Robert and Ethel, as always, and Senator Birch Bayh and his wife, Marvella, were staying with Ted and his wife, Joan. When we all split up one afternoon for an impromptu boat race—Robert against Ted in their identical small sailing yachts—I somehow unfortunately wound up as a member of Ted's crew.

I told Ted in advance that I knew nothing whatsoever about sailing. True, I said with a nervous laugh, I'd been a member of the Sea Scouts in Walters, Oklahoma, when I was in junior high school, but the only vessel we'd ever been piped aboard in those days, at each Tuesday night meeting, was a fake one, laid out in outline on the floor of the American Legion hall located over Calhoun's Grocery. I should have taken note, right then, that Ted Kennedy did not laugh at any of this.

That calm, hot summer afternoon in Hyannis Port was virtually windless, and the bay was prairie smooth. On a signal, our two boats set sail. Robert and Ted began to work feverishly to catch every stray breath of the laggardly breeze. Joseph Kennedy's motor launch, the Honey Fitz, cruised alongside the two sailboats, carrying family members and friends who cheered one or the other of the astonishingly intense racing captains.

On our boat, Ted Kennedy was a virtual Captain Ahab, utterly engrossed in his goal, barking orders in a rudely commanding voice. For me, some of the orders might as well have been in Swahili. As Robert's boat started to slowly inch ahead of ours, Ted became almost frighteningly agitated.

"Set the spinnaker! Set the spinnaker!" he suddenly, and furiously, yelled at me at one point.

"The spinnaker?" I repeated phonetically, a word I could not remember ever hearing before.

"Get that line, there, for Christ's sake!" Ted Kennedy shouted, pointing toward the rope that he wanted pulled to lift the sail in question from its basket.

"Line?" In Oklahoma, we called a rope a rope.

"Line! Line! That one in the bow. The spinnaker's in the basket!"

I lurched first one way and then another, trying to follow Ted Kennedy's pointing and his increasingly impatient and unintelligible instructions. His face grew redder and redder. "Can't you see they're getting ahead of us?" he shouted at me.

As Ted became even more frantic, I wondered seriously whether there was any federal penalty for mutiny on a private sailing vessel. At one point, he yelled toward the Honey Fitz, motioning wildly, "Move off! Move off! You're in our wind!"

Our boat did not win the race. Back on shore, over cocktails that evening, I tried to make a joke about the experience, but there had not really been anything very funny about it for me.

By contrast, I sailed the next day as a member of Robert Kennedy's crew in a Hyannis Yacht Club race. Robert's son Joe and a young friend of Joe's were also in the crew. Robert proved to be both a daring sailor and a patient captain. On the leg going out, he explained that I would have the job of handling the spinnaker when it was set on the inbound, downwind leg of the race. He showed me in advance how to hold the spinnaker line, once the sail was up, and how to fly the sail like a kite, keeping it full of air.

It seemed odd to me that when every other boat had turned and begun to reach crosswind, Robert kept going on out to sea. He said we would catch the incoming tide and the wind just right when we headed back toward the bay and the finish line. And his knowledge of the tide and wind, and his skill and daring, paid off. When at last we headed home, running before the wind, we really moved. On order, I properly set the spinnaker, and this huge ballooning blue-and-white striped sail billowed out in front of us. Under Robert's encouragement, I kept the spinnaker full in the strong wind, and we sliced past the other boats, some still tacking, and won the race with yards and yards of blue water to spare.

His work done, Robert gave the wheel to young Joe, stripped off his shirt and shoes, and jumped off the stern of the boat into the cold bay water, holding onto a trailing rope. He yelled for me to join him, and I was foolish enough to do so.

Clinging to the end of the dragline, Robert and I were pulled headlong through the surging, foamy bay waters behind the boat, which was still under full sail. Then, responding nimbly to a cry from the crew that we were coming into a cluster of jellyfish, Robert moved hand over hand up the rope, against the force of the water, and neatly climbed into the boat with no great trouble. It took me twice as long, and I needed a little help at the last. For several minutes after I had finally reached the security of the deck, I lay there panting, pondering the trials of an underachiever. I was glad that I had not been born a competitive Kennedy.

Competitive as they were, even with each other, the Kennedys had an impressive closeness, too. You cannot think about Robert Kennedy without thinking also of the members of his family. They constituted for him an enveloping and almost self-sufficient environment of warmth, loyalty, and enjoyment. Robert Kennedy's brother and sisters appeared to be his best friends, and he theirs. He laughed and teased with them, but he trusted them and their judgment, and they were equally and confidently dependent on him.

When I first visited Hyannis Port, Joseph Kennedy was still a central figure in the family, despite the stroke that had silenced him and left him paralyzed. The old man's eyes still seemed to see everything, but he could not talk and could move only his left hand, a little. I found it difficult to picture the Kennedy patriarch as the brusque, domineering, aggressive figure described by earlier news reports and biographies I had read, but you could catch some indication of what Joseph Kennedy had been from the way Robert Kennedy treated him—with great deference and evidence of a touching love. Just before dinner each evening at Hyannis Port, for example, Robert always went next door to his parent's house for a kind of one-sided conversation with Joseph Kennedy that could last a half hour or more.

In Hyannis Port, a light-hearted sibling rivalry among the Kennedys manifested itself in at least a couple of ways. Frequent guest Art Buchwald once wrote that there was a pecking order for weekend guests at the Kennedy compound. Your rank was determined by which of the brothers or sisters had invited you. Robert's guests, Buchwald wrote, ranked highest. They invariably flew back and forth between Washington and Hyannis Port in the Kennedy plane, the Caroline, a two-motored prop plane outfitted with a sofa, a work table, and a few individual passenger seats. Buchwald said that guests could get an idea of their rank by learning whether or not there was room for them on the Caroline, especially for the trip back to Washington at the end of a weekend. If you were Robert's house guest, you always made the Caroline, he wrote, which was true, but if you were sister Jean Smith's, say, you couldn't even find out when the plane was scheduled to leave and were reduced to watching carefully for any telltale packing activity in Robert's house so that you could hurry and try to edge onto the Caroline and not have to take an airline flight back.

Kennedy sibling rivalry was evident at Hyannis Port in another way: Who had invited the most interesting weekend guests? Sister Eunice Shriver generally lost, other family members said, because being seriously involved in the field of mental retardation and related subjects, she was always likely to bring with her an entourage of what some thought were relatively stodgy doctors and psychologists. Ted and Joan Kennedy, though, were always in the running, such as when they invited singer Andy Williams and his wife one weekend when LaDonna and I were there.

LaDonna and I always stayed with Robert and Ethel, of course. Their white clapboard house, much like the larger house of his parents next door, was in the center of the Kennedy compound. At the end of the day, the brothers and sisters and their guests would generally gather at Robert's, or Eunice's, or Ted's, or Jean's, or Pat's for cocktails and fun, then return to the separate houses for dinner.

On our first trip to Hyannis Port, LaDonna and I met Jacqueline Kennedy at dinner at Robert's house. She had a kind of withdrawn, wistful manner, and she spoke very quietly, with a little-girl breathlessness that reminded me of Marilyn Monroe. As soon as I was introduced to her that time, she said, "I am so glad to meet you, because you are the man who defeated Bud Wilkinson." Ribbing Robert a little in the process, Jacqueline and Ethel then told us that they had not shared Robert and John's obsession with big-time college football and that they had wanted their husbands to know, as they said they knew, that Wilkinson, whom President Kennedy had appointed to head the national physical-fitness program, was a disloyal conservative who said derogatory things about the president in private. "Ethel and I kept trying to figure out how to get Jack to see this," Jacqueline said. "We even considered writing him an anonymous letter about it, but then Wilkinson finally resigned to run for the Senate, and the problem took care of itself." How interesting. But I found it odd, and a little sad, that Jacqueline Kennedy would admit that she was unable or unwilling to speak to her husband directly about such a thing.

Robert Kennedy could be unbelievably charming, and not just with adults—with children and young people, too. Among other things, he liked to ask them somewhat bantering questions, individually and in groups. Once, I had him come to Tulsa to speak at a human rights meeting, and afterward, on our way to the airport by car, we passed a grade-school playground where the kids, apparently let out of class, were pressed up against a cyclone fence to catch a glimpse of him. Robert had the car stopped, and he got out with a bullhorn.

"What's the name of this school?" he called out. The kids yelled back their answer. "Do you know who I am?" he then asked.

"Yes," they said in a chorus.

"What's my name?"

"Kennedy!" they shouted.

"Do you know who this is with me?" he asked, gesturing toward me. There was confusion. Some yelled "Yes!" Most yelled "No!"

Robert turned away from the bullhorn and said to me, "Fred, I don't see how you ever got elected in Oklahoma."

I remember reading about a similar episode that took place when he was campaigning for president in a town in Indiana, possibly Elkhart. "Are you going to vote for me for president?" Robert called out to a group of grade-school kids.

"Yes!" they yelled back.

"Are you going to get your parents to vote for me?"

"Yes!"

"Have you read my book *To Seek a Newer World*?"

"Yes!"

"You lie in Elkhart, Indiana," he said.

Another time, in a crowd at the University of Oklahoma, where I had brought Kennedy, a student asked him, "Do you favor lowering the voting age, and if so, to what level?"

"Yes, I do," Robert answered, "and I think twelve would be about right. After that, I seem to start losing them."

Liking kids was good, but I thought Robert Kennedy was a little too fond of dogs. I've never been keen on having dogs in the house. My grandfather Pa Harris was crazy about them, but they were dogs that could hunt. I grew up among people who believed that dogs were supposed to *do* something, and that they were not supposed to live in the same house with humans. In Robert Kennedy's household, there always seemed to be at least three dogs underfoot.

The most noticeable of these dogs was Brumus, a black Newfoundland almost as big as a small Shetland pony. Brumus, though, seemed to think of himself as a small puppy. He bounded around a living room like one, despite his woolly-mammoth size. He was the scourge of the neighborhood trash cans in McLean, Virginia, and he once sidled up and peed on a woman's leg at a Kennedy pet show.

One weekend in Hyannis Port, Brumus clambered right into the Kennedy family convertible with a bunch of us who were headed to a local horse show, in which assorted Kennedy and Shriver children had been entered. There, parents and other human spectators stayed outside the fence, but not Brumus.

Brumus preferred the excitement and action in the show ring, and he spent a lot of time there, to the great annoyance of the somewhat pompous ringmaster. When this official—and some of the horses—could apparently stand Brumus no longer, the ringmaster finally undertook to shoo him back outside the fence, using his foot to gently nudge him along. Robert Kennedy leaped over the fence in an instant and took Brumus by the collar to lead him off, saying in genuine anger, "Don't kick the dog!"

"I didn't kick him," the flustered ringmaster said.

"I saw you, and don't do that again," Robert said icily, white-faced.

The rest of us watched, a little embarrassed. And when Robert had led Brumus back to the family group, outside the fence, Jacqueline Kennedy broke the ice by saying, laughingly, "Bobby, there goes the chance any of our children had to win ribbons today!"

One afternoon at Hickory Hill, when LaDonna and I were gathered with Robert and Ethel in their little sitting room to hear Robert read, for our comment, his first major speech breaking with President Johnson on the Vietnam War, Brumus slobbered all over our teacakes.

—∞— —∞— —∞—

In 1967, Robert Kennedy and I teamed up to try to improve a Social Security bill that included some highly punitive and regressive welfare provisions, the bill that Johnson wanted passed in spite of the provisions. I took the lead on the Senate floor because I was a member of the Finance Committee, which had jurisdiction over the bill, but Kennedy was right beside me at every step. He and I lined up other supporting senators, parceled out among them our sixteen proposed amendments to improve the bill, and carefully organized our floor strategy and arguments. We won. The Senate adopted fifteen of our sixteen amendments.

But our victory was short-lived. A conference committee was appointed to reconcile the differences between the House and Senate versions of the bill. In those days, Senate conferees on a particular bill were automatically appointed from among the most senior members of the relevant committee—in this case, the Finance Committee—whether or not they had voted with the Senate majority. (That practice was later changed as a result of Senate adoption of one of the recommendations made by the Democratic Reform Committee, which I chaired.) The Senate conferees on the bill, which Robert Kennedy and I had worked so hard on the Senate floor to make more progressive, were all senators who had bitterly opposed our amendments, and though bound in principle to support the Senate position, in Senate parlance, they "dropped the Senate amendments as soon as they walked out the Senate door." The bill came back to the Senate from the conference in its worst possible form.

Most of our allies in the Senate felt Kennedy and I should give up the fight at this stage because it appeared hopeless. This was in December 1967, and everyone was looking forward to congressional adjournment. Also, the bill included a 7 percent increase in benefits for Social Security recipients, and senators did not want that increase delayed.

Among those who were determined that the Social Security increases should go into effect at once were President Johnson, of course, and Majority Leader Mansfield. The president sent three of his aides—Lawrence O'Brien, Joe Califano, and Douglas Cater—to pressure me in Senator Mansfield's office. They argued, as did Senator Russell Long, chair of the

Finance Committee, and others, that there was simply no way to get Representative Wilbur Mills, then head of the Ways and Means Committee, the Senate Finance Committee's House counterpart, to back down from the House version of the bill.

Privately, Robert Kennedy said to me, "This is the time for some moxie," a word I had not heard much. What he meant was that we could probably bluff our opponents down by threatening to hold up the Social Security bill and delay adjournment until we'd had our way. So, although five or six of our Senate supporters were shaky at best, we decided to be obstinate—and obstructionist. I rose in the Senate and said, "The pending bill presents such a crisis of conscience for all of us and such a moral matter for many of us that we cannot stand and let it pass without being heard." This meant that we intended to be "heard" in the Senate at length—that is, we were going to undertake a sort of mini-filibuster.

Mansfield asked Kennedy and me to a meeting in his office with all the senators who would be seeking reelection in the coming year, including my colleague from Oklahoma, Mike Monroney. One by one, these senators said to me and Kennedy that we were going to cause them very serious reelection problems if we delayed the Social Security benefits increase by blocking passage of the conference-report bill that authorized it. Kennedy and I felt sorely put upon by this unusual procedure. Speaking for both of us, in as few words as possible, I simply pointed out that he and I were adamantly determined to do everything we could to block adoption of the conference report. I suggested that the majority leader and the other senators were putting pressure on the wrong people. I said that they should take the bill back to conference, drop the welfare provisions altogether—thus postponing consideration of them until the first of the next year—and bring the bill back to the Senate simply as a measure for increasing Social Security benefits.

The senators replied in a virtual chorus that nobody could make Wilbur Mills back down. "Then," I said, "he is the one who will have to take responsibility for delaying the increase in Social Security benefits." The senators tried another tack: they promised that if Kennedy and I would allow the bill to pass in its conference-report form, they would join with us and the White House in trying to eliminate its regressive features later on, during the next session. We said that was unacceptable. The meeting broke up and, with what few troops we had, Kennedy and I began to gear up for what the Senate politely calls "extended debate."

And we would have eventually won, too. Moxie would have worked except for a bizarre lapse of attention by one of our Senate supporters, Joseph Tydings of Maryland. In the closing days of a Senate session there is such a rush of legislation that nothing can really be accomplished without unanimous consent, so one determined senator alone can gum up the works. That is the obstructive power that Kennedy and I, with the help of a few Senate supporters, set out to exercise. The job of each member of our team was to be present and alert on the floor of the Senate to object whenever necessary to the Senate's even taking up the conference report on the Social Security bill. Our strategy was that simple. Joe Tydings was assigned the first day's floor duty. I went to the chamber that day just to make sure that he was on the job, and he was—sitting in the back, reading his mail.

Senator Mansfield came up to me while I was on the Senate floor and informed me that some senators intended to prevent the Senate from taking up any business except the Social Security conference report, to put more pressure on Kennedy and me to give in. He pointed out that if such a delay of pending legislation occurred, it would mean, among other things, that the appropriations bill for the Office of Economic Opportunity would not be passed in time to pay the salaries of that agency's employees. I told him that this made no difference to Robert and me, that we intended to hold out until the Social Security bill was sent back to conference and stripped of its regressive provisions. Privately, however, I felt that this news was so serious that it should be communicated at once to my principal collaborator. So, first reminding Senator Tydings that he was in charge and that he was not to allow the conference report to be taken up for consideration, I left the Senate floor and went out into the adjoining lobby to call Robert Kennedy, who was in a committee meeting.

I had just gotten Kennedy on the telephone when Charles Ferris, of the Senate staff, rushed out from the floor and shouted to me, "They've passed it!"

I put the phone aside. "Passed what?" I asked Ferris, afraid I already knew the answer.

"They passed the conference report!"

"Where was Joe Tydings?" By now *I* was shouting.

"Sitting on his ass" was the response.

I lay down the phone and rushed back into the Senate, only to find that what Ferris had reported was unfortunately true. I learned that at the back of the chamber, Senator Tydings had been going through his mail and messages while the assistant majority leader, Robert Byrd of West Virginia, took the Senate through its routine housekeeping procedures—approving the preceding day's *Journal*, adopting a motion to allow certain committees to meet during the Senate session, and disposing of other such mundane matters. Then, apparently in the same dull and unexciting voice, and by previous arrangement with Senator Russell Long, Senator Byrd had called up the conference report for consideration. There was no objection. Tydings was deep into his mail and took no notice. The conference report was then quickly adopted without objection. Worse than that, in a kind of parliamentary lock of finality, Senator Long rapidly moved to reconsider the action on the report, Senator Byrd moved to lay that motion on the table, and the presiding officer declared that the motion to table was adopted. There was no way to reopen the proceedings and reverse the Senate action except by unanimous consent.

After learning all this, I raced back to the telephone and told Robert Kennedy what had happened. He was as incensed as I was. He was with me later on the floor when Mansfield rose and angrily lectured senators Byrd and Long for their unfair tactics. But the damage was irreparably done. Joe Tydings took his medicine, publicly accepting responsibility for what had occurred, but that did not change the result. Robert Kennedy made a bitter speech, attacking Senator Long. Long responded, not without justification, I thought, that if you "live by the sword, you must be prepared to die by the sword," meaning that if senators were going to take advantage of the rules to block legislation supported by a majority of the Senate, they should be prepared to have the same rules used against them.

Ours was a disappointing and unnecessary loss, but I was glad to have been associated with Robert Kennedy in what I saw as a worthy fight (though standing up for welfare recipients was not a very politically helpful act for either of us). And I lived to see the day when most of the punitive welfare provisions of that Social Security bill were later stricken from the law.

I have never forgotten how many sick jokes there were about John F. Kennedy while he was president, and some of them persisted even after his assassination. In some ways, I believe, the mean jokes and comments about Robert Kennedy were even worse. I got awfully tired of hearing talk about the length of Robert Kennedy's hair, for example, this minor criticism masking a deeper kind of anger that many people felt toward him. I knew that one reason for this anger was Robert Kennedy's stand on civil rights. I was the object of some of the same kind of anger in Oklahoma, and for the same reason.

More than any other senator, Robert Kennedy fought to move the country toward equal rights for African Americans and other minorities. He praised publicly the findings of facts and recommendations in the 1968 report of the Kerner Commission. Back when President Johnson appointed the commission, it came under attack almost at once from all sides. A number of activists, black and white, charged that our report would wind up being too conservative and would not really amount to anything. Conservatives, on the other hand, predicted that the commission's members would prove to be apologists for African American rioters and that our eventual report would have the effect of encouraging more violence.

Robert Kennedy was at first one of those who expected the report to be bland and inconsequential. He joined with Senator Abraham Ribicoff in a declaration on the floor of the Senate that what was needed in urban America was action, not more studies. And Kennedy privately thought that Mayor John Lindsay of New York, vice chair of the commission and the member who would be my closest collaborator on it, was a lightweight and a dilettante. Sitting next to me in the Senate one day, Robert asked me, "How do you like working with John Lindsay?" His question was accompanied with a kind of laugh, and his tone made clear that his regard for Lindsay was not very high, an attitude bolstered some, I imagine, by the fact that John Lindsay was something of a Kennedy rival for public and press attention in New York. When I answered that John Lindsay was one of the most sensitive and hardworking members of the Kerner Commission and that the two of us were working together very closely to make sure the report would be tough, factual, and fundamental, Kennedy was surprised.

Nevertheless, when the Kerner Commission's hard-hitting report was finally released and received harshly negative comments from President

Johnson and a lot of other politicians around the country, Robert Kennedy joined Senator Joseph Clark of Pennsylvania in calling public hearings in the Senate to receive our report and to hear explanations and a defense of it by me and some of the other commissioners. Attendance was so great that the hearings had to be moved to a large auditorium in the new Senate Office Building. Although the hearings were held when Robert Kennedy was on the verge of announcing as a candidate for president, he still spoke out very strongly in favor of the report.

In addition to his recognition as a civil rights advocate, Robert Kennedy became a central symbol of America's agony over the Vietnam War. I presume that as a member of his brother's cabinet, he had supported America's initial intervention. And it was quite a while after Lyndon Johnson became president, and a while after I had become acquainted with Robert Kennedy, before he finally spoke out against the war. I know that he agonized over his decision to do so, as the country would agonize more and more over what should be done in Vietnam.

During the last half of 1967 and the early part of 1968, I was so focused on urban and racial problems and so engrossed in the work of the Kerner Commission that I did not give the kind of close attention I should have to America's immoral and impractical involvement in Southeast Asia. Back then, when I spoke at all on the subject, I employed almost reflexively the hawkish phrases then popular in Oklahoma and repeated the arguments that I heard often in White House briefings by secretaries McNamara and Rusk and President Johnson.

One weekend afternoon, Robert Kennedy asked LaDonna and me to come over to his house, to give him our opinion of a speech he was planning to make, for the first time breaking with the Johnson administration on Vietnam. The four of us—Robert, Ethel, LaDonna, and I—gathered in the small sitting room at Hickory Hill. The speech was beautifully written and passionately argued. Robert asked me about his principal worry at the time: whether it would be charged that he was breaking with the Johnson policy for political reasons only. I said he should not be deterred by that concern. He obviously felt deeply that the war had to be de-escalated, and he should go ahead and say so.

A while later, at a time when Premier Alexei Kosygin of the Soviet Union was visiting the British prime minister, Harold Wilson, in London, Robert Kennedy asked me to try to get President Johnson to make, through Wilson, some private overture to Kosygin toward settlement of the Vietnam War. Kennedy told me that he had reason to believe such an overture could prove fruitful. Soon after this conversation, LaDonna and I were at an intimate family dinner with the Johnsons at the White House. As the president was showing me and a couple of other people through the Queen's Bedroom, I mentioned to him that I had "heard" that a peace proposal, such as an offer of a bombing halt, delivered through Prime Minister Wilson to Premier Kosygin while the latter was in London, might be favorably received. President Johnson reacted quickly and negatively. He said that a cable containing a message to that effect had just come from Prime Minister Wilson, but that he had rejected the suggestion out of hand. The president added, rather sarcastically, that if Prime Minister Wilson'd had some troops on the ground in South Vietnam, he might be a good deal less willing to take away their air cover by proposing a bombing halt. And that was that.

After the completion and release of the Kerner Commission Report in March 1968, I began at last to turn my attention to the Vietnam War. At about the same time as Clark Clifford was changing his mind on the war, Robert Kennedy and I and a few others got together in his office for one of our skull-practice sessions to hear from Roger Hilsman, a former State Department official who had just returned from a visit to South Vietnam and from the ongoing talks in Paris with representatives of the North Vietnamese. Hilsman told us that the massive bombing in Vietnam was not working and, as a matter of fact, was probably serving to solidify North Vietnamese resistance, as well as world opinion, against the United States. I found Hilsman's report highly persuasive, and I began to change my mind about the war.

At about this time, I had Robert Kennedy come to the University of Oklahoma to speak at an American Indian youth conference sponsored by an organization that LaDonna and I had founded, Oklahomans for Indian Opportunity. After that appearance, I took him over to address five thousand wildly enthusiastic University of Oklahoma students, gathered in the jam-packed OU field house. Kennedy was generously introduced there by OU's great president George L. Cross. When Kennedy stepped up to the microphone, he began by saying, "That's the best thing any president has said about me in a long time." He made a brief speech and then answered questions from the huge crowd.

One of the first students to get to a microphone asked whether Kennedy supported automatic draft deferments for college students. He promptly and firmly stated that he did not favor such automatic deferments, particularly as long as some people were unable to attend college because they could not afford to. This answer was greeted with general hissing and booing. His answers to other questions brought warm applause and cheers.

"Now let me ask you a few questions," Robert Kennedy said at last. "How many of you agree with me about automatic student exemptions from the draft?" Again, there were loud hisses and boos. "How many of you disagree, and think students should automatically be deferred?" Resounding cheers and applause echoed through the barnlike sports arena.

"How many of you want to see a unilateral withdrawal from Vietnam?" A minority.

"How many of you support President Johnson's position on the war—continuing to muddle through?" A slightly larger minority.

"How many of you support my position, calling for a bombing halt and de-escalation?" A somewhat larger group, but still a minority.

"How many of you are for escalation of the war?" Very strong applause from at least a plurality of the students, perhaps a majority.

Then rapidly: "How many of you who voted to escalate the war also voted for automatic student deferments?" There was a giant gasp throughout the field house as students suddenly realized what they had just done—voted for a larger war as long as they didn't have to fight in it. Then came an overwhelming tide of applause, partly in approval of Kennedy's implied point, I think, and partly in admiration of the deft way in which he had made it.

Later, when we were alone, I asked Kennedy whether that was the first time he had used the war and draft-deferment questions, juxtaposed like that, before a student audience. He said he did it all the time. I asked him whether the way most of the OU students had voted—to widen the war—was different from what he had found elsewhere. He said it was always about the same, but he believed that the antiwar minority at the time, as author Jack Newfield had recently put it, was a "prophetic minority," that they would eventually lead the rest of the country's young people, and the country itself, toward ending the Vietnam War. He was right.

But the war increasingly began to cause terrible inner conflicts for Robert Kennedy. On the one hand, practical politician that he was, he had more than once endorsed the seemingly inevitable reelection of Lyndon Johnson and Hubert Humphrey. On the other hand, his criticism of Johnson's war policy was, every day, becoming more and more bitter. I remember seeing, about this time, live television coverage of an appearance Kennedy made before the U.S. Chamber of Commerce. He spoke in the most outraged moral terms against the Vietnam War, and yet, when asked what he intended to do about ending the war besides continuing to make speeches, he was at a loss for a satisfactory answer. Something had to give. As it turned out, although we did not know it at the time, LaDonna and I were at Robert Kennedy's house on the very evening he decided to become a candidate for president. I had already signed on to head "Town and Country for Johnson and Humphrey" when, in the spring of 1968, Robert and Ethel asked LaDonna and me to come over and help liven up an obligatory dinner they sponsored each year for upstate, mostly conservative, New York newspaper editors. We went.

Robert Kennedy was in a particularly whimsical mood that night, and it was the first time I ever heard him refer to his brother John by his first name. He had always said "my brother" or "President Kennedy." Standing to make a brief toast, Robert took note of the fact that President Kennedy's dark blue president's flag was, unusually, just behind his chair. "There is no significance in the fact that John Kennedy's flag is so openly on display here," Robert said, his eyes twinkling at this allusion to growing rumors of his own impending announcement.

The press had speculated a great deal that Robert Kennedy was inching closer to becoming a presidential candidate. Once, earlier, the subject had come up when a group of us were weekending together in Hyannis Port. Aboard the Honey Fitz, we were idling along in the bay. Robert and I were sitting off by ourselves, talking about the New York political situation, while Ethel, LaDonna, and others, including some newspaper people, were engaged in a separate conversation that somehow turned to the possibility of Robert's running against President Johnson. Suddenly, Ethel called out, "Bobby, tell them how difficult it is for a person to challenge a president of his own party!"

Everyone immediately became breathlessly quiet, and the press people particularly strained to hear what they thought might be Robert's momentous answer. "Oh, you must be referring to General McClellan's challenge to Lincoln," he responded, getting off stage in the resulting burst of laughter without having to answer the question.

As the dinner at Hickory Hill for the New York State editors drew to a close, LaDonna and I said our good-byes all around, and Ethel and Robert followed us out into the entrance hall. Jim Whitaker, the mountain climber, was also there, leaving. Teasingly, Ethel said to Whitaker, "Jim, Fred here, you know, is Lyndon Johnson's campaign manager." We all laughed.

I took the occasion to say a serious word to Robert. I had seen his senior staff people gathering in another room for a meeting that obviously was to follow the social occasion. Now, as I shook hands with him, I said solemnly, "You know I can't be of any help to you in your decision, but do what your heart tells you, and that will be the right thing." That was the last time I saw Robert Kennedy alive.

LaDonna and I talked the situation over on the way home. We knew that Kennedy could not support Lyndon Johnson's reelection, but both of us doubted that he would actually become a candidate himself. We were aware that Kennedy did not like Senator Eugene McCarthy, already an antiwar candidate for president, but we thought that, nevertheless, he would probably endorse McCarthy as a kind of halfway solution to his dilemma.

But he decided to go all the way.

Deciding to support Humphrey was not the hardest decision I ever had to make, and I guess I would make it again. It was, though, the one that caused me the most anguish. But what if Kennedy had not been assassinated on the night of the California primary? I believe that Hubert Humphrey would nevertheless have been nominated at the Democratic convention in Chicago, and that in those circumstances he would probably have been elected president that fall.

Robert Kennedy was growing and developing, becoming better able to be president every day of his campaign, but the polls showed him losing public favor in the process. The polls indicated that many people were put off—even frightened—by the frenzy of the crowds that mobbed Kennedy everywhere he went. Although Humphrey was avoiding the primaries—partly because he'd had to start his campaign too late and partly because of a bad decision—he was, from the first, ahead in the public opinion polls, as well as in the rather closed Democratic Party delegate-selection process that governed at the time. And his lead kept growing, up until Robert Kennedy's death. From that moment on, however, Humphrey's standing in the polls plummeted. It seemed as if everything that had been said against him up to that date was permanently chiseled in granite. Humphrey told me later that the tragic bullet that killed Robert Kennedy also politically wounded him.

I was plunged into despair by Robert Kennedy's death. So was the nation. So was Humphrey. And his campaign never recovered. I believe that had Robert Kennedy lived but lost the nomination, he would have stood up with Humphrey and endorsed him at the 1968 convention, presuming that Humphrey would have stuck with his antiwar position at the convention, rather than announcing it later in Salt Lake. With Robert Kennedy's close ties to Mayor Richard Daley and with so many of the peace activists, he might even have helped to prevent, or at least quell, the Chicago police violence and calm the street demonstrations outside the 1968 convention hall. And being a practical politician, Kennedy would, I believe, have helped thereafter to legitimize the Humphrey-Muskie campaign.

But none of this was to be. America lost one of its greatest ever, most compassionate, most courageous voices for good.

I sat near the casket under the high, vaulted ceiling of Saint Patrick's Cathedral in New York City and listened tearfully to Senator Edward Kennedy's brave eulogy: "My brother need not be idealized or enlarged in death beyond what he was in life. He should be remembered simply as a good and decent man who saw wrong and tried to right it, saw suffering and tried to heal it, saw war and tried to stop it." Ted Kennedy quoted the George Bernard Shaw lines that, reworked a little, had earlier come to be a kind of campaign-speech mantra of Robert Kennedy's: "Some men see things that are and ask why. I see things that never were and ask why not."

I cannot express how deeply I wish that Robert Kennedy had been able to go on asking that kind of question. Our country today would be so much the better for it.

9

—∞—

Going National

SOMEWHAT RADICALIZED BY MY EXPERIENCES on the Kerner Commission, hit hard by the deaths of Robert Kennedy and Martin Luther King, Jr., frustrated that more wasn't being done about race and poverty in the country or toward stopping the war in Vietnam, I became more and more an uncompromising fighter for what I believed in. That is the way I used my last years in the U.S. Senate.

Then I decided not to run for reelection in 1972 and instead to run for president. I did not make this decision because I thought I could not get elected again to the Senate. I believed I could, and an Associated Press poll showed I could.

But I was a controversial figure in some circles in Oklahoma after eight years in Washington. I had become an outspoken critic of the giant oil companies and their unfair tax privileges. As national head of the Democratic Party, I had helped push through changes in party rules that in the past had, among other things, allowed Oklahoma officials simply to appoint half of the state's national convention delegates. Alone among the members of the Oklahoma congressional delegation, I had become a vigorous opponent of the Vietnam War. I was the most ardent national advocate of measures to end racism in the country, as recommended in the Kerner Commission Report.

My senatorial interests and activities had grown to include a wide span of concerns, from broadening East-West trade to prohibiting the killing of ocean mammals. Comparing my Oklahoma colleague, Republican Senator Henry Bellmon, and me, an editor of a conservative Oklahoma weekly newspaper wrote, "Oklahoma has two United States Senators; one doesn't do anything, and the other does too damn much." It was clear that I was the one he thought did "too damn much."

I decided against running again for the Senate in 1972 because I would have had to spend a whole year of my life doing nothing but campaigning, and I did not think it was worth it. I had been in the Senate for eight years, and the country did not seem to have changed for the better very much, if at all, during that period. I thought that even a good *campaign* for president could help move the country more in the right direction.

As it turned out, I did not so much run for president that year as sort of jog. I had grossly underestimated the difficulty of raising money to finance a campaign focused on the goal of more fairly distributing wealth, income, and power in America. Too, I waited far too long to announce. By the time I finally did, Senator George McGovern, who would wind up as our nominee that year, had long since secured for himself much of the backing and support I was hoping to count on.

So, I went broke rather quickly in the campaign for the 1972 Democratic nomination for president and pulled out even before the first primaries. David Broder, of the *Washington Post*, wrote that it was a great shame the only reason Senator Henry Jackson of Washington could continue as a candidate that year, and I could not, was money. Ironically, my withdrawal announcement in 1972 probably received more press attention than did my short campaign. I joked that if I could have just kept on withdrawing about once a week, I might have eventually caught on.

But the fact was that I did not catch on. So, I finished my Senate term, fighting against monopolies, strip mining, and runaway plants and for land reform, welfare reform, and tax reform.

Once out of the Senate, I went around the country a lot, speaking and lecturing for a fee to earn the money to pay off the debt I had accumulated. I formed a Washington-based private group, called New Populist Action, to continue to push for tax reform, and I became a citizen activist in a number of other public-interest groups and causes. I traveled to Kentucky, for example, to support the embattled mine workers there who were striking against the coal companies, and I wrote an article about this fight for the *Atlantic Monthly*. I went to Montana to stand with the Northern Cheyennes against strip-mining and the building of a coal-gasification plant on their reservation. Ralph Nader and I each bought one share in General Motors so that we could argue—unsuccessfully, as it turned out—for five minority-stockholder proposals we made at the corporation's annual meeting, including to require that General Motors adopt the same pay scale for workers of color as for white workers in their plants in South Africa and to ask them, in this country, to voluntarily break themselves up into five human-size and competing corporations. Nader and I also produced a public-interest television commercial in which I, as spokesman, answered a paid commercial in which the railroads sought more federal subsidies and protection from competition. I also began teaching a course of my own devising, New Populist Studies, at Washington's American University. LaDonna worked full time as president and CEO of Americans for Indian Opportunity, a Washington-based American Indian advocacy organization that she had formed, with my support and backing.

The Watergate burglary by operatives hired and directed by President Richard Nixon's Committee to Reelect the President (CREEP) only flared into full, front-page scandal in 1973, after I was out of the Senate, a private citizen.

The actual break-in at the Watergate offices of Democratic Party national chair Lawrence O'Brien (offices that had previously been mine) had occurred earlier, during Nixon's successful 1972 reelection campaign against George McGovern. It did not become big news until much later—unfortunately too late to affect the election's outcome. But from the very first newspaper report I read about the burglary, I knew—and told people—that Nixon was a goner, that he would inevitably be driven from office by the fallout from the crime.

Why? I knew that once the Watergate burglary had become the subject of a criminal investigation, there would be no way, under our system, for anyone to suppress that investigation, no matter where it might lead. I also knew that the break-in simply could not have been some "third-rate burglary," as the Nixon people were claiming. Nothing as serious as that would ever have been undertaken during a campaign without highest-level authorization and direction.

And I knew Nixon—surely one of the most peculiar people ever to serve in American public office.

He was a politician who didn't like to be around people. When he could, he limited his contact with others to his closest aides. By contrast, senators, including me, had seen almost *too* much of Nixon's predecessor, Lyndon Johnson—briefings, receptions, dinners, personal audiences. You saw Johnson just about every time you turned around. It was the opposite with Nixon, something I once remarked about to a Republican Senate colleague, thinking that it was only Democratic senators whom Nixon was shunning. Not so, this senator responded, shaking his head in puzzlement. "We [Republicans] hardly ever see him, either."

Mel Elfin, a reporter who covered Nixon for *Newsweek*, once told me that he was sure Nixon was manic-depressive, what is now called bipolar. Elfin might have been right, though some of Nixon's strange behavior also could have been the result of too much drinking. We were later to learn from former aides' revelations that Nixon was doing a lot of that, particularly late in his time in office.

At any rate, I saw Nixon when he seemed abnormally hyper, manic. For example, at a breakfast once in the East Room of the White House, he first went around to every separate table personally, engaging each senator present in a one-way, rapid-fire babbling of inanities, mostly about sports. To me, he said, "What about those Sooners?" then rattled on quite specifically about a previous Saturday's game when the Oklahoma football team had been down on the twenty-yard line, or some such, and had run what he described as a terrific play. He could not stop talking.

And I saw Nixon when he seemed to be in a darkly withdrawn and depressed state, once in the Roosevelt Room at a rather intimate White House bill-signing ceremony. Though most of the few senators there were people Nixon knew well as former colleagues, he did not shake hands with any of us or even acknowledge our individual presence, never made eye contact with any of us, even as, at the end, head down, he peremptorily handed each of us one of the pens with which he had just signed the legislation.

Nixon was hateful and vindictive, a lifelong dirty-tricks campaigner with a mean practice of always trying to "screw" his enemies. I was on his famous Enemies List that the *New York Times* somehow got hold of and published. The publication of that list, as well as the Watergate scandal and similar revelations, caused me to think again at the time about three earlier, and odd, office burglaries that I had been the victim of. In all three, no suspect was ever found and nothing of value was taken. Further, in each instance, it was apparent that no effort had been made to cover up the crime. Indeed, it seemed that the perpetrator, or perpetrators, had wanted the fact of the break-in and burglary to be obvious, perhaps as kind of warning or threat.

The first of these three incidents occurred in 1971, after I had launched a first, very brief, presidential campaign. One morning, my press secretary, Sherry Jones, entered her fourth-floor office in the brick R Street townhouse we had rented in Washington as a headquarters and found that her desk drawers had been rifled and left open. Papers and files were strewn around. But valuable taping and other electronic devices were still in the same drawers, untouched. Nothing had been stolen.

The two other incidents both occurred in 1973, after I had left the Senate. A secretary in the law office I affiliated with for a short time came to work one morning to find a drawer of my personal file cabinet, always locked, standing wide open. Nothing in the office was missing. The only thing gone from my personal file drawer, we found on close inspection, was a fat folder that contained all the material and documents that backed up my 1972 federal income tax return. For the next four years, I feared that I would be audited by Internal Revenue and wouldn't have the necessary receipts, vouchers, canceled checks, and other records to defend my filing. Luckily, no such audit ever came.

The third incident occurred at about the same time as the second one. When former Senate staff members of mine, Sherry Jones and Jim Rosapepe, and I formed New Populist Action, we rented second-floor space for it in a slightly rundown Washington office building. When I moved into the sparsely furnished room that would be my personal office there, I found that a previous tenant had left a small combination safe on the floor of the room. The safe's door was open and the combination for it was written on a piece left inside, so I used the safe, storing papers in it from time to time, though nothing of real importance. I kept the safe's door locked. Coming in one early morning, I found it fully open and my papers spread out on the floor in front of it like a fan, as if someone had arranged them to be photographed.

Was the Nixon crowd responsible for these odd break-ins? I came to think so at the time, and I pretty much still do. That was the kind of stuff they did.

A federal grand jury was convened in Washington to look into the Watergate burglary. A Senate subcommittee also began a full public investigation. And one day, I received a mysterious, hush-hush call from my friend Washington attorney Robert McCandless, who asked for an urgent and secret meeting with me.

We soon got together like two revolution plotters, in a dark and out-of-the-way Washington bar. McCandless, constantly looking over his shoulder to be sure he was not being watched or overheard, told me that he was representing White House counsel John Dean, who had been subpoenaed by both the Watergate federal grand jury and the Senate subcommittee. McCandless wanted my advice concerning his representation of Dean. The two of them, I knew, were former brothers-in-law; their first wives were sisters, daughters of a Missouri senator.

McCandless was at pains not to reveal confidential client information, but at the same time, he tried to tell me enough so that I could give him useful advice. "The main thing," I finally said, "is that if Dean's going to testify, he's got to tell the truth; he damned sure doesn't want to escalate any trouble he's in to the level of a felony, by committing perjury."

McCandless instantly agreed, but then he asked, "How high up the ladder should Dean go in implicating people?"

"Well, how high do the facts go?" I asked.

"About as high as they *can* go," McCandless said. I knew that without directly saying so he meant Nixon.

"Dean's got to tell the truth, no matter what," I said. And that's what Dean did. His testimony at the Senate subcommittee hearings particularly put a noose around Nixon's neck. His memory about relevant facts and conversations proved to be uncannily accurate, before he or nearly anyone else knew that the president had taped everything said in the Oval Office during his term. When finally produced, the tapes, even with one long erasure, completely corroborated Dean's testimony and sealed Nixon's fate.

Nixon resigned. He had to or he would have been impeached and convicted. Except for incoming President Gerald Ford's broad pardon of him, Nixon would also have been tried and convicted in federal court of at least the crime of obstruction of justice.

Knowing Nixon, I think he actually *authorized* the Watergate burglary, not just tried to cover it up after the fact. Perhaps the reason behind the erasure of a portion of the presidential tapes was to eliminate proof of that authorization. We will never know.

And we will never know for sure why the Watergate break-in was ordered in the first place, whether by Nixon or whomever. I think *I* know the reason. I think the break-in was designed to put Democratic chair Lawrence O'Brien on notice that the Nixon people knew, from O'Brien's papers they intended to find and copy, that O'Brien was on the payroll of eccentric billionaire Howard Hughes, to discourage O'Brien and the Democrats from using against Nixon in the 1972 presidential campaign the evidence they had that Nixon had once received a big sum of money from Hughes. It was a payment disguised as a loan to Nixon's brother, a loan never repaid.

Walter Mondale and I, back when we cochaired Hubert Humphrey's 1968 Democratic presidential campaign, were primarily responsible for bringing O'Brien in as the Humphrey preconvention campaign czar. And later, at the Democratic Convention in Chicago, after Humphrey had been nominated, I sat in with him on a meeting with O'Brien at which Humphrey successfully talked O'Brien into becoming national chair of the Democratic Party, to run the Humphrey-Muskie general election campaign. On that occasion, O'Brien at first demurred. He told us confidentially that he was then receiving an annual retainer of $140,000 from Howard Hughes, ostensibly for political advice, and that the money was being run through a New York–based consulting firm. O'Brien said that he could not afford to forgo this income in order to take the party job. Humphrey said he did not have to; he could keep the retainer and nobody would have to know about it.

Years later, in Albuquerque, on an anniversary of Nixon's death, I appeared as a member of a televised panel to discuss and assess the Nixon presidency. Former White House aide John Erlichman, out of prison by then and living in Santa Fe, was also on that panel. At the end of the program, while the cameras were still on us as the credits were rolling, but the sound was off in the studio, I abruptly turned to Erlichman and asked him, "Were the Watergate burglars looking for proof that Larry O'Brien was on Howard Hughes's payroll?"

"No," Erlichman said immediately, and dismissively. "We already knew all about that; we had O'Brien's tax returns."

Just then, the television program director yelled, "Clear on the set!" The lights went off. The cameras were shut down. And it was not until I was outside and walking to my car that I suddenly thought, *Why didn't I say, 'Well, what were you looking for, then?'* We will never know what Erlichman might have answered.

In the spring of 1974, I began to think about the central importance for the country's future of the upcoming 1976 presidential race, and I decided to write a lengthy memorandum to my friend Senator Mondale, a presumed Democratic presidential candidate whom I expected to support, to give him my most thoughtful advice about what kind of campaign, and on what issues, he should run in order to win.

I worked on the Mondale presidential-campaign memorandum, off and on, for almost a month, but about the time I had it finished, Mondale suddenly announced that he would not run for president after all. "So, what did you decide to do, then, Fred? Write your own name on the memo, instead of Mondale's?" Robert McCandless later asked me. And I guess what I did do was something akin to that.

I redrafted the memorandum, no longer addressing it to Mondale, but simply calling it "A Model 1976 Presidential Campaign." I had copies printed in quantity. And in June 1974, still without committing myself to run, and not sure what the response might be, I mailed the memorandum to several hundred friends and other potential supporters throughout the country, asking for their comments. The responses were overwhelmingly enthusiastic. My best friend, Jim Hightower, for example, then heading up a Nader-like operation in Washington, the Agribusiness Accountability Project (and later to be elected Texas agriculture commissioner and, still later, to become a highly effective national populist advocate and commentator) told me at once that, if I would run for president, he would take a year out of his life to help me do it. My friend Peter Barnes, West Coast editor of the *New Republic* (and later to form Working Assets and continue to work for progressive causes), also made an immediate commitment to my candidacy.

So, suddenly, I was running for president again, but this campaign would be very different from my brief 1972 run. The central issues were crisply refined from the first. So were the underlying assumptions of the campaign, the strategy, and the style. All these were stated plainly in my 1974 memorandum. As the campaign unfolded, we followed that memorandum almost to the letter. And we came close to making it work.

I had learned, as I said in the memorandum, that "in the American tradition, the most effective way to raise issues is through elective politics, and a Democratic presidential campaign is the best vehicle." Emphasis on this point was particularly necessary if I was to have any chance of involving public-interest activists around the country, many of whom had come to feel, with good reason, that fighting utility companies at the local level, for example, or working to end mortgage-company redlining (that rejected loans for housing in poor and minority areas) was a more effective way of using their time and energies than taking part in electoral politics. Most of these activists had seen too many months and too many minds used up in political campaigns that went nowhere and left no lasting trace. I hoped mine would be different, and said so.

In August and September of 1974, I began to hold a series of private-home coffees around the country, starting in California and New Hampshire, asking people to sign written support cards. A majority of those at each coffee did sign up.

But then and throughout the campaign, the toughest problem I found was that a lot of people really did not believe that democracy could be made to work. "You should win, and I hope you do," they would say, "but *can* you? Will they let you—the party powers and the wealthy and corporate interests?"

I always explained how party reforms that were launched when I was the national Democratic Party chair had given ordinary people a fighting chance. "If we want to be, you and I *are* the Democratic Party," I said, and I reminded my listeners that Senator McGovern's untrained but committed volunteers, outsiders, had handily beaten the party powers in 1972.

Frequently, my argument along those lines knocked down one reason for reluctance to support me only to cause another. "But look what happened to McGovern; he lost [in the general election]," a potential supporter would say.

I pointed out that a new 1974 campaign-financing law—limiting contributions to one thousand dollars and providing for federal matching funds in the primaries and full federal financing in the general election—had cut down to size the rich and the friends of the rich and had made it possible for us to put into practice the principle of "one person, one vote." "In the past," I said, "some people had more than one vote, because they had the money."

"A lot of big shots are waiting to see which way the wind is going to blow," I would say toward the end of each gathering where I spoke, just before asking people to sign support cards. "I'm asking you to decide which way the wind will blow. If you say 'I know Fred Harris, he's the best person in this race, I'm for him, and he's going to win'—and you have to say 'He's going to win'—if you say that often enough and strongly enough, you yourself will make it come to pass." Invariably, half or more of those who heard the message signed up immediately. A highly skilled and gifted staff member, Frank Greer, who had stepped away from his San Francisco public-interest advertising business to volunteer full time in my presidential campaign, produced a sound and slide show of my whole in-person presentation, and soon committed supporters around the country began to show the slides and conduct their own coffees, signing up new supporters themselves.

We all came to call the support cards, which were the lifeblood of my campaign, green cards because that was the color of paper the original batch was printed on. Whipping out a green card to sign up anyone who expressed support became an almost automatic reflex for everybody in my organization. During the campaign, our older daughter, Kathryn, married Manuel Tijerina. Our other daughter, Laura, then fifteen, was the bridesmaid. As the wedding party waited nervously for our time to enter and walk down the aisle of the little Deyo Mission Indian church near our old hometown of Lawton, Oklahoma, Laura peeped into the packed sanctuary, then turned back to me and playfully said, "It's a good crowd, Daddy; do you want me to pass out green cards at the end?"

Two basic assumptions underlay my presidential campaign. The first, as stated in the 1974 memorandum, was that "the fundamental ideal of the American experiment is the widespread diffusion of economic and political power." The second was that "people are smart enough to govern themselves." These fundamental assumptions were stated over and over, in the campaign literature and by me at coffees, until everyone began to repeat them, word for word, like a mantra. It's the kind of thing that always happens with the words and phrases much employed in any particular campaign, often, after a while, causing insiders to get into a kind of giddy and joking use of them. One night in California, for example, I was being driven from one coffee to another, led by three local supporters in a car ahead of the one I was in, when, after we'd had to turn around and backtrack for the third time, the three leaders finally stopped under a street light and got out to study a city map. I stuck my head out the window and in some exasperation yelled, "Are we lost?"

"No," one of the three answered without looking up, "we're just having a little debate about whether people really are smart enough to govern themselves."

The campaign memorandum said, "People can be expected to do the right thing, to act in their own best interests—if they have the facts and are given real choices." I still think that's true.

Mine was always an issues campaign. I did not see the presidency as some kind of Man of the Year award. I had already received all the awards a person ought to have. I wanted to be president because I felt deeply about the issues. As I put it in my original memorandum, "Too few people have all the money and power; most people have little or none."

"The campaign must address the real day-to-day problems of people—heavy and unfair taxes; bad or nonexistent housing; inadequate and costly medical care; inflated food, utility, and other prices; high interest rates; exorbitant military expenditures and waste; cynical and interventionist foreign policy; low wages and unemployment—in terms of how economic and political privilege thwarts the will of the people." That's what the memorandum said.

Because of my emphasis on these issues, I was able to enlist many dedicated, like-minded supporters from diverse backgrounds. But I found to my surprise that some people who thought of themselves as issue-oriented liberals professed more interest in my issues at first than they demonstrated later on. In the beginning, some of these people were quoted to the effect that they liked what I said, and they agreed that I could stir a crowd, but they wondered about my "depth." In due time, televised forums were set up all around the country, at which the presidential candidates appeared together and answered questions on the issues, and when it was agreed, and reported, that I invariably came off strongest at these events and got the most enthusiastic response from the audience, some of the same liberals began to say I was too good on the issues. "Of course, you're the best on the issues," one sponsor of an issues forum told me when it was over, "but you just can't get elected talking like that, and I'm tired of getting beat."

Another longtime liberal activist—a wealthy one—whose principal policy interest had always been in breaking up the vertically integrated oil companies, a key plank in my platform, expressed the same pragmatic concern to me. He said he would not make a commitment to me because he was afraid I could not win. And, interestingly, he was later to endorse one of the other presidential candidates, former governor Jimmy Carter of Georgia, who, of course, ultimately went on to win the 1976 nomination and election, at a time when Carter was the only moderate-to-liberal candidate in the race who had not taken a strong stand on curbing oil-company power.

With this experience in mind, I later asked Eugene McCarthy how he explained that some of his own most dedicated and reform-minded 1968 supporters had turned into some of George McGovern's most Machiavellian manipulators of credentials and platform issues at the 1972 Democratic convention, opposing, for example, a platform minority report I advocated at that convention in favor of fundamental tax reform. "Idealists should be limited by law to involvement in one campaign only," McCarthy replied. "After that, they tend to get too interested in power." Perhaps there is some truth in that.

An early problem in my campaign was that I found myself tagged a radical by *Time* magazine, Walter Cronkite (who, incidentally, later told me on the night before the New Hampshire primary, following a great campaign rally for me, "Fred, you're going to win this thing!"), and others. This was not malicious. Reporters were seeking a quick label for me, and I am hard to categorize. I never was a traditional liberal. I believe, as Thomas Jefferson did, in the widespread diffusion of economic and political power, and it was in those terms that I defined the New Populism that I advocated. That kind of widespread diffusion of power would require no change in the Constitution or in our basic principles and very little change in our laws. Basically, it would mean putting into practice what we say we believe in. So, as I said to every crowd and gathering during the presidential campaign, we ought to have a true graduated income tax, rather than graduated loopholes; we ought to break up the monopolies that overcharge us; and we ought to commit ourselves to full employment and mean it. "There is plenty of money to do what needs to be done, if we take the rich off welfare," I would also say. I often pointed out that Nelson Rockefeller, for example, had admitted to a congressional committee that he paid no individual federal income tax in 1971, and I would conclude, "We ought to sue him for nonsupport."

My kind of talk had not been heard much since Harry Truman had reminded the country that the Ford and Carnegie fortunes—and foundations—had been built out of the mangled bodies and the blood of exploited working people. I was, of course, advocating a return to basic American principles, but people simply had not heard this message in so long that it sounded too radical to some of them at first.

That had also been true to some extent during my short-lived 1972 presidential campaign. One morning back then, I was explaining at a breakfast with Washington reporters how I hoped to get free press attention on specific issues of mine by holding a series of outdoor, on-site press conferences at various locations in the country. I had already held such a conference in front of the General Motors Building in New York City to say that, as president, I would move vigorously to enforce antitrust laws against the automobile industry. Peter Lisagor, a first-rate reporter for the *Chicago Daily News*, asked a question in intentionally provocative form: "But Fred, isn't there a limit to how many places you can stand on your head and make outrageous statements?"

"First, I don't believe I'm making outrageous statements—" I began.

"You know what I mean," Lisagor interrupted.

Before I could continue my answer, veteran conservative columnist Roscoe Drummond, then aging considerably and apparently a little hard of hearing, caused an explosion of laughter that practically broke up the meeting when he leaned over to Lisagor and said in a voice he obviously intended to be a confidential whisper but that could be heard to the corners of the room, "Well, *I* think he's making outrageous statements!"

This view was less prevalent in 1976. "When Mr. Harris began to campaign in the summer of 1974, there seemed to be several possible outcomes," Charles Mohr wrote in the *New York Times*. "One of the most likely was that, sooner or later, commentators and politicians would begin to denounce him as a radical. Another possibility was that he would make no significant impact at all and would go unheard. Instead, something quite different happened. Rather than 'ex-communicating' Mr. Harris, many liberals in his party embraced his populist doctrines."

So did some of the other presidential candidates that year. Once, on the CBS television program *Face the Nation,* I said, alluding to Jimmy Carter's famous smile and his lack at that time of specific proposals for tax reform, that he was like a horse trader who would show you *his* teeth but not the horse's. By Tuesday night, Governor George Wallace of Alabama was using those exact words as his own to describe Carter.

Political columnist and book author Jules Whitcover, writing about me in the *Washington Post,* observed that "other candidates, notably Carter and Udall, often picked up his themes, in sometimes toned-down phrases, sometimes in identical ones, delivered with less aggressiveness."

Mohr described this same phenomenon in a *Times* article. "Other liberals, such as Representative Morris K. Udall of Arizona and Senator Birch Bayh of Indiana, echoed many of the words and even some of the rhythms of the Harris campaign, particularly his unrelenting attacks on monopolistic power wielded by 'giant corporations,' his appeals for more equality of opportunity and his demands for social justice," Mohr wrote. "Even more conservative candidates, such as Senator Henry M. Jackson of Washington and former Governor Jimmy Carter of Georgia, seemed to borrow elements of the Harris gospel."

This was a development we had not planned on. When I decided to seek the 1976 Democratic nomination, I knew that I would be outspent by the other candidates in Iowa and New Hampshire—and this, of course, proved to be true. But I thought this handicap would be balanced out some by my being so distinctive on the issues. What actually happened was that many of us presidential candidates began to sound a great deal alike.

That was good for the country. It was a major breakthrough that all the leading candidates, for example, came to endorse full employment and expressed enough support for the Humphrey-Hawkins bill to bring it about. All of the leading candidates, too, soon spoke out for tax reform. Most of them, as I did, condemned covert actions by the Central Intelligence Agency. Most of them called for breaking up the monopolistic (or more technically, oligopolistic) oil companies. Most came to favor granting the president at least stand-by power to control prices in such monopolistic industries.

And that is what a good campaign *should* do—focus the attention of the country on the issues and educate the candidates. That is what makes a campaign worth undertaking. Some of my friends—writer Elizabeth Drew and Senator Walter Mondale, for example—have said that it is unnecessarily grueling and demeaning for presidential candidates to have to go through the present, long, drawn-out nominating process. I do not agree. For one thing, I never found running for president that grueling. As I've sometimes said—jokingly, but truthfully—I used to pick cotton for a living, and I find campaigning much easier. Some people get up in the morning and go to work at a steel mill. Presidential candidates get up in the morning and go to Boston or Milwaukee to make a speech. It's not all that hard.

This was especially true for me in light of the style of my campaign, a natural outgrowth of its basic assumptions and central issues. My 1974 memorandum set forth the general pattern: "No limousines and drivers for the candidate. He must campaign like other people live. Buses. Public transportation. Coffees in homes. Personal contact. Staying in people's homes. No campaign jets and big staffs. These will not be gimmicks; they will be financial necessities."

When Senator Mondale announced that he would no longer be a candidate for president, he said that he could not face the prospect of having to stay in Holiday Inns for a year. I did not have to worry about such a prospect, because I stayed in private homes. This practice saved money of course, but it also made the campaign better and more enjoyable, and I learned a lot in the process.

I carried my own bags, and later on, so did the press people who followed me, although some of them had been accustomed in other campaigns to being waited on like movie reviewers, which, in a way, they were. When Peter Lisagor first heard that my campaign did not intend to handle lodging, baggage, and other arrangements for the press, he said—only half jokingly, I think—"Fred, we thought it was sort of quaintly attractive that you planned to carry your own bags, but we never had any idea that you wanted *us* to do that, too."

One of the most effective and enjoyable parts of the whole campaign was traveling coast to coast in a big Winnebago camper, during July and August of 1974. We started with a huge rally in Lafayette Square, across the street from the White House, then headed west and wound up crossing the Golden Gate Bridge into San Francisco five weeks and 5,400 miles later. Along on this trip in the Winnebago were our younger daughter, Laura; her young cousin Alexis Gover; two wonderful staff members, Mimi Mager, later a Washington consultant and powerhouse, who handled press and other meeting arrangements, and Don Grissom, who went on to become a video expert and political activist; the driver; the trip director; and the photographer. Alexis and Laura distributed the green cards and took up the contributions at each stop. I did all the cooking, as well as all the speaking. LaDonna joined us intermittently for two or three days at a stretch, when she could get loose from her duties at Americans for Indian Opportunity.

We called the trip "On the Road to the White House," and this phrase, along with "Fred Harris for President," was emblazoned on the sides of our Winnebago. I always had to explain that I knew we were heading away from the White House, but that this was because I believed that the right way to get to the White House was to first go out to the people. The camper trip was well advanced. Long before we left Washington, some fifty-five well-planned and advertised picnics, rallies, coffees, and other gatherings had been scheduled along our thirteen-state route. We depended primarily on our local supporters for arrangements, but two volunteer staff members, driving a van, arrived at each point a week ahead of us, like a circus advance team, to help the local people. Two other volunteer staff people were flown in specially a couple of times to places where extra advance help with arrangements was needed.

The camper trip was about the most effective part of my whole campaign. It helped us intensify our organizing efforts in the states we visited. It was well covered by the press, a number of reporters even traveling with me for stretches, and it gave me and the campaign our first real burst of national publicity. The camper trip projected an image of me that stuck, too; months later, some people thought I was still riding around the country in a camper. Indeed, we did rent other campers on several later occasions for particular brief in-state swings just before the voting in Iowa, Oklahoma, New Hampshire, and Massachusetts.

The original Winnebago journey was great fun, and many funny things happened along the way. When it began, before our publicity began to get out ahead of us, not many people had heard of me or the trip. Later on, that changed, but during the first week especially, I had more than a slight identity problem. Once, for example, an entire busload of high school students pulled alongside the camper on the highway and, leaning out the windows, shouted in unison, "Who's Fred Harris?" Luckily, no press people were with us at the time to report this.

But the Associated Press did somehow pick up and publish a report of a similar incident, which occurred at a campground shower one evening. I was undressing to go into the shower as another man emerged from it, toweling off. "I see we have a presidential candidate in the camp," he said to me, obviously not knowing who I was.

"Uh huh," I said, trying to hurry my undressing, not wanting to get involved. It seemed to be less than an ideal time and place to shake hands and pass out literature.

"They say his name's Fred Harris. You ever hear of him?"

"Huh uh."

"A person would almost have to be beside himself to want to be president these days. Don't you agree?"

"Uh huh."

"Well, I guess anybody would be better than the one we got."

"Right," I said, and quickly escaped at last into the shower.

From the first, I envisioned that my 1976 campaign organization and staff would consist of volunteers. "One enthusiastic volunteer, with a clear understanding of the theme, style, basic assumptions, and strategy of the campaign, is worth three lukewarm paid workers," I wrote in the original memorandum. "If the campaign starts paying people, other than a small central office, there will be no end to the paying; people won't volunteer to do the same work for nothing that other people are paid to do. People with no experience, if they understand the nature of the campaign and come to it with enthusiasm, can be taught the necessary skills—press, radio, canvassing, organization. Most of them must be able to live off the land, or their own resources, in order to do so."

That concept worked marvelously well, with one very important exception. We came to feel that we should have, months in advance, put a skilled organizer into each major state that had an early caucus or primary. But at that time, we had neither the skilled organizers among our volunteers nor the money to hire some. We had to grow our own. That lost us vital time we could never make up, damaging delays in key organizing that we could never overcome. Local volunteers can go only so far. They need the assistance and guidance of a full-time staff. In no state were we able to provide this help early enough.

The great joy of my 1976 presidential campaign was in associating with our dedicated and effective staff, volunteers, and supporters—in the national office and throughout the country. The Washington-based staff consisted of a mixture of superb professionals, including Jim Hightower, who did an excellent job as campaign manager and treasurer; and media expert Frank Greer, who later went on to head the firm of Greer Margolis, which handled Bill Clinton's successful presidential campaigns and many others; as well as extremely fast learners, like Barbara Shailor, then of Denver, who took a leave of absence as a senior flight attendant for United Airlines to head our delegate operation and later went on to become vice president for international affairs of the AFL-CIO. Most of the staff worked without salaries. As Charles Mohr wrote in the *New York Times*, "Mr. Harris had one of the largest—and most gifted—staffs in politics, and his staff members worked for nothing or next to it."

We were all very close—literally close for the first nine or ten months because our national office was then located in my McLean, Virginia, home. In the beginning, the campaign used only the basement there, which we converted into a bustling office, but before long, the campaign expanded into the ground-floor living room, dining room, and den. Next, the two-car garage was fixed up for use by the financial and printing sections of the campaign. By then, the bedrooms and kitchen were all that were left in our home as exclusively family quarters. And finally, just prior to our campaign operation moving into downtown Washington, where we took over a couple of floors in the seedy Ambassador Hotel, we even rolled two construction-office trailers into our backyard. Campaigning out of our home was like living up over your store, and this early close arrangement gave the members of the campaign staff a uniquely warm feeling for each other that was never lost, even after there were more than 150 full-time people, at the national office and in the field.

—⚘— —⚘— —⚘—

I believe people ought to be able to laugh a little, at themselves and at the world. That keeps things in perspective. I was pleased when *Time* magazine's Hugh Sidey said in a syndicated television commentary, "Harris supplied more than his share of the campaign humor, which was not exactly in oversupply."

From the first, I told campaign audiences that while the 1976 issues were terribly serious, there was no reason why we had to be solemn all the time. Most people did not know, or had forgotten, that presidential campaigns could be fun. "Can you imagine old Scoop Jackson ever laughing?" I used to ask early crowds. They could not, and most of them thought the attempt would probably break his jaw. One columnist at the time wrote that if Jackson got elected president and, like Franklin Roosevelt, gave a fireside chat, the fire would go out.

Jim Hightower is a laugher, and he helped us keep perspective. Once, early on, as we were finishing a scheduling meeting, Hightower suddenly remembered that we had set aside no dates for me to make initial organizing appearances in Illinois. "Here it is, right here in the middle of the country," he said, pointing at a map of the United States. "Can't you just see

Theodore White's next making-of-the-president book? 'No doubt Fred Harris would have been elected president of the United States except for the fact that he and his crack staff forgot about Illinois until it was too late.'"

Leading off as master of ceremonies in early meetings of our supporters, Hightower sometimes used to point to me and tell the crowd, "Unlike the other campaigns, we've got the issues on our side; our candidate is not just another pretty face—as you can plainly see." Maybe there ought to be a limit, I sometimes thought, to how far a person should go to get a laugh.

Another advantage we had in my presidential campaign that none other could match was LaDonna—and people knew it. Both in New York and in California, separately and spontaneously, my supporters almost at once brought out "LaDonna Harris for First Lady" buttons. Soon we could not print enough of them. In introducing LaDonna, I used to say that she belonged to the national board of directors of every organization anyone had ever heard of—from Common Cause to the National Organization for Women. I called her a "nonprofit conglomerate." And I said, with some truth, that people in Oklahoma used to tell me, "If LaDonna can't come, why don't you come yourself."

Once the campaign was in full swing, LaDonna took a leave of absence from Americans for Indian Opportunity and began to spend a large part of her time working in the campaign. We liked to travel together, and we generally did so during the campaign, sometimes splitting up for separate appearances during the day, then getting back together at night. LaDonna spoke on the issues with particular emphasis on those in which she was most interested—human rights and health, including mental health. I liked having her speak to a new audience just ahead of me. Remarkably warm and personal, she helped to humanize me for our audiences and make me more believable.

LaDonna liked to tell about our children, too. She would say that Byron, recently graduated from high school, was working for a filmmaker in New York, that Kathryn, who had been an early demonstrator against the Vietnam War, was fresh out of Stanford Law School and working in my campaign, and that Laura, who had already been a demonstrator for virtually every cause in America, from civil rights to support for farm workers, had just entered high school but was active in the campaign, too. And LaDonna always mentioned that I was the only member of our family who was not a Comanche Indian.

Until almost the end of my presidential campaign, I declined Secret Service protection. I felt that their presence would inevitably diminish the open, spontaneous, and personal character of the campaign. But one morning, a strange man confronted me with a drawn pistol as I exited a downtown Chicago building where I had just done a live television interview. Frank Greer courageously shielded me and quickly grabbed the man's pistol hand, saying to him, "Now, you don't want to do that." The man jerked away, turned, and ran down the street, never to be identified nor found after that. But at my direction, Greer made an immediate telephone call to the Chicago office of the Secret Service and told them we were now ready to accept their protection.

The agents proved to be a good bunch, and we got along well with them. Some of them had previously been assigned to Senator Birch Bayh. After looking over the diverse mixture of people in our crowds—long haired, short haired; old, young; white, black, Hispanic, American Indian; blue collar, professionals—one agent confided to Fred Droz, my highly competent director of advance, "A lot of the people in your crowds are the kind we were worried about keeping away from Bayh's."

The most beautiful mixture of people we ever got into the same room during the campaign came together in a packed ballroom in a Jackson, Mississippi, hotel. The huge crowd included some of my local African American friends, some of my progressive white friends, a large contingent from the Choctaw Indian reservation in that state, and as I used to say, telling about it later, "a whole lot of my redneck Mississippi kinfolk." At first, there was some tension among the people in that Jackson meeting, but I put them at ease when I told them what I had said in Madison, Wisconsin, the preceding day. "I told those people in Madison yesterday," I began, "that I was on my way to Jackson, and that I was either going to put together in one room the most beautiful mixture of people who ever got together here, or the damnedest race riot, one or the other."

The people in the meeting began to nudge each other and laugh, and then we got down to my populist talk about issue positions that I knew were in the best interests of all kinds of people—black, white, or whatever. I said that there were white people in that state who thought it was all right for a black woman to work all day, cleaning a white person's house, for a jar of green beans and a bucket of syrup, without realizing that that was why the white person was still earning only a dollar an hour for his or her own work. I said, "Black people and white people don't have to love each other. I wish they would, but they don't have to. All they have to do is realize that it's in their own interests to get together, and, if they do, they're a majority." That kind of talk worked in Mississippi, just as it did everywhere else. Afterward, an eighty-year-old great-aunt of mine came up to me and said, "Well, Fredie, I guess we're just going to have to be for you." And a sixty-five-year-old great-uncle of mine took my hand and held it a long time, and tears came to his eyes when he said, "I've waited forty years to hear something like that."

I wish we could have been as successful at gathering money as we were at assembling our great staff and volunteers. Luckily, with a volunteer staff, we did not need as much money as the other campaigns did. Our first financial goal was to raise at least five thousand dollars in each of at least twenty states so that we could qualify under the public-financing law for dollar-for-dollar federal matching funds. It was a great day when we passed that tough hurdle. Thereafter, every dime we raised became two. But the going was still slow. We took up collections at every meeting. Our supporters held garage sales and bake sales. We sponsored simultaneous "Neighbors Night" fund-raising coffees throughout the country, and I spoke to the participants in a nationwide radio hookup. We solicited contributions cold, by mail. Toward the end of the campaign, the great singers Pete Seeger and Tom Paxton, and some others, entertained at our fund-raisers, and Arlo Guthrie and his band, Shenandoah, did twenty-seven concerts for me at which a campaign contribution was the price of admission. Most of all, we kept going back to our list of green card supporters, which had grown to about fifty thousand names by the time I had to quit. Looking back now, I think we should probably have put more early emphasis on direct-mail appeals and on concerts, but direct mail, in its initial rounds, costs you more money than it brings in, and we did not have sufficient cash at first to invest enough in this fund-raising method. Also, in the beginning, we thought that the Federal Election Commission would match only the net amount raised from concerts. The commission finally, for that 1976 campaign only, as it turned out, decided to match the gross amount collected at the concerts, and that saved our campaign's life for a while.

But really, raising money is not a separate activity from campaigning. They are intertwined parts of the same thing. My 1974 presidential campaign memorandum had described this correctly: "A people's campaign will generate its own money; peck sacks of money won't save a bad campaign." I was not surprised, then, when that year's lavishly financed presidential-campaign efforts of Senator Lloyd Bentsen of Texas and Governor George Wallace began to fizzle.

Mine was not a bad campaign. It was a good one. But getting contributions became almost impossible after my disappointing showings in the first few state contests for delegates. The campaign died, and so did our ability to raise the necessary money to resurrect it.

There was nothing wrong with my original strategy, and had I received a few percentage points more in the voting in the first key states, we would have soon been answering the question "How in the world did you do it?" instead of "What in the world went wrong?"

My goal, as stated in the original memo, was to place among the top three candidates in the first two contests, the caucuses in Iowa and the New Hampshire primary; to emerge in the top two in the middle contests, such as the one in Wisconsin; and then to run first in the last contests, in states like California and Ohio, for example. "The candidate does not have to run number one in the New Hampshire primary, because the 'conventional wisdom' of the national press and political officials and observers will be that he will not even make a showing there," I'd written in the 1974 memo, going on to say, "History indicates that the conventional political wisdom is always wrong—not sometimes wrong, but always wrong." Unfortunately, in 1976, it was wrong about Jimmy Carter, not about me.

I knew from the first, as I wrote, that the winning Democratic candidate would have to beat the expectations. Initially I did that, running second to Senator Birch Bayh for the endorsement of the New Democratic Coalition in New York and coming in first in the voting of two other progressive groups, Massachusetts Citizens for Participation in Political Action and Texas Democrats. I eventually beat the expectations, too, by coming in a respectable third in the Iowa precinct caucuses, after which I rightly said in a press conference there that night, "The winnowing-out process has begun, and I've been winnowed in." That statement was true, but not for long.

I held on through the Oklahoma caucuses, staying alive even though I was attacking the oil companies on their home ground, and running against George Wallace, Lloyd Bentsen, and Jimmy Carter, who was backed locally by David L. Boren, the governor of Oklahoma, a state not known lately as a hotbed of liberalism. I ran a squeaky-close second there to Carter, and this result was regarded as acceptable only because I was no longer a senator from Oklahoma and indeed, by then, no longer had a home in the state.

Then came the New Hampshire Democratic primary. Morris Udall had been able to revive his campaign there, after a poor showing in Iowa, while I was tied up in Oklahoma, a state that he did not compete in. He ran second to Jimmy Carter in New Hampshire. I received just 11 percent of the New Hampshire vote, a "lower than the expectations" fourth place, though it was a large field. The handwriting was on the wall, and we all knew it that night. I tried to be as cheerful as possible under the circumstances, saying to my gathered supporters, when the results were in, "Ours was a campaign for the 'little people,' but the problem was that they couldn't reach the levers"—a statement that probably became the most famous thing about my 1976 campaign and that people all over the country, even now, often quote back to me. I went on to laughingly say that same night in New Hampshire that we would just have to make sure there *were* stools available in the voting booths in the state contests that would soon follow.

Because of my losing showing in New Hampshire, I was instantly out of the news, as I knew would happen. I lost the contingent of television and newspaper reporters who had been traveling with me. The New Hampshire winner, Jimmy Carter, by contrast, had to put on an extra plane for the press now covering him, and his photograph was on the next week's covers of *Time* and *Newsweek,* though the actual New Hampshire vote difference between us had been small. My campaign contributions trickled down to a drip. People, no matter how much they like you, do not want to throw good money after bad.

So, I couldn't advance my campaign in the free media. I couldn't buy much paid advertising to speak of, either. And there proved to be no stools in the voting booths in Massachusetts the week following New Hampshire. I got only 9 percent of the Massachusetts vote and ran no better than fifth. Although I placed ahead of Senator Birch Bayh and former Peace Corp director Sargent Shriver, my Massachusetts showing was not nearly good enough. Like both of them, I was really finished then, although I tried my best to keep on going.

I decided to skip the Illinois, Wisconsin, and New York primaries and make a stand somewhat later, in Pennsylvania, but long before the day of the Keystone-state primary, the ground had clearly fallen out from under me. So I announced out.

My staff and supporters would never have forgiven me if I had quit any earlier. Had I made my announcement before it became obvious to most of them, too, that everything was over, they would have felt betrayed, that all their work had been thrown away. It was tough enough as it was to convince some of them that I had no choice other than to withdraw when I did from active campaigning. The Service Employees International Union, which had supported me strongly, begged me to stay in the race, as I did, at least through the date of the Wisconsin primary. Quite a few supporters never gave up. But most had seen the campaign's demise coming for a long time, so there was not nearly so much sadness and recrimination at the end of my campaign as usually characterizes such losing efforts.

Although the crowd of friends and supporters that gathered in the ballroom of the Ambassador Hotel in Washington on April 8, 1976, to hear my withdrawal statement was not exactly a festive one, neither was it overly hangdog. There were tears, to be sure, especially when LaDonna spoke and when I finished reading my prepared statement, but there was laughter too, and by and large, those who had worked in the campaign felt good about it and about themselves. "There was considerable potential for tears as Mr. Harris stood before his followers and friends, but he did not let his full-scale campaign end that way," Charles Mohr reported in the *New York Times*. "Mr. Harris turned the occasion into an unusual—but, for him characteristic—moment of emotion, warmth and unpretentious retrospection." That is, indeed, what I tried for.

"Neither I nor my campaign have come to the attention of enough people," I said. "There are probably several reasons for this, the most important of which was lack of money, a fundamental problem made worse by the delay in reconstituting the Federal Election Commission." (For several crucial months, the Federal Election Commission would not pay out our matching federal funds because the constitutionality of the act creating the commission, and providing for the public funding, was being challenged in the courts.)

I then told that group of supporters that it was too soon for solid assessments and too late for might-have-beens: "It is enough for now to say that you and I shared a vision of what kind of country this ought to be, that we did what we could toward making that vision a reality, that we had some effect on our country's thinking and future, and that we may yet have more before we're through."

I knew that America could be put back together again—across race, age, sex, and regional lines—because we had begun to do so in my campaign. What was required, I said, was first to get people's attention, and then give them a glimpse of what kind of country this could be: a country where a young married couple would not have to worry about how they were going to pay their baby's doctor bills, where an older person would not have to give up lunch or breakfast to be able to buy medicines, where everyone willing and able to work would have a useful job at decent pay, and where our foreign policy, once again, would be based on our ideals, so that our people would have renewed cause for pride in calling themselves Americans. I still believe that.

A reporter then asked me when my decision to withdraw had been made. I said that it had become final on the morning after the New York and Wisconsin primaries; I had spent no money or effort in those contests but had mistakenly hoped that I might nevertheless gain at least a handful of delegates in them. I explained that after Massachusetts, I had planned on leapfrogging the intervening contests to devote all our resources, staff, and effort to the Pennsylvania primary, but that, reluctantly, we had finally been forced to conclude that the campaign just could not be revived. "We didn't do well enough in the early contests to call it victory," I said, "and we didn't do so poorly as to call it defeat; we ran just well enough to keep going. We didn't know *what* to call it, so we just decided to call it quits." Those words, paraphrasing a country and western song, dried up most of the tears, some of which, I noted, were actually in the eyes of more than one reporter.

What went wrong? Not much, really, I answered. My position on the issues did not prove to be as distinctive as I had expected, and I was therefore less able to overcome the handicap of being outspent by the leading candidates, but I thought that it was a plus for the country that other candidates had picked up my issues. I said that we had somehow not taken proper account in our campaign planning of the time and effort I would have to spend in Oklahoma between the Iowa caucuses and the New Hampshire and Massachusetts primaries.

The day before I made my withdrawal announcement, I had gone to tell the 1972 Democratic presidential nominee, George McGovern, and the 1968

Democratic presidential and vice-presidential nominees, Senator Hubert Humphrey and Senator Ed Muskie, what I was about to do. I also talked with Representative Morris Udall, who was still in the 1976 race, by telephone. McGovern and I discussed how Udall's close, second-place finish behind Jimmy Carter in Wisconsin would have been viewed by the press as a victory if Udall had not stated in advance that he needed to run first there. "The perception *is* the reality in presidential campaigns," I said to McGovern. And I said the same thing fifteen minutes later when talking to Muskie.

"I know it well," Muskie responded. "The press killed me in New Hampshire [in 1972, when he ran unsuccessfully for a short while against McGovern], even though I clearly won there."

"That's right," I said. "You got 46 percent of the vote, and McGovern got only 37 percent."

Afterward, I thought Muskie must have wondered how I had those exact figures so readily in mind, but at the time, what occurred to me was a story Morris Udall had told during his campaign. Udall said that he went into a barbershop in New Hampshire one day and shook hands with the barber and his customer, saying, "Hi, I'm Mo Udall; I'm running for president," and the barber responded, "Yeah, we were just laughing about that yesterday." When Ed Muskie spoke about how the press had killed him in New Hampshire, though he had won, I was tempted for a fleeting second to say, "Yeah, we were just laughing about that a few minutes ago."

At that final Ambassador Hotel press conference, I suggested, somewhat tentatively, that the harsh effect of the expectations system—and the disproportionate influence of the early primaries—might be ameliorated somewhat if the law required that free or minimum-cost television time be made available to those presidential candidates who had qualified for federal matching funds, no matter how they did in the first contests.

I was asked whether I would I throw my support to any of the remaining Democratic presidential candidates. I responded that it seemed there was not all that much support to throw, and that I felt about that question the same as I had felt after my poor showing in Massachusetts, having earlier taken on Secret Service protection. The situation, I said, reminded me of the story about the guy in my home county who'd run for sheriff and got barely enough votes to count. The next day, he nevertheless showed up on his little hometown's main street with a pistol strapped to his hip. When someone said to him, "Woody, why are you carrying that gun; you didn't get elected sheriff?" he replied, "Listen, anybody who doesn't have any more friends than I do needs all the protection he can get."

—ᴥ— —ᴥ— —ᴥ—

I was in Madison Square Garden for the Democratic convention that nominated Jimmy Carter—to see a lot of good friends, to say thanks to those who had helped out in my campaign, and to show my public support for Carter. I felt good about Carter and the convention. After Jimmy Carter had accepted the nomination, I was pleased that all those who had contested him in the primaries now stood with him on the convention platform as supporters. There was Senator Birch Bayh, a good man with Little League hustle, maybe a trifle light on the issues, but making up for this with friendliness and sincerity. There was Representative Morris Udall, a man I thought was especially suited to be president, having grown tougher in his outspokenness on the issues as the primaries had progressed. I was sorry that Udall had announced earlier, in the heat of the presidential campaign, that he would under no circumstances be a candidate for the Senate opening in his home state of Arizona, and I was concerned about reports that he had incurred a lot of personal debts in financing his campaign.

There was Sargent Shriver, too, truly a kind of Hubert Humphrey, Jr., as someone had put it—bubbly, committed, cheerful. There was Terry Sanford, a solid man whose public career did not end when he left the North Carolina governor's office. There was Milton Shapp, who did not go anywhere at all in presidential politics but as governor of Pennsylvania had shown quite a bit of guts. There was Senator Henry Jackson, who basically was just as he appeared to be—a little too conservative and a trifle stodgy but prepared in depth on all the issues. There was latecomer Senator Frank Church of Idaho, who came across on television as slightly stilted but whose heart, and head, were in the right place. There was governor Jerry Brown of California; he had not said much in detail on the issues, but he seemed to be a serious person with a fresh outlook, a person, I correctly thought, who would continue in public life.

Before Carter's acceptance speech, there had been the acceptance speech by the vice-presidential nominee, Senator Mondale. Nothing so became Jimmy Carter, I thought, as did his selection of Mondale as his running mate. I had earlier sent Carter a telegram supporting Mondale, saying that he was clean, honest, correct in his views on the issues, and fully qualified himself to be president. I was right about that, and I would come to regret deeply that Mondale was not elected president when he was nominated in 1984.

I thought Carter grew during the campaign, though he was already a prepared, disciplined, determined person—not bad qualities for a prospective president. He came to endorse full employment as a specific national goal. A part of his acceptance speech adopted populist rhetoric and solutions, and after the 1976 Democratic convention, he even began to speak of himself as a populist. I left New York feeling that the Carter-Mondale ticket was a good one, a strong one, and one that ought to be elected. I did all I could toward that end. And I am sorry Carter did not wind up being as successful as a president as he would later be as an ex-president.

In Washington, at a great picnic of friends and supporters on the summer day in 1976 that LaDonna and I and our daughter Laura left Washington for good, I looked out over a crowded flower bed of familiar faces. "We will be of good cheer," I said. "LaDonna and I are proud of our association with each of you."

Then we flew off to our new home state, New Mexico—and a new life.

10

—◦◦—

A New Life

I'VE ALWAYS THOUGHT THAT PEOPLE ought to be like snakes and shed their skins every now and then. In a way, that's what I did when I left Oklahoma for Washington in 1964. And that's what I did again when I left Washington for New Mexico in 1976.

Why New Mexico? In the summer of 1956, an Oklahoma State Senate colleague of mine offered me the use of his family's old vacation place, which he had not visited since he was a boy, for a trip I wanted to make to New Mexico with my own family. He showed me on a map how to get there. It was east of Santa Fe, up in the pine-forested Sangre de Cristo Mountains. I loaded up my bunch in Lawton, Oklahoma, and we drove to what turned out to be a rustic little log cabin, perched most picturesquely on the west bank of the Pecos River, which was there a beautiful, rushing, tree-lined mountain stream.

We made that cabin our central headquarters—and what a lovely one it was. Then on some days, we made forays to other New Mexico places and sights that drew our interest. We drove up to Taos, especially to visit Taos Pueblo. Somehow, there in that little Indian village's magic plaza with its multistoried tan adobe apartment-like structures, situated both to the north and south of the mountain stream that runs right through the village, I instantly felt like I was coming home. When I was in third grade, we had made a model of Taos Pueblo, with mud-plastered boxes. (And one of my most important, and most satisfying, U.S. Senate accomplishments was getting the Pueblo back its sacred forty-eight-thousand-acre Blue Lake lands; the resultant friendship and gratitude of the gentle and generous people of that village have been a lasting blessing for me in all the years afterward.)

One night on that 1956 New Mexico trip, we stayed over, as you could do then, at Bandelier National Monument. There, the next day, we clambered through the ancient ruins and cave houses of Frijoles Canyon and rode horseback up a precarious mountain trail to a high nearby ridge and back. We drove into Santa Fe and roamed its historic old plaza and Palace of the Governors Museum, were captivated forever by the paintings of the Taos School of artists that hung in the Museum of Fine Arts. We stayed on that night for the already famous Santa Fe Opera, nestled in juniper-clad hills under a jillion stars, and saw a thrilling performance of *Carmen*, the great arias of which I had been in love with since my OU days. We ate our first fiery bowl of nearly habit-forming green-chile stew (not Tex-Mex chili). We attended an unbelievably impressive and mystical green corn dance at Santo Domingo Pueblo that must have involved 750 intensely focused and traditionally costumed men and women dancers.

This is the most exotic place I've ever been to, I thought. And I still think that. New Mexico's not called The Land of Enchantment for nothing.

My family and I vacationed out there every summer after that 1956 trip. Somewhere in the back of my mind, I began early to form a kind of unspoken resolve that, if and when I ever retired, which at that time seemed well off in the future, I would think seriously about retiring to New Mexico.

Then the day came. I had retired as a U.S. senator in January 1973, and after losing in the 1976 presidential race, I was retired as a national politician, too; anybody really has only one good shot at running for president. I had lived in Washington for twelve years; my close friend Jim Hightower had lived there that long or longer. He and I both decided that it was time we made a geographic change and got ourselves back out in the country. Hightower went home to Texas. I went to a new home, and a new life, in New Mexico.

I felt I could start afresh in a place where I had long been thinking I would ultimately wind up, where I would still be close to my beloved native Oklahoma, just across the line east. I would be able to go back and forth a lot, but without having to get mixed up again in old Sooner-state political divisions and conflicts.

I was still licensed to practice law in Oklahoma and in the District of Columbia, but I had no interest in taking the bar exam and opening up a New Mexico law office. I was thinking that instead I would primarily occupy myself with paid lecturing and writing. Then, as so often had been the case in my life, serendipity suddenly showed up once more.

I had just sold our house in McLean, Virginia (for three times what I had paid for it, thus surprisingly providing myself with useable capital that I did not earlier realize I had). We were packing one morning, getting ready for the movers, when I got an unexpected telephone call from a longtime Lakota Indian friend of mine, Pat Locke (who would later get a MacArthur genius grant for her work preserving her tribe's language and who has since passed away).

Pat Locke told me that she had just attended a regular meeting, in Denver, of the Western Interstate Commission on Higher Education (WICHE) and that she had told another WICHE member, William E. Bud Davis, president of the University of New Mexico (UNM), that I was moving to New Mexico. Bud Davis, she reported, immediately said, "Why, we ought to get him to teach at UNM." As I would later learn, Davis was quite interested in politics and government and had run unsuccessfully as a Democratic candidate for the U.S. Senate from Idaho. He knew who I was and had followed my political career.

After Pat Locke's report to me, I made a typically instinctive and almost instantaneous decision: I would become a university professor. I had barely hung up the telephone after the call from Pat when I grabbed it up again and called the UNM president. He offered me a job as a UNM political science professor. I said I would take it, at first on a half-time basis; I was still working on finishing a book I was writing, *Potomac Fever*, about my Washington years and running for president.

President Davis put me in touch with the outgoing and incoming chairmen of UNM's Political Science Department. I flew to Albuquerque to see them. They said they would be pleased to have me as a professor (one important reason being that President Davis had given the department an extra salary line for use in hiring me). We shook hands on the deal, and I had a new profession, which would begin in just a couple of months, that very fall semester, 1976.

I really liked the UNM Political Science Department and the University of New Mexico, and they liked me. At the end of my first year there, they offered me a full, and full-time, professorship, with instant tenure. I took it, with gratitude and great pleasure. In some ways, I had always been a teacher. I had always felt that if I could understand something, I could explain it in such a way that other people could understand it, too. And I really enjoyed doing that. What I knew best, what I understood best, were politics and government. Now I had a chance to teach it to others full time.

My life changed in other ways. My thirty-three-year marriage to LaDonna, who had been my great and valuable partner in politics and activism, did not long survive the move to New Mexico. Ours was simply, and very sadly for both of us, one of those growing-apart stories. She and I continued to be friends. I went on serving as an international adviser and supporter of Americans for Indian Opportunity, of which she is still chair; our daughter Laura is now the quite successful executive vice president and CEO of that important national Indian-advocacy and Indian leadership-training organization.

Margaret Elliston has been my loved and loving wife, my partner in social activism and politics, my inspiration, my joyful fellow world traveler, and my personal trainer for twenty-five years (a milestone that she says marks our "silver" anniversary, and I say "linoleum"). Born in Manhattan, raised in Houston, and educated in California, Margaret is an early-childhood expert; a longtime Rio Grande–banks resident of Corrales, New Mexico, where we live; and a recently retired administrator in the New Mexico State Department of Children, Youth, and Families. I gave up tobacco and alcohol and got in better physical shape. With Margaret, I took up bicycle touring (including in France, Germany, Austria, and northern Italy), cross-country skiing (one year winning in my age group a blue ribbon in a five-kilometer race, The Chama Chile Classic.), snowshoeing, and mountain hiking. I took up serious vegetable gardening, well remembered from my boyhood, and even did a little canning. A canned taco sauce I made from homegrown ingredients and entered in the New Mexico State Fair won a third-place ribbon (causing a local super-Mex friend of mine to complain: "Must have been a bunch of Okie judges!")

There have been other members of Congress who first were professors, but I think I'm the only one who ever went the other direction full time. After leaving the Senate, I worked hard at converting myself into an academician. I not only regularly taught a large first-year introductory class on American government and a fairly large upperclass-level course on Congress, but also, from time to time, taught courses on political parties, Native Americans and tribal governments, and U.S.-Mexico relations. My classes were always full, usually with a waiting list. One year, the UNM

Alumni Association named me as the Outstanding Faculty Member. And the New Mexico Commission on Higher Education designated me an Eminent Scholar. I attended and took part in numerous professional political science meetings and did a good deal of political science research and writing. Scott Foresman and Company—the originators of the grade-school textbook characters Dick, Jane, and Spot, whose portraits, hanging in the corporate boardroom, company officials were soon to show me proudly—offered me what turned out to be a remunerative contract to write their first college-level introductory American government text. It did well and went through four editions. I produced three other textbooks for Scott Foresman and their successor corporations.

I had always been highly interested in Mexico and Latin America and had traveled extensively there while in the Senate. At the University of New Mexico, I decided to prepare to teach a course on Mexico, but first, I launched into the study of Spanish, which I'd had only a year of, a long time earlier, in high school. At UNM, I took an initial Spanish course for faculty members. Then I went to Cuernavaca, Mexico, one summer for a one-month intensive-language course and went back to take similar courses twice more, once in Cuernavaca again, once in Mexico City. I became fluent in Spanish, and, unusually, without an American accent. I taught the Mexico course, U.S.-Mexico relations, for several years, on the UNM campus as well as on site for groups of UNM students I took to Mexico—one summer in Guadalajara and two in Xalapa—and to Costa Rica, twice. During two additional summers, I took UNM students to Granada, Spain, and taught special courses for them there.

Other activities developed from my Spanish-language facility. I lectured extensively in Spanish for the U.S. State Department in a number of Latin American countries, including Mexico, Guatemala, El Salvador, Honduras, Costa Rica, and Uruguay, as well as in Spain. I was a Fulbright Scholar in Mexico. (Upon hearing about my being selected for a Fulbright, former senator William Fulbright of Arkansas, the program's originator, told my friend Senator Jim Abourezk of South Dakota, "I wish I could get one of those!") I was a visiting professor for one semester at Mexico's national university in Mexico City. I edited one book in Spanish and coauthored another. At UNM, I directed a U.S. Information Agency program that brought five Guatemalan professors to our campus for graduate study; I chaired the Spanish-language Ph.D. dissertation committee of a

Mexican scholar; and I frequently lectured in Spanish to various groups of State Department–sponsored Latin American visitors.

My academic credentials gave me a lot of other great opportunities for travel, which I love. At one time or another, I lectured in France, Spain, England, and the Netherlands. As a visiting adjunct professor in OU's public administration master's degree program, I taught short courses on Congress a number of times in Japan and South Korea under OU's U.S. military-base contracts. My wife and I traveled together to give separate lectures for the U.S. State Department in several different cities in Japan and India and also in Bangladesh and Sri Lanka.

Nationally and locally, I naturally stayed very interested and active in politics and political issues. I took part in a number of statewide campaigns in New Mexico and served as state chair of Howard Dean's 2004 presidential campaign. I was state chair of the New Mexico Democratic Party in 1998 and 1999, and I pushed for campaign-finance reform and open government as state chair of New Mexico Common Cause. I served as the chair of the New Mexico Governor's Commission on Higher Education and went on the national governing board of Common Cause, fighting there for a number of government-accountability measures and against the American war in Iraq. With a grant from the Century Fund, I went to Washington, made a thorough study of the U.S. Senate, and wrote up my recommendations for reform in a book published by the Oxford University Press. I became chair of the board of trustees of the Milton S. Eisenhower Foundation, in Washington, and in that capacity produced seminars and conferences, and books, two updating the Kerner Report and one defending Social Security and opposing the demonization of Mexican immigrants.

I kept on writing a lot. In truth, I am a little embarrassed to report that I have produced enough books, as somebody said, to cause a small forest or two to be cut down. This memoir, is my twenty-first book. It is my eighteenth nonfiction book (including nine I authored alone, four I coauthored, and five I edited or coedited).

More lately, I have turned my hand to fiction. (A too-funny friend I first told that to said, "I thought you'd *always* been writing fiction.") I'd always thought I would write novels when I got to the stage in life where I felt free to do that. As a matter of fact, I wrote a novel during my junior year at OU. I sat down that summer, without a whole lot else to do, and typed out a historical novel with a Comanche Indian protagonist and a viewpoint from the inside of that tribe and culture, of which I was an avid student. Then law school started for me the following fall, and I put the finished novel in a box and laid it aside, never submitting it anywhere.

When I later became administrative assistant to the dean of the OU College of Law, I not only handled a lot of his correspondence, but also often acted for him as the lawyer for the great University of Oklahoma Press. I soon got to know quite well, and like very much, the press's outstanding director, Savoie Lottinville. Lottinville always tipped me for my law work for him by giving me books from the OU Press's western and Indian collection, for which the press was justly famous. One day, knowing about my interest in and knowledge of things Comanche, Lottinville proposed to me that I write a nonfiction book for him about the history and culture of that tribe. I was intrigued. He gave me another OU book, Alice Marriott's now-classic *The Ten Grandmothers*, about the Kiowas, and told me to pattern my Comanche book after it.

I went home and read Marriott's terrific book—and was totally intimidated by it. I soon went back and told Lottinville that there was no way I could write a book about the Comanches that was anywhere near as good as Marriott's. I told him, though, in passing, about my earlier Comanche novel. The OU Press did not then publish fiction, but Lottinville asked to see my novel anyway. With great trepidation, I brought him the manuscript and, with even greater trepidation, went back later at his request to discuss it. In his office, I squirmed while Lottinville first told me what he thought was wrong with the novel. Then he mentioned an agent friend of his in New York, Maurice Crain, and said, "I send him all my fiction, and he sends me all his nonfiction." Lottinville said that, with work, he thought my novel could be turned into another *Big Sky* (by A. B. Guthrie). Lord! He wanted to send the manuscript to Crain, but I was focused on a career in law and politics, and I did not think an image as a novelist would fit well into that picture. So, I filed the Comanche novel away again, never sent it off, never looked through it again.

By the late 1990s, though still a university professor and still active in politics, I decided it was finally time for me to start writing fiction. I should start, I thought, with mysteries. My friend, the excellent, bestselling novelist Tony Hillerman, had told me that he had wanted, at first, to write the great American novel but had decided to start with mysteries, since, as he put it, self-deprecatingly, "They're short and formulaic." I decided to do the same thing. But what was my schtick, as an old Borscht Belt comedian might put it? Not Navajos; Hillerman was already doing that. I still had all that research I had done for the 1930s-Oklahoma non-fiction book "Before the World Changed," which I had planned but never written. That was it, I decided.

I set *Coyote Revenge* in 1938 Oklahoma, in a small town I called Vernon, which looked suspiciously like my hometown of Walters. Some Oklahomans have always said that John Steinbeck in *Grapes of Wrath* "made us look bad." I never agreed. I think Steinbeck showed Oklahomans of that period the way they were: good people pushed down by forces beyond their control and trying their best to keep body and soul together in hardscrabble times. I tried to write true, too, about those people and their times.

The manuscript for my first novel finished, I followed all the rules about what you are supposed to do. I studied how-to-sell-your-novel books, wrote a good query letter, and soon got a New York City agent. He sold the novel to HarperCollins, in a two-book deal. The reviews—in the *New York Times, Washington Post, Chicago Tribune,* and elsewhere—were great. *Coyote Revenge* won the Nero Wolfe Award (the first time ever for a first novel), and when I accepted the award at a Manhattan banquet, I felt like gushing, the same as Sally Fields at the Academy Awards, "You like me! You really like me!"

My second-in-a-series mystery, *Easy Pickin's,* was published in 2000, and it got generally good reviews, too. My third novel, *Following the Harvest,* was a coming-of-age novel set in 1943 Oklahoma and north.

I found I loved writing fiction—and I may do some more of it. For one thing, you can make people do what you want them to do and draw on your most important life experiences, the most unforgettable characters you've met, and the deepest feelings you've had, though all these, of course, must be reworked and mixed up and fictionalized.

So, in New Mexico from 1976 on, my life changed. My high school history teacher, though, would surely say that I still have too many irons in the fire. But that is the way I have always lived, and the way I like to live. At the end of 2005, I formally retired from the University of New Mexico, though I entered into a contract with them to keep my office there and continue to teach one course, which has turned out to be supervising each semester a group of UNM students interning in Washington with members of Congress, in a program now called the Fred Harris Congressional Internship Program.

And all the time since I have been in New Mexico, I have traveled to Oklahoma once or twice every two or three months to lecture or speak somewhere or get an award. People give you awards when you live to be my age. I like that. Not only did the OU Journalism School give me their outstanding journalism alumnus award, even though I had never taken a journalism course, I was also selected by the OU College of Arts and Sciences as an outstanding alumnus, by the OU Communications Department to give the first annual Senator Josh Lee Lecture, and by the OU History Department to give the sixth or seventh annual Fred Harris Lecture in History, endowed by a former Senate intern of mine.

Oklahoma has been good to me. So has New Mexico. And so, too, has life itself.

Epilogue
This At Least Was Good

One time, at a small dinner party at the Washington home of my friend Averell Harriman, the great foreign policy adviser to many presidents and a former New York governor, his first wife, Marie, seated me next to the host, then in his eighties, so that I could press him at Marie's request to write his memoirs. She said he had been resisting doing that. So, between the main course and dessert, I spoke up. "Governor, with all the great experiences you've had, you ought to write your memoirs." Harriman instantly bristled. It was obvious that this was a sore subject with him. Huffily, he said, "I'm still more interested in *making* history than I am in writing it!"

Well, I could probably have said the same thing when I was asked to write my own memoirs. I am still active in politics, still teaching, still writing. But the two tasks, making history and writing it, do not have to be mutually exclusive. That's why I agreed that this would be as good a time as any to review my life and write this book. And I've enjoyed doing it, too.

I have learned a little in the process. Looking over my life, I have been struck by how often the most important opportunities, life-changing opportunities, that have opened up for me through the years have appeared suddenly and serendipitously, but that my being at the right time and place to take advantage of those opportunities, which I often decided almost instinctively and instantaneously to do, was the result not of accident but of planning and preparation. I have been struck, too, by how many times serendipity showed up in my life in the company of an actual person, a friend, and how indebted I am to those friends.

The great old cowboy painter Charlie Russell wrote in his book *Trails Plowed Under*, which came out after his death, "I had friends when I didn't have anything else." That's me. I wish I could name them all here and thank them personally. A good many of them worked for me as staff people at one time or another—like a number I've mentioned earlier in this book—as well as great people like television producer Sherry Jones, retired publisher Jim Monroe, lawyer and dealmaker Fred Gipson, the late H. B. "Boots" Taliaferro, Jr., whom I brought to Washington to work on the Kerner Commission staff, and the late Gary Dage, who became an expert on agriculture and politics. I hope they all know how much they have meant to me.

I count my children among my best friends, too. They are people I like and like to be with: Kathryn Harris Tijerina, Santa Fe, a University of Phoenix senior official, and her state-lawyer husband, Manuel Tijerina; Byron Harris, who's made a great success working in television production in Hollywood, or Hollyweird, as he calls it; and Laura Harris, in Albuquerque, who heads up Americans for Indian Opportunity so well, and her college son, my grandson, Sam Fred Goodhope. They all share—go figure!—my own politics, political views, peculiar interest in archaeology and the Discovery Channel, and sense of humor. I can say the same thing, and do, about my stepchildren, Margaret's daughter and son whom I helped raise, and their families: Amanda Elliston and her husband, John Gray, both great teachers, and their wonderful new son, Reuben Mark Elliston; and Los Angeles dot.com wizard Amos Elliston and his gifted author and humorist wife, Wendy Spero.

During my life, I have been able to meet virtually everyone I ever wanted to meet, and I got to be friends with many of them. Once, for example, at a small dinner at the Merrywood home of NBC television reporter Nancy Dickerson, who interviewed me a lot on the *Today Show,* I told another guest, publisher and author Bennett Cerf, that the living person I'd never met but would most like to was Willie Morris, the author of one of the very best books I had ever read, *North Toward Home.* Bennett Cerf and his wife, Phyllis, soon put together a small dinner in their Manhattan home just so Morris and I could get together—and their other guests on that occasion were also pretty impressive, including authors Philip Roth and William Manchester and actresses Claudette Colbert and Lauren Bacall.

Katherine Graham, the publisher of the *Washington Post,* was a friend I valued. I was in her home a good bit when I was in the Senate, and she once called me up to say that I looked like I was working too hard, then invited my family and me to spend a weekend by ourselves at her nearby country farm. Norman Lear, the television producer of *All in the Family* and other programs, founder of People for the American Way, was a friend and a terrific supporter of my presidential campaign, as were Dennis Weaver of *Gunsmoke* and *McCloud* and Will Geer, Grandpa on *The Waltons,* who had been a great Depression-era activist and a friend of Woody Guthrie's.

When John Kerry first returned from Vietnam, I had him out to my house in McLean, Virginia, where we talked about the historic testimony he was about to give against the Vietnam War before the Senate Foreign Relations Committee. I first knew Al Gore as the son of Albert Gore, Sr., a senator from Tennessee with whom I served on the Finance Committee. I first met Michael Dukakis when he was lieutenant governor of Massachusetts and chaired a syndicated public television program out of Boston, *The Advocates,* on which I appeared several times after I left the Senate. And I first met Bill Clinton, as he was later to remind me, when I was in New York City for a late-night radio call-in show and he and I somehow ran into each other when he drove down there from Yale to see an old girlfriend.

Teaching full time for over thirty years, I have had some terrific students, and people ask me what I say to today's young people, what kind of advice I give them. Here's what I said to some of them in my remarks as the May 2006 graduation speaker at the University of New Mexico Political Science convocation (remarks that contain a couple of sentiments or stories that appear elsewhere in this book):

> I'm happy to be here at the graduation of this terrific political science class. We're glad to have had you as students. We're proud of you. We express our warmest congratulations to you—and, not only to you, but to your friends and family who've helped you so much to get to this important milestone of achievement.
>
> I'm here to make predictions. That's what graduation speakers are expected to do, and I'm no exception. Here are two of my confident predictions for you: first, the future is headed this way, and you might as well get ready for it; and second, the future for each of you can be pretty much what you make of it.
>
> That's especially true if you take to heart four pieces of advice that I'm about to give you—and giving advice is another thing graduation speakers are expected to do.

First, keep on learning. In my thirty years of university teaching, I've found that the deepest need of students is to understand themselves, their world, and their place in it. Isn't that what all of us need, and want?

Christopher Morley wrote that "Life is a foreign language." That's certainly true. We're not born understanding life. We have to study it, and we have to keep on studying it.

It's my hope that in your stay here at UNM each of you has become a true intellectual—and the way I define an intellectual is as a person who is curious about everything, who keeps on asking questions and finding answers for them: How do things work? How does the world work? How do I fit in? An intellectual is a person who keeps on learning.

A folksinger I saw one time seemed to spend about as much time tuning his guitar as he did singing, and as a part of his patter, filling the time, he said: "If I ever get this thing tuned again, I'm going to weld it." But, as we know, it doesn't work that way with guitars, and it doesn't work that way with life, either. Things change. The world changes.

Frank Carey, when he was head of IBM, said, "Our company is not just looking for people with technical competence; we want people who have learned how to learn." That's what I want for each of you. I hope that, here at UNM, you have learned how to learn, and that you keep on learning.

Second, let's remember our debt to others. I am a good example of the fact that there is no such thing as a self-made man or a self-made woman. We all owe a lot to others, more than we can repay—to parents, teachers, and taxpayers. And we ought to at least pay back a little of the interest on that debt.

Frances Lappe, author of *Diet for a Small Planet*, wrote, "It is in interaction with and service to others that we are truly human." I believe that. None of us is fully, truly human unless we accept and act upon a profound realization that we as humans are bound to each other, are a part of each other, and that, as has been said, "Service to others is the best work of life."

It was John Donne, who more than 350 years ago wrote, "No man is an island, entire of itself; every man is a piece of the continent, a part of the main; if a clod be washed away by the sea, Europe is the less, as well as if a promontory were, as well as if a manor of thy friends or thine own were; any man's death diminishes me, because I am involved in mankind; and therefore never send to know for whom the bell tolls; it tolls for thee."

And I believe that government should be an instrument through which each of us may do what we can do to help others. Which leads me to my third piece of advice:

Participate. Take part in civic affairs. I'm told that the word "idiot" comes from a Greek word that has to do with a person who takes no part in civic affairs.

Here at UNM, you majored in political science. A task force of the American Political Science Association [APSA] once recommended that political science study should "aim at turning politically interested and concerned students into politically literate college graduates, whatever their career plans or their interests." As my friend political scientist Nelson Polsby has put it, a political science major should be able to understand political news and happenings like a radiologist can read an x-ray. That task force of the APSA went on to say that majoring in political science should maximize the capacity of students to analyze and interpret political events and processes, and equip them "not merely to understand or to manage their effects on society and on them individually, but also to evaluate and seek to shape them." To take part, to participate.

In my own political science classes, we've always asked the question: What does it mean to be an American? What does America stand for? And we've seen that the answer was stated a long time ago, and well, in the Declaration of Independence: America stands for human rights, equality, and self-government.

John Fitzgerald Kennedy said, "If a free society cannot help the many who are poor, it cannot save the few who are rich." Dr. Martin Luther King, Jr., said, "Injustice anywhere is a threat to justice everywhere." That's why we take part, why we should take part, in politics and government. To help America, as Dr. King put it, "live out the meaning of its creed." And right now that means, for example, that we ought to resist current and strong efforts to demonize the immigrants among us—especially here in, as John Kennedy called us, this "nation of immigrants."

Fourth, go for it. Or, as the Nike slogan says, "Just Do It." I grew up working in the fields with my dad's brothers, my uncles, who were actually like brothers to me. I learned a lot from them, particularly my Uncle Ralph Harris. He ran away from home when he was seventeen. In the depths of the Great Depression, he hitchhiked his way from Oklahoma out to Los Angeles, looking for work, which proved to be mighty scarce. One day, broke and hungry, he made his way out to a site where they were building a dam, where he'd heard they were looking for another person to run a fresno—a horse-drawn dirt mover, sort of the bulldozer of those days. The foreman looked over Ralph's skinny frame and said, "Son, people who work for me have to move such and such cubic yards of dirt a day. What do you say to that?" And, Ralph told me, he replied: "Does people do it? If people does it, I can do it."

That's got to be *your* attitude, too. You're as good as anybody else—better than some. You've got a first-rate education. Whatever the challenge—whether you're going on for more education, right now, or straight on out into the world—believe in yourself and say, "If people does it, I can do it."

Take risks. I like a country and western singer, Lee Ann Womack. I liked her hit song of a few years back, "I Hope You Dance." In the video, incidentally, the daughter she's giving the song's advice to is my grand-niece. Lee Ann Womack sings, "When you have the chance to sit it out or dance, I hope you dance."

That's my final piece of advice to you: I hope you dance. Go for it! Don't worry about failing. As the late Dr. Benjamin Mays of Morehouse College wrote, "It isn't a tragedy to die with dreams unfulfilled, but it is a calamity not to dream. . . . It is no disgrace not to reach the stars, but it is a disgrace to have no stars to reach for. Not failing but low aim is sin." Dare to dream.

Congratulations to each of you on this important achievement and on this commencement. You well know that, as you go forth from here, there are today many tough problems in our country and in our world. But be assured that these are problems that were not caused by circumstance or bad luck. They were caused by people, and people—people like us—must face our problems and solve them, as each generation before us has faced and solved its own. With our education, we're privileged, you and I—and with privilege, comes obligation, an obligation to take part, to lead.

So, I say to you, in the words of John Fitzgerald Kennedy: "With a good conscience our only sure reward, with history the final judge of our deeds, let us go forth to lead the land we love, asking His blessing and His help, but knowing that, here on earth, God's work must truly be our own."

Old Charlie Russell also wrote in *Trails Plowed Under*, "Any man who can make a living doing what he likes is lucky. I've been that, and anytime I cash in now, I'm ahead of the game." That's me, too. I've been lucky to have had several careers—lawyer, politician, professor, and writer. One has led to the other. They've sometimes overlapped. And I've enjoyed them all.

I made some missteps along the way, which I haven't mentioned here, but I can say that I've been able to go nearly everywhere I wanted to go, see nearly everything I wanted to see, live out most of my fantasies, and do nearly everything I ever wanted to do. I wrote a poem in 1963 that still expresses my feeling about life—and *my* life. It's a good way, I think, to close out this memoir:

To a Butterfly

No songbird, you,
No thing for capture,
Nor for cage.
No owing grasp your fragile
        self survives.
I even fear the lightest touch
        of tenderness
May still your flight,
For magic dust removed.

What have you been?
What are you now, save
Beauty in a pleasing form?
What may you yet become,
When metamorphosis works its
        will again,
And you, like all, shall change
Once more in unknown ways?

Dark future shrouds her secrets well.
Our hopes cannot the fact of change withstand.
So, let us love this stage
And change, itself,
And say, what else may come,
That this, at least, was good.

Acknowledgments

Just as a I owe more than I can repay to many good people for what I may have done in my life up to now, I owe a lot, too, to many good people who helped me get this memoir put together and into print.

My wife, Margaret Elliston, in particular has been, as always, a loving and inspirational "M and D"—muse and driver.

I am grateful, too, to the wonderful Teresa Miller of the Oklahoma Center for Poets and Writers, in Tulsa. She first came up with the idea for this book, and she gave me warm and generous encouragement from its start to its finish.

Many thanks, too, to John Drayton, director; Alice Stanton, special projects editor; Kirk Bjornsgaard, acquisitions editor; and all the other great people at the marvelous University of Oklahoma Press. It has been a pleasure to work with them.

I should also say that when, a year or so ago, I told a friend that I was going to write my memoirs, he said, "I thought you'd already done that." The friend was right, of course. I *have* done at least several pieces of my memoirs in several books. So, I wrote into my publishing contract with the University of Oklahoma Press that, for this book, I could "recycle, rework, and reuse" material previously written and published by the author.

That is some portion of what I have done here—revised and reused certain material that I earlier wrote in other books, now long out of print, namely, *Alarms and Hopes*, 1968, my first book, which grew out of my experiences on the Kerner Commission; and extensively, *Potomac Fever*, 1977, about my years in Washington and running for president. I thank everybody who had anything to do with those books and others I have written through the years.

I also express great gratitude to the University of Oklahoma Political Science Department and its chair, Greg Russell, for inviting me to the campus and giving me a temporary Oklahoma academic home while I also worked on this book. And I should say, finally, that the University of New Mexico and its Political Science Department, chaired by Mark Peceny, have always given me support without measure. Many thanks.

Index

Page numbers in italics refer to illustrations.

Harris, Fred. R. (Presidential
campaign—1976): and borrowing
of themes by others, 184–85, 196;
campaign strategies for, 180–81;
campaign style of, 186; and demise
of campaign, 193–95; and fund-
raising, 192–93; and humor,
189–90, 194, 197–98; identity
problems of, 187–88; issues of, 181–
82; and Jackson, Miss., 191–92; and
LaDonna's support, 190; and
liberal label, 183; photo of, *103*;
populist message of, 183–84; and
the press, 196–97; Secret Service
protection for, 191; volunteer staff
of, 188–89, 192; and Winnebago
journey, 186–87; withdrawal from
race by, 195–96
Harris, Fred R. (U.S. Senator):
campaign for, 73–74, 80, 83, 90;
contender as Humphrey VP, 137–
39; as controversial figure, 172;
decision not to run in 1972, 172–73;
decision to run for Kerr's seat, 69–
70; as Democratic primary winner,
78; election themes, 75–76, 78; and
Harris' office burglaries, 175–76;
and Humphrey, *100*, *101*, 116–17;
and Johnson's endorsement, 93, *99*;
and Johnson's taped conversation,
87–88; and Lindsay, *100*, 106, 109–
10, 112, 165; and Mondale, 98,
106–107, 131, 179; nomination of
Muskie for VP by, 139; presidential
"jog" in 1972, 172–73, 184; publicity
in election, 76–77; and Robert
Kennedy, *98*, 105–106, 146–47; and
victory, 84, 93–94; and Vietnam
War, 114–15, 135–36, 172; and
Wilkinson debate, 83–88. *See also*
Kerner Commission; Wilkerson,
Charles B. ("Bud")
Harris, Irene (sister), 6, *97*
Harris, Kathryn (daughter). *See*
Tijerina, Kathryn Harris
Harris, Kathryn (sister): birth of, 4;
chores of, 21; family-history sketch
of, 5; and parents, 14–15; photo of,
97; unhappiness of, 13, 14
Harris, LaDonna Crawford (wife):
and Americans for Indian

Opportunity, 174; as asset in
Harris' campaigns, 79, 86, 190; as
civil rights advocate, 42; courtship
and marriage of, 28–29, 36; and
dissolution of marriage, 203; and
Ethel Kennedy, 150; as Harris'
emissary, 46; and Humphrey, 122–
23, 125, 130, 137; and Johnson, 121;
and Oklahomans for Indian
Opportunity, 167; photos of, *98*,
103; and presidential campaign,
186, 190
Harris, Laura (daughter): and
Americans for Indian Opportunity,
203, 210; as bridesmaid at sister's
wedding, 181; and Johnson
phonecall, 108; and King's
assassination, 152; and presidential
campaign, *103*, 186, 190
Harris, Loretta Sue (sister), 4, 6, 8, *97*
Harris, Margaret Elliston (wife), 3,
104, 203
Harris, Newcombe, Redman, and
Doolin law firm, 45
Harris, Ralph (uncle), *97*
Harris Grocery, 20
Harris/LBJ bumper stickers, 83, 90
Harry E. Bailey Turnpike, 49
Hawks, Marshall Rex ("Hawkeye"),
55
Haybaling Harrises, 15
Hays, Burl, 60, 72
"Hermit of Shark Tooth Shoal"
(Paramore), 51
Hightower, Jim, 179, 188, 189–90
Hill, Lister, 95
Hillerman, Tony, 206–207
Hilsman, Roger, 167
Hoodenpyle, Ernest, Jr., 28
Hoopes, Townsend, 119
Howard, Frances, 125
Hughes, Howard, 178
Hughes, Richard, 135
Human Rights Commission, 80
Humphrey, Hubert H.: characteristics
of, 122–26; and Democratic
nomination (1968), 137; election
to Senate of, 126; FBI file of, 127–
28; and Harris as cochair of
presidential campaign for, *100*,
131–32, 101.; Johnson's criticism of,

O'Brien, Lawrence, *101*, 135, 136, 139–
40, 177–78
O'Hara, James, 137
Oklahoma Daily, 33
Oklahoma Human Rights
Commission, 46
Oklahomans for Indian Opportunity,
167
Oklahoma Turnpike Authority, 47
"Onward Oklahoma!" (campaign
slogan), 54
OU. *See* University of Oklahoma
Ozarks Regional Development
Commission, 96

Paramore, Edward, 51
Paxton, Tom, 192
Peace Corps, 122
Peden, Katherine G., *100*, 109
Penn, John, 26–27, 42
People for the American Way, 211
Permanent Investigating
Subcommittee, 149
Person, Leroy, 5
Persons, Alene (mother). *See* Harris,
Alene Persons
Phi Beta Kappa, 38
Potomac Fever (Harris), 202
Poverty issue, progress in, 110–11,
113–14, 122
Presidential run in 1972, 171–72
Prohibition, repeal of in Oklahoma,
49–50

Race issue, progress in, 113–14, 192
Rayburn, Sam, 91
Reagan, Ronald, 113–14
Reciprocal Trade Act, 60, 94
Recitations by Baldwin, 51, 52–53
Reischauer, Edwin, 135
Reynolds, Bill, 72
Ribicoff, Abraham, 149, 153
Riots problem. *See* Kerner
Commission
Robert Dean Bass Memorial
Scholarship, 36–37
Rockefeller, Nelson, 183
Rogers, Cleeta John, 39, 40
Roosevelt, Eleanor, 95–96
Roosevelt, Franklin, 58–59

Rusk, Dean, 96, 120
Russell, Charlie, 209, 214
Russell, Richard, 95

Salinger, Pierre, 83
Salinger-Murphy effect, 83
Sanford, Terry, 135, 198
Seeger, Pete, 192
Senate Journal, 48
Senator Josh Lee Lecture, 208
Sexton, Bill, 69
Shailor, Barbara, 188
Shapp, Milton, 198
Shepler, Ned, 43, 46, 48, 53, 64–65, 70–
71
Shriver, Eunice (Mrs. Sargent), 158
Shriver, Sargent, 135, 198
Sidey, Hugh, 189
Smith, Jean Kennedy, 158
Sneed, Earl, 39
Snuff Ridge, 4
Social Security bill, opposition to, 114,
161–64
Southwest turnpike. *See* Turnpike bills
Spero, Wendy (daughter-in-law), 210
Spivak, Lawrence, 83–84
Stauffer, Loretta Sue Harris (sister), 4,
6, 8, *97*
Steinbeck, John, 207
Stephenson, Malvina, 106
Stevenson, Adlai, 82
Sullivant, Otis, 47

Tabbytite, 30–31
Taliaferro, H. B. ("Boots"), 210
Talmadge, Herman, 95
Taylor, Barbara, 7
Television and politics, 60
Temple Tribune, 26
Ten Grandmothers, The (Marriott), 206
Thomas, Elmer, 59
Thornton, Charles ("Tex"), *100*, 109,
113
Thurmond, Strom, 80, 81
Tijerina, Kathryn Harris (Mrs.
Manuel) (daughter), 36, 134, 137,
181, 190, 210
Tijerina, Manuel, 181, 210
Time magazine, 183, 189
Titchywy, Mickey, 28

CPSIA information can be obtained
at www.ICGtesting.com
Printed in the USA
LVHW051537230422
717055LV00006B/94